Gaston Crunelle and Flute Playing in Twentieth-Century France

flute, flute maker, and the last holdout at the Paris Conservatory against the modern Boehm flute. Bernard's classmates included Johannès Donjon (1839–1912), who later played flute in the Opéra and composed *Pan* and *Offertoire*, two works with a firm place in the flute repertoire. Bernard, Tulou noted on his official record, "has facility and has made noticeable progress."[10] Although Bernard later learned the modern flute developed by Theobald Boehm, he still played a Tulou wooden flute with eight keys. He played flute at the Paris Opéra from about 1860 until 1870.[11] In Douai, Bernard lived next to the conservatory, at 12 rue de Paris. When he died in 1915, Douai's mayor Charles Bertin paid special tribute to him:

> Mr. Bernard, flute teacher at the National Conservatory of Douai, died a few days ago. First Prize at the Paris Conservatory, for forty-two years, as a teacher, as a member of the Municipal Band and various musical societies of the city, he has manifested a great devotion, never sparing in his contributions that his talent made precious.[12]

The young Crunelle could have heard or met one of the most important flutists in France, Jules Herman (1830–1911), who himself was born in Douai and studied at its conservatory. Like Bernard, Herman earned a first prize with Tulou at the Paris Conservatory in 1849 and became music director at the National Theater of Lille and professor of flute at the Lille Conservatory.[13] He is best known for his transcription of Paganini's twenty-four caprices, but he also wrote opera fantasies for flute and piano.

Another musician Crunelle might have met was composer Victor Gallois (1880–1941). Born in Douai, he studied first at its conservatory and then at the Paris Conservatory. He won the Premier Prix de Rome in 1905, and all of Douai showed up to welcome him for a grand celebration in his native city. In 1917, he became the director of the Douai Conservatory, which is now named in his honor. Years later, Crunelle would return to Douai with Henri Dutilleux, who studied harmony, counterpoint, and piano with Gallois, to perform Dutilleux's Sonatina at a concert honoring Gallois on March 17, 1951.[14]

Just shy of his sixteenth birthday, Gaston earned a prize in flute from the Douai Conservatory and performed at the prize ceremony in the Douai Hôtel de Ville (town hall) on July 25, 1914 (see Figure 1).[15] He played the *Fantaisie* by Georges Hüe (1858–1948), written only a year earlier for the Paris Conservatory's annual competition. In solfège, he was awarded presented operas. The Douai Conservatory, founded in 1806, was the first regional conservatory in France, and later in the nineteenth century became a *succursale*, or branch, of the Paris Conservatory. Paul Cuenelaere (1851–1923) was its director from 1881 to 1917—encompassing Crunelle's time there—and founded the Société des concerts symphoniques du Conservatoire de Douai. Many great wind players have come from the north of France because of the tradition of *Harmonie*, or wind bands. For instance, Crunelle's first teacher in Paris, Adolphe Hennebains (1862–1914), grew up playing in wind bands in Saint Omer, nearly eighty kilometers northwest of Douai.[4] The Harmonie municipale of Douai won competitions during the nineteenth century.[5]

Gaston was born soon after the marriage of his father, Léon Gaston Crunelle (b. 1875),[6] and mother, Gabrielle Julie, née Mars (1876–1957), on November 24, 1897. Both sides of the family had lived in the area for generations, and the Crunelle lineage goes back at least eight generations to Balthazar Crunelle, who died in Douai in 1681.[7] Gaston's ancestors were working class: day laborers, farmers, millers, game wardens, boatmen, innkeepers, brewers, bakers, sellers of hemp, carpenters, blacksmiths, spinners, and dressmakers—there was not a professional musician among them. His mother Gabrielle was a shopkeeper,[8] and his father Léon continued his own father's trade as a coachman and a *loueur de voitures*, or coach lender. In the late nineteenth century, *voiture* still meant a horse-drawn carriage or coach, as motor vehicles only became common in the following decades. The family was probably prosperous, although the carriage trade would soon become obsolete.

The 1906 census listed three generations of the family living together at 3 rue Morel, an eight-minute walk from Douai's belfry.[9] Gaston's maternal grandfather, Florent Mars (b. 1847), an *ajusteur arsenal*, or fitter of military equipment, was head of the household, which included Gaston's grandmother, Virginie née Coppin (b. 1852), his aunt Noémie Mars (b. 1878), his uncle Charles Mars (b. 1890), his father Léon Crunelle, his mother, Gabrielle Mars, Gaston, and his sister, Suzanne (1904–1944). There was a salesman (*représentant de commerce*) named Dutilleux next door at 1 rue Morel.

At the Douai Conservatory, then at 16 Place d'Armes, just down the street from the famous belfry, Gaston had an excellent flute teacher, Auguste-Charles Bernard (1837–1915), who had won a first prize at the Paris Conservatory in 1855, studying with Jean-Louis Tulou (1786–1865). Tulou was solo flutist at the Paris Opéra, composer of numerous works for solo

2

Early Years

Douai

Among the first sounds Gaston Gabriel Crunelle would have heard was the carillon of Douai's imposing Gothic belfry, built in 1380. The composer Henri Dutilleux, who also grew up in Douai, had nostalgic memories of its chime:

> The carillon in the belfry sounds the hours, the half-hours, and so on. In addition, a bell-ringer used to come on Sunday and those sounds excited my imagination. They have very individual timbres, full of rich harmonies.[1]

Crunelle was born in the town on Thursday, August 18, 1898. At the time, Douai had a population of about 32,000—not much less than today, although now much of the surrounding area is built up. Located on the Scarpe River in the Nord Department of France, forty kilometers south of Lille and 190 kilometers north of Paris, Douai was settled in the seventh century and became a hub for textiles and wheat through the Middle Ages and for coal, industry, and breweries in the nineteenth century. Originally Flemish, Douai became part of France when Louis XIV captured it in 1667. As well as being a military outpost, it was also a religious, intellectual, and artistic center. The letters patent establishing the University of Douai dates from 1562.[2] It was the second-largest university in France in the eighteenth century; after its suppression during the French Revolution, it was subsequently re-established but moved to Lille in 1887. Among many local artists was painter Constant Dutilleux (1807–1865), great-grandfather of the composer Henri Dutilleux, who was born in Angers but moved to Douai at age three and then studied at its conservatory.

The town had an active musical life.[3] Charles Luce-Varlet (1781–1853), who had studied violin with Pierre Baillot (1771–1842), harmony with Charles-Simon Catel (1773–1830), and counterpoint with François-Joseph Gossec (1734–1829) at the Paris Conservatory, led the Douai Philharmonic Society from 1806 until 1853, developing an excellent regional orchestra that hosted Liszt and Paganini. The beautiful Théâtre à l'italienne de Douai

Gaston Crunelle and Flute Playing in Twentieth-Century France. Leonard Garrison, Oxford University Press.
© Oxford University Press 2024. DOI: 10.1093/9780197778579.003.0002

recordings, and even appeared on *The Tonight Show* and *The Muppet Show*. Rampal performed and taught a vastly expanded solo repertoire and used a more flexible sound. Although Rampal's career emphasized solo playing, his tone production, like that of Crunelle's, was based on embouchure finesse and purity of sound, traits many current French flutists share. A greater break from the traditional French sound came with Moyse, who modeled his playing on operatic singing, and this dramatic style influenced William Bennett (1936–2022), Sir James Galway, and Trevor Wye (b. 1935) in the British Isles, and Paula Robison (b. 1941) and Carol Wincenc (b. 1949) in America. Rampal's characterization of Moyse's playing is revealing: "He attacked the flute with a force that was almost bellicose."[10] Elsewhere, Rampal wrote that Moyse "was someone who wanted to play the flute 'differently.' To do so, he was obliged to change the school itself, more or less; this is fatal."[11]

Crunelle, on the other hand, was true to the traditions established by his predecessors. His experiences provide a window to a forgotten era in French musical life—actually, several eras, as he experienced so many important events in France from World War I through May 1968. This book reveals the scope of his activities, the excellence of his playing and teaching, and the reach of his influence. It includes discographies for both Crunelle and the QIP, and presents a full account of the ensemble's activities, including a list of the repertoire written for it (see Appendix 2).

Galway (b. 1939), Christian Lardé (1930–2012), Maxence Larrieu (b. 1934), and Jean-Pierre Rampal (1922–2000).[5] He was principal flutist in both the Orchestre Pasdeloup, one of four major Parisian orchestras of his era, and in the Opéra-Comique. He was a member of the Quintette instrumental de Paris (QIP), also known as the Quintette Pierre Jamet (QPJ), an acclaimed chamber ensemble consisting of flute, harp, and string trio. He performed in numerous other chamber music concerts, broadcasts, and recordings.

Despite Crunelle's renown during his lifetime, there are several reasons why he is not better known today. Since his wife, Raymonde Crunelle, née Martinet (1899–1977), preceded him in death by thirteen years, and his only child, Éliane Crunelle (1925–2009), had no interest in music, he had no one to curate his legacy. His papers and mementos have disappeared; thus, his life and career have had to be reconstructed for this book through archival research and oral histories.[6] Other French flutists of his generation enjoy greater posthumous reputations. Unlike René Le Roy (1898–1985), Crunelle was modest and shied away from self-promotion. He did not form any chamber groups, and although many composers dedicated conservatory *morceaux de concours* to him, he did not commission new works. Unlike Marcel Moyse (1889–1984), who compiled thirty-seven volumes of flute études and technical studies, including his *Enseignement complet de la flûte* series for Alphonse Leduc, Crunelle published only one minor book of orchestral excerpts and no editions of flute music.[7] While Crunelle taught a handful of students from outside France, Moyse developed an international following, teaching classes in flute and chamber music both in Europe and the United States. The Marcel Moyse Society sponsors events and releases recordings, videos, and publications, but the Gaston Crunelle Association died with its founder, Crunelle's former student Jean-Claude Diot (1933–2016).[8]

By the end of his long life, Crunelle's style of teaching and playing had gone out of fashion:

> In terms of style, Crunelle was a key transitional figure in French flute playing, a bridge from the brilliant technique and bright silvery sound that was prominent in Paris before the war, toward a new, rich, colorful tone and light *détaché* that evolved in Paris during the 1950s.[9]

The preeminent exemplar of the new approach was Jean-Pierre Rampal, Crunelle's successor at the Paris Conservatory. As the first flutist to become an international soloist and celebrity, he toured widely, released around 400

1

Introduction

This is the story of a man who rose from humble beginnings to become one of the most prominent musicians in France, performing and teaching at the top of his profession and living in comfort. He lived through two world wars, participated in dramatic events during the German Occupation of Paris, and like his compatriots, faced difficult choices in wartime. He has since been almost forgotten but deserves recognition.

Many flutists today have a vague recollection of the name Gaston Crunelle (1898–1990). They may remember having seen him as a dedicatee on their scores to sonatinas by Henri Dutilleux (1916–2013) and Pierre Sancan (1916–2008) and the *Chant de Linos* by André Jolivet (1905–1974). A few recall that their teachers had once studied with him. Before now, there have been no books about him, only several short articles.[1] He is absent from a widely read book, *The French Flute School, 1860–1950* by Claude Dorgeuille, except for his inclusion on the list of first-prize winners from the Paris Conservatory; even there, important flutists are distinguished in bold type, but not Crunelle.[2] In fact, by focusing on the period 1860–1950, the book de-legitimizes the playing and teaching of later French flutists, including Crunelle, whose career reached its pinnacle after World War II. Dorgeuille, writing in 1983, summarizes his view of the French flute school:

> Its existence . . . is undeniable; unanimously born out by the evidence assembled here and by the legacy of recordings which enable us to appreciate the quality and originality of this School. Its total disappearance today seems to me to be no less incontestable.[3]

This neglect of Crunelle is puzzling, for he was a beloved pedagogue and remarkable flutist, widely admired in his lifetime. He held the most prestigious teaching position in France—professor of flute at the Paris Conservatory—for a longer period (1941–1969) and taught more first-prize winners than any other flute professor in the institution's history.[4] His students, over 200 altogether, included international artists Michel Debost (b. 1934), Sir James

Gaston Crunelle and Flute Playing in Twentieth-Century France. Leonard Garrison, Oxford University Press.

Abbreviations

AFAA   Association française d'action artistique
ANF   Archives nationales de France
BNF   Bibliothèque nationale de France
INA   Institut national de l'audiovisuel
OFF   Association française des orchestres
PTT   Les Postes, Télégraphes et Téléphones
QIP   Quintette instrumental de Paris
QPJ   Quintette Pierre Jamet
SMI   Société musicale indépendante
SN   Société nationale de musique
STO   Service du travail obligatoire

Buyse, Isabelle Chapuis, Jean-Claude Dhainaut, Odette Ernest Dias, Reynaud François, Gabriel Fumet, Gérard Grognet, Eric Groussard, Marie-Claire Jamet, Gérard Jemain, Maxence Larrieu, Carlos Leresche, Guy-Claude Luypaerts, Betty Bang Mather, Alexander Murray, Bernard Pierreuse, Michael Scott, Francette Venay, and Tim Wilson. France Ménard and Angèle Roze helped me transcribe the interviews in French.

Archivists and librarians in France were extremely helpful, especially Sophie Lévy, archivist of the Paris Conservatory; Corine Morel and Adeline Quillard, librarians of the Médiathèque Hector Berlioz at the Paris Conservatory; and Karen Schmidt, librarian of the Orchestre Pasdeloup. Gilles Milleville, President of the Centre d'études généalogiques du Douaisis, was extraordinarily welcoming and productive.

Many shared their research with me, including Melissa Colgin-Abeln, whose dissertation on *morceaux de concours* I have admired for years; Pascal Gresset, editor of *Tempo flûte* and former editor of *Traversières*; Javier Rodriguez, alumnus of the Paris Conservatory, who shared his thesis on the Quintette Pierre Jamet; Lucie Kayas, Professor of musicology at the Paris Conservatory; and Anne Ricquebourg, Professor of harp at the Conservatory of Boulogne-Billancourt.

Finally, a heartfelt thanks to my loving family: my wife, Shannon Scott, who suffered through my enthusiasms about Crunelle and shared many great French meals and an overstuffed Paris apartment to make this project a success; and my son, Arthur Scott Garrison, who will never forgive my French accent and will never think my homemade baguettes are good enough.

Acknowledgments

It takes a village. This book would not be possible without the many people who helped.

Many thanks to my colleagues at the University of Idaho. Sean Quinlan, Dean of the College of Letters, Arts, and Social Sciences, and Vanessa Sielert, Director of the Lionel Hampton School of Music, approved my sabbatical leave twice, once before the COVID-19 pandemic, and once after. My French became more tolerable with the steady guidance of Sarah Nelson, Associate Professor of French, and Anne Perriguey, Senior Instructor of French. My writing improved thanks to input from Carol Padgham Albrecht, Emerita Professor of Music, and Miranda Wilson, Professor of Music. Thanks also to Nancy Holmes, Proposal Development Specialist in the Office of Research and Faculty Development, for suggesting revisions to my book proposal.

I am indebted to my editors at Oxford University Press—Michelle Chen, Rada Radojicic, and Hinduja Dhanasegaran—who guided a neophyte through the process of publishing a book. Philippe Bernold, Professor of Flute at the Paris Conservatory, Leone Buyse, Joseph and Ida Kirkland Professor Emerita of Music in the Shepherd School of Music at Rice University, and Kyle Dzapo, Caterpillar Professor of Music at Bradley University, also offered valuable advice on my manuscript. No one worked harder on this project than Susan Nelson, unsurpassed in her knowledge of the history of flute recordings. Nancy Toff, author and editor at Oxford University Press, shared much wisdom in her vast knowledge of research in France, writing, and publishing. Jane Fulcher, Professor of Musicology at the University of Michigan, and her former student Jessica Grimmer offered advice on research in France.

Three people connected me with many others in France: Sandra Howard, freelance flutist in Paris and teacher at the École Koenig; Patricia Nagle, Professor of flute at the École normale de musique; and Denis Verroust, former President of the Association française de la flûte, Professor of flute at the Palaiseau Conservatory, and President of the Association Jean-Pierre Rampal.

I deeply appreciate those who sat with me for interviews: Pierre-Yves Artaud, Jean-Louis Beaumadier, Edward Beckett, Brigitte Buxtorf, Leone

Contents

Oxford University Press is a department of the University of Oxford.
It furthers the University's objective of excellence in research, scholarship,
and education by publishing worldwide. Oxford is a registered trade mark of
Oxford University Press in the UK and in certain other countries.

Published in the United States of America by Oxford University Press
198 Madison Avenue, New York, NY 10016, United States of America.

CIP data is on file at the Library of Congress

ISBN 9780197778548 (pbk)
ISBN 9780197778531 (hbk)

DOI: 10.1093/9780197778579.001.0001

Gaston Crunelle and Flute Playing in Twentieth-Century France

LEONARD GARRISON

OXFORD
UNIVERSITY PRESS

premiers accessits (certificates of merit) in theory, transposition, and dictation and a *deuxième accessit* in sight singing.

France, England, and Germany declared war on August 4, a few days after the concert in Douai. The town was soon behind enemy lines, and its inhabitants experienced many privations, but by the end of August, the Crunelle family had moved to Paris.

Paris

In the capital city, Crunelle gained access to the great tradition of flute teaching at the Paris Conservatory, the most prestigious music school in France. Musical studies in France, except for musicology, are at conservatories, not in elementary or secondary schools or universities. The Paris Conservatory has always been a state institution with subsidized tuition for French students. Most French cities and towns have conservatories, but the Paris Conservatory was the only national school of music until 1980, when the Lyon Conservatory attained the same status. Many other conservatories, including the one in Douai, are *succursales*, regional institutions where students begin their studies prior to finishing in Paris if they attain a level of musicianship sufficient to enter the more prestigious school.

Claude Dorgeuille uses the phrase "the French Flute School" in a narrow sense to describe the playing of Paul Taffanel, Philippe Gaubert, Marcel Moyse, René Le Roy, and a few other late nineteenth-century and early twentieth-century flutists. A more useful perspective is to explore a continuous evolution from Michel Blavet (1700–1768) to the present, accounting for both changing styles and continuities. In 1947, the English-born American pianist Harold Bauer (1873–1951), who lived in Paris and served on the juries of the Paris Conservatory piano *concours* for many years starting in 1906, identified hallmarks of the French tradition of performers: "Clarity, elegance, proportion, logic. To these we may add such factors as fluency, wit (in the French sense of *esprit*), and above all, order."[16] The best French flutists have always demonstrated a high level of technical skill, a tone that is delicate, pure, refined, and flexible—capable of producing a variety of colors— respect for the score, and an emphasis on vocal phrasing. The establishment of a national school of music in Paris during the French Revolution created a uniformity in flute playing in France, and the adoption of the flute invented by Theobald Boehm in the mid-nineteenth century set France ahead of other nations, which did not take up the Boehm flute widely until the twentieth century.

The Paris Conservatory[17] was founded in 1795 as a merger of several schools: the École royale de chant et de déclamation, established in 1784 to train vocal and instrumental musicians for the Paris Opéra and for music for the court at Versailles; the École royale dramatique, established in 1786 for studies in theater; the École de musique du garde national, established in 1792 to train military musicians; and the Institut national de musique, established in 1792 to offer instruction in a wide variety of musical subjects. The Conservatory initially enrolled 600 students—men and women—and included studies in music and the dramatic arts until 1947, when a separate institution, the Conservatoire national supérieur d'art dramatique, was established. The founding documents mandated a library and collection of musical instruments:

> A national music library is formed in the Conservatory; it is made up of a complete collection of scores and works dealing with this art, antique or foreign instruments, and those for our uses which can serve as models through their perfection.[18]

By the beginning of the twentieth century, the Conservatory had the largest music library in Europe, but a 1935 law made the collection part of the Bibliothèque nationale de France (BNF), and it was transferred from the Conservatory to the BNF Richelieu site in 1964.[19] Since then, the Conservatory itself has built up a significant collection of scores, books, and recordings in its library, now known as the Médiathèque Hector Berlioz. The Conservatory's musical instrument museum was greatly augmented with the collection of composer and violinist Louis Clapisson (1808–1866) in 1864.[20] It is now a separate institution, one of the world's best museums of its kind, across a plaza from the Conservatory in the Cité de la musique complex at La Villette.

Until 1911, the Conservatory was in the former Hôtel des menus-plaisirs—responsible for royal banquets and ceremonies—at what is now 2 rue du Conservatoire at the corner of rue Bergère in the ninth arrondissement. The neighborhood, dating from the Middle Ages, was known as the Faubourg-Poissonnière, as it had originally been dominated by fishmongers.

The school's directors from its founding in 1795 to the present day are listed in Table 2.1.

Table 2.1 Directors of the Paris Conservatory

Director	Tenure
Bernard Sarrette (1765–1858)	1795–1822
Luigi Cherubini (1760–1842)	1822–42
Daniel Auber (1782–1871)	1842–71
Ambroise Thomas (1811–1896)	1871–96
Théodore Dubois (1837–1924)	1896–1905
Gabriel Fauré (1845–1924)	1905–20
Henri Rabaud (1872–1949)	1921–41
Claude Delvincourt (1888–1954)	1941–54
Marcel Dupré (1886–1971)	1954–56
Raymond Loucheur (1899–1979)	1956–62
Raymond Gallois-Montbrun (1918–1994)	1962–83
Marc Bleuse (b. 1937)	1984–86
Alain Louvier (b. 1945)	1986–91
Xavier Darasse (1934–1992)	1991–92
Marc-Olivier Dupin (b. 1954)	1993–2000
Alain Poirier (b. 1954)	2000–09
Pascal Dumay (b. 1951)	2009
Bruno Mantovani (b. 1974)	2010–19
Émilie Delorme (b. 1975)	2020–

The nineteenth century saw many changes in the structure, name, and policies of the institution.[21] It flourished during the Napoleonic years. Over the course of the century its emphasis was on training for professional careers in opera, and its directors Cherubini, Auber, Thomas, and Dubois were primarily composers of opera, although Dubois also wrote oratorios, masses, and music for organ.

There are several words for "class" in French, each translating directly to English: *cours*, *leçon*, and *classe*. A distinguishing feature of the Conservatory throughout its history is the emphasis on *la classe* or group of students.[22] Unlike in many other countries, there are no individual lessons, and each subject, including instrumental study, is taught through group meetings, often for many hours each week. Each class develops a strong sense of community, with a respect for the professor, who was called *maître* until the last couple of decades. A tradition of the Conservatory is the annual class photograph with the professor and all students, preserved in the school's archives.

From the first years of the Conservatory, solfège has always dominated the curriculum, and since students start solfège at an early age and continue through the end of their studies, they become fluent. This emphasis on sight-reading also figures in instrumental studies; entrance and exit exams or *concours* for the Conservatory include *déchiffrages*, or short sight-reading pieces with piano accompaniment, usually written by one of the faculty.

The flute professors of the Conservatory since its foundation are listed in Table 2.2.

Of the founding flute professors, the best known today is François Devienne, a prolific composer. His *Nouvelle Méthode théorique et pratique pour la flûte* (1794) has been translated and edited numerous times and

Table 2.2 Flute Professors of the Paris Conservatory

Professor	Tenure
François Devienne (1759–1803)	1795–1803
Antoine Hugot (1761–1803)	1795–1803
Johann George Wunderlich (1755–1819)	1795–1819
Nicolas Duverger	1795–1802
Jacques Schneitzhoeffer (1754–1829)	1795–1802
Joseph Guillou (1787–1853)	1816–28
Jean-Louis Tulou (1786–1865)	1829–60
Victor Coche (1806–1881)	1831–41 (assistant)
Louis Dorus (1813–1896)	1860–68
Joseph-Henri Altès (1826–1895)	1868–93
Paul Taffanel (1844–1908)	1893–1908
Adolphe Hennebains (1862–1914)	1909–14
Léopold Lafleurance (1865–1953)	1914–19
Philippe Gaubert (1879–1941)	1919–32
Marcel Moyse (1889–1984)	1932–40; 1946–49
Gaston Crunelle (1989–1990)	1941–69
Roger Cortet (1910–1953)	1949–53
Jean-Pierre Rampal (1922–2000)	1969–81
Alain Marion (1938–1998)	1977–98
Michel Debost (b. 1934)	1981–90
Pierre-Yves Artaud (b. 1946)	1991–2014
Sophie Cherrier (b. 1959)	1998–
Philippe Bernold (b. 1960)	2014–

is still used. Hugot and Wunderlich also wrote an official method that the Conservatory adopted in its early years. The original professors played the one-key wooden flute, and their successors Guillou, Tulou, and Coche were also devoted to old-system flutes with added keys. Tulou, discussed above, wrote a *Méthode de flûte* (1835) that became the official flute method of the Conservatory and composed the *morceaux de concours* used as examination pieces for the end-of-year competitions throughout most of the nineteenth century. Virtuoso showpieces, including opera fantasies and theme and variations, dominated the solo flute repertoire at this time.

Flute playing in France underwent a sea change with Louis Dorus, the first professor to require students to learn the Boehm flute. He studied with Guillou and won a first prize at the Conservatory in 1828. Dorus, for decades principal flutist in the Paris Opéra and the Société des concerts du conservatoire, was a close friend of Theobald Boehm (1794–1881) and early adopter of the 1833 conical Boehm flute and then the 1847 cylindrical Boehm flute with Dorus's innovation of a closed G-sharp key that is now the international standard.[23] When he became the flute professor at the Conservatory in 1860, the school adopted the silver Boehm flute as its official instrument.

One of the longest-serving professors was Joseph-Henri Altès, immortalized in Edgard Degas's painting, *The Orchestra at the Opera* (ca.1870). After receiving a first prize in 1842 under Tulou, Altès switched to the Boehm flute. His teaching emphasized technical development, and his *Méthode complète de flûte* (1880), the first based on the Boehm flute, is still studied, especially the twenty-six études extracted from it.[24] Many of these studies focus on the use of alternate fingerings to facilitate technique.

Paul Taffanel, who won a first prize under Dorus in 1860, is often called the founder of the French flute school, and no doubt his influence is unsurpassed. He was solo flutist of the Opéra-Comique (1862–1864) and then the Orchestre de la société des concerts du conservatoire (1865–1892), the leading orchestra in France from 1828 through 1967.[25] As professor at the Paris Conservatory, Taffanel transformed flute playing and teaching, developed a style based on vocal models, and brought a new seriousness to the solo flute repertoire by reviving Bach's flute sonatas and Mozart's flute concertos and commissioning pieces by his friend Camille Saint-Saëns (1835–1921) and other leading composers. Rather than recycling the contest solos by Tulou and Altès, he convinced Théodore Dubois to commission new *morceaux de concours* for instruments with limited solo repertoire, starting in 1897.[26] These commissions were the purview of the Conservatory director, but Dubois

Table 2.3 *Morceaux de concours*, 1898–1908

Year	Composer and Title
1898	Gabriel Fauré (1845–1924), *Fantaisie*, op. 79
1899	Alphonse Duvernoy (1842–1907), Concertino
1901	Louis Ganne (1862–1923), *Andante et Scherzo*
1902	Cécile Chaminade (1857–1944), Concertino, op. 107
1903	Albert Périlhou (1846–1936), *Ballade*
1904	George Enescu (1881–1955), *Cantabile et Presto*
1906	Philippe Gaubert, *Nocturne and Allegro scherzando*
1907	Paul Taffanel, *Andante pastorale et Scherzettino*
1908	Henri Büsser (1872–1973), *Prélude et Scherzo*, op. 35

seems to have given Taffanel free rein on the choice of composers, and Edward Blakeman quotes detailed correspondence between Taffanel and several of them. Table 2.3 shows works written during Taffanel's tenure; Crunelle would teach them in his class, and they are still standard repertoire.

Taffanel planned a comprehensive flute method, left unfinished at the time of his death. His pupil Gaubert completed the book and had it published in 1923. It is not known how much of the material is by Taffanel, but he developed technical exercises that students were required to copy from his manuscripts and memorize. Gaubert retained this practice when Crunelle was in his class in 1919–20,[27] and the exercises became Part IV of the *Complete Method* and the *Seventeen Daily Exercises* omnipresent today.[28] The Taffanel–Gaubert exercises became the core of Crunelle's teaching of technique.

In 1914, Crunelle studied briefly with Adolphe Hennebains, a pupil of both Altès and Taffanel and their successor as flute professor at the Conservatory and principal flutist of the Paris Opéra, but Hennebains had a fatal heart attack on September 17 of that year. Gaston then took lessons with Léopold Lafleurance, also a student of Taffanel and Altès, who the Conservatory named as its temporary flute professor. Lucy Dragon (1897–1992), who studied with both Hennebains and Lafleurance, compared their approaches:

He [Lafleurance] was very tough, very demanding. He never smiled. He spoke very frankly, and that wasn't always pleasant. Hennebains would play a lot during class. He played so well that I only wanted one thing, to end up playing like him. With Lafleurance, it was very different. He played some during class, but much less, and in any case, we didn't want to imitate him. He played harshly and didn't have the luminous sound that Hennebains had.[29]

Crunelle had great respect for Lafleurance, who made his students work hard and who, despite Dragon's dislike of his tone, always insisted that his students play with a good sound and even technique.[30] But Crunelle admitted that Lafleurance "was not an artist of the first rank. His personality was very changeable (affable/angry). His teaching method was very rigid. He always started a lesson with scales and had a preoccupation with fingering technique."[31] At this time, Gaston lived at 9 rue Ambroise Thomas, close to the old Conservatory, and his first audition for the Conservatory on October 8, 1915, was unsuccessful, but his second attempt on October 9, 1916, gained him admission into the exclusive flute class at the maximum age of eighteen (see Figure 2); he was one of nineteen wind players accepted out of thirty-four who auditioned.[32] At his 1915 audition, he performed the *Fantaisie*, op. 79 by Gabriel Fauré and *La Flûte de Pan* by Jules Mouquet (1867–1946).

When Crunelle entered the Conservatory, it had recently (in 1911) moved from its original location to 14 rue de Madrid in the eighth arrondissement, where it was to remain until relocating into a modern building in 1990.[33] The facility on rue de Madrid was more spacious than the original one (6,000 square meters as opposed to 3,550 in the Menus-Plaisirs) with twenty-eight rooms.[34] Its neighborhood, called the *quartier d'Europe* because the streets are named for European capitals, is relatively modern, dominated by the Gare St. Lazarre, the city's first train station, which opened in 1837. The rue de Madrid was only completed in 1867, and the Conservatory building was originally the Jesuit collège St. Ignace.[35]

During Crunelle's student years at the Conservatory, its director was Gabriel Fauré, the first person in the post not to have attended the school, as he studied at the École Niedermeyer, founded in 1853 by Louis Niedermeyer (1802–1861). Fauré instituted many changes, causing consternation and some resignations among the conservative faculty.[36] He enlarged the governing body, *le conseil supérieur d'enseignement*; he expanded the curriculum, adding new classes in harmony, counterpoint, and fugue separate from composition classes; he reformed vocal studies by requiring a firmer technical foundation and including repertoire outside of opera, including French, German, and Italian art songs; he abolished January exams to make room for more study of orchestral and chamber music; and he changed the system of *concours*, or entrance and exit exams. The director of the Conservatory chaired the *concours* juries, which included specialists from outside the Conservatory and outside the discipline of the jury. Initially, Fauré forbade the professor of the class from serving on its entrance and exit *concours*. The entrance audition was held in September or October, just before the beginning of the school year. Students who were accepted had little time to arrange for housing if they were from outside of Paris. The entrance *concours* were in two rounds, both with piano accompaniment, and always included a required piece, usually an existing *morceau de concours*.

The end-of-year *concours* was held in June and widely reported in the press until World War II.[37] With their professor's blessing, students could participate in the *concours* no matter how many years they had been at the Conservatory. Those who were awarded a first prize had attained a certain standard and had finished their studies; thus, there could be more than one first prize in any area of study. Those who earned second prizes could receive their diploma or continue to study toward a first prize. Other awards were the *premier* and *deuxième accessits*. At the end-of-year *concours*, each candidate performed from memory a new *morceau de concours imposé*, a required contest piece commissioned by the Conservatory director. As we have seen, in the nineteenth century, these pieces had been written by the flute professors, but starting in 1898 with Fauré's *Fantaisie*, they were by professional composers.

Crunelle took solfège for male instrumentalists with composer Paul Rougnon (1846–1934), who was a professor at the Conservatory from 1873 to 1921; his solfège manuals are still used in France today. Rougnon embodied the heritage of the Conservatory and published a memoir about his sixty years there, going back to his student years starting in 1861.[38] Also in his class were flutists Georges Boo (b. 1898), Pierre Castel, Jean Chefnay (b. 1903), who became principal flutist of the Orchestre Colonne and later played piccolo with Crunelle in the Opéra-Comique, Achille Glizon,[39] and René Le Roy, founder of the Quintette instrumental de Paris (QIP). Bassoonist Fernand Oubradous (1903–1986), who later revived Taffanel's Société des instruments à vent, a concert series in Paris originally focused on wind music, was also in the class. The exercises studied under Rougnon were undoubtedly complex; Rémy Campos writes of the state of solfège instruction at the Conservatory in the late nineteenth century:

It is a time of gratuitous virtuosity, with authors [of official Conservatory solfège texts] taking cruel pleasure in accumulating difficulties that one never encounters in this form in normal musical life: key changes, rhythmic traps, hazards of intonation, metric pitfalls, and other ambushes.[40]

Crunelle would have taken the obligatory class in music history with composer Maurice Emmanuel (1862–1938), who had studied composition with Léo Délibes (1836–1891), wrote a dissertation on ancient Greek music and published a text on music history.[41] One of Fauré's reforms was to require all Conservatory students to perform music of many eras and genres in the class.[42]

The flute class of 1916–17 was smaller than usual, as many were on military leave. At the *concours* on June 26, 1917, Gaston earned second prizes in flute and solfège and performed the required solo, *Promenades et danses nocturnes* by Alfred Bachelet (1864–1944), director of the conservatory in Nancy.[43] For the first time in history, a woman—Lucy Dragon—won a first prize, as did René Bigerelle.[44] André Delaître also received a second prize, René Le Roy received a *premier accessit*, and Pierre Castel a *deuxième accessit*.

Despite its proximity to the war zone, life in Paris was relatively normal, at least until the Germans employed the "Paris gun," a long-range siege gun that menaced the city between March and August 1918. After his first year of study, Gaston joined the army, as all males who had reached twenty were required to serve full-time in the military for three years. He was granted a leave from the Conservatory for the 1917–18 and 1918–19 years and served in the 84th, 114th, and 166th Infantry Regiments of the army.[45] He was fortunately not among the 1.5 million French men to die in battle, 18 percent of those mobilized. He also was unscathed by the influenza epidemic that killed between 125,000 and 250,000 civilians and 30,000 soldiers in France in 1918–19.[46]

At the age of twenty-one, Gaston returned to the Conservatory for the 1919–20 year, when the flute professor was Philippe Gaubert (1879–1941), who had also served in the war from 1914 to 1917. One of the great figures of French music, Gaubert was among the earliest flutists to be recorded, and his playing was stunning; his sound was resonant and flexible, and he played with great freedom. Devoted to his teacher Taffanel, Gaubert followed him as principal flutist in the Paris Opéra and the Orchestre de la société des concerts du conservatoire, then became the principal conductor of both organizations and a prolific composer.

Between 1919 and 1931, Gaubert taught a generation of flutists (see Chapter 3), including Marcel Moyse, who had studied with him earlier.

Moyse was Gaubert's assistant, teaching the class when he was absent, and in fact claimed Crunelle as a student.[47] Penelope Fischer summarizes recollections of Gaubert's teaching:

> Gaubert was not an organized teacher . . . [he] apparently used no teaching methods, as Taffanel and Hennebains had before him. He taught primarily by demonstration and through performance, but did not verbally elaborate . . . Gaubert was such a naturally gifted flutist that he may not have had to analyze why certain playing problems existed and the possible solutions for them.[48]

Gaubert's beautiful sound came naturally, and as Robert Hériché relates, he was unable to explain how to produce it. When a student asked him how he developed his tone, he quoted Taffanel: "Philippe, you have a lovely sound; look after it well!"[49]

Crunelle's own reminiscences accord with these descriptions:

> Gaubert was immensely, and naturally, gifted himself as a player and liked the very good students. He did not really understand problems with playing, did not explain very much, and was easily bored. He liked to hear students attempting really difficult things and could not be interested in working with a student on a Handel sonata.
>
> Crunelle said Gaubert was a tremendously busy man—and not just as a flute player. He really inclined more towards conducting and composing. There were always people wanting to see him during the class time, waiting for him to be free—he was very occupied with all sorts of musical matters.[50]

At the *concours* on June 25, 1920, thirteen flutists performed the required piece, Gaubert's *Fantaisie*, which had been written and published in 1912 and dedicated to Léopold Lafleurance. The work begins with a lyrical, quasi-improvisatory section followed by a scherzo, similar in style and difficulty to other *morceaux de concours* from the first two decades of the century. The members of the jury were:

Gabriel Fauré, chair
Guillaume Balay (1871–1943), composer
André Bloch (1873–1960), professor of harmony
Georges Corroyez (18–1950), composer

Louis Costes (1881–1932), principal clarinetist of the Orchestre de la
société des concerts du conservatoire

Edouard Flament (1880–1958), professor of bassoon

Fernand Gillet (1882–1980), principal oboist of the Concerts Lamoureux
and the Paris Opéra

Louis Hamburg (b. 1867), bassoonist in the Opéra-Comique

Marcel Moyse

Gabriel Parès (1862–1934), conductor of the Garde républicaine, the
French army band and orchestra

Paul Vidal (1863–1931), composer

Fernand Bourgeat (1851–1932), secretary general of the Conservatory.[51]

Le Ménestrel praised Gaston Crunelle as "an accomplished virtuoso who
by way of instant bravos earned the *prix d'excellence*."[52] This prize, only
awarded for a few years, meant that Crunelle received a unanimous vote
from the committee. Georges Boo, Marcel Welsch (b. 1893), and Alfred
Beuchat (b. 1899) also won first prizes. Second prizes were awarded to Pierre
Castel and Crunelle's sister, Suzanne, who would win a first prize in 1921.[53]
Robert Hériché, Armand Dubos, and Roger Désormière (1898–1963), later a
world-renowned conductor, garnered *premiers accessits*, and Achille Glizon
and Roger Cortet, who would take over Moyse's class at the Conservatory in
1949, received *seconds accessits*. *Le Figaro*, *Le Temps*, and *Le Monde musical*
also reported the results of the *concours*, and Jean Poeigh wrote in *Comœdia*,

> A magnificent bunch of thirteen flutes for the price of a dozen, presented
> by Mr. Ph. Gaubert, composer, moreover, of the competition piece. Among
> those who best captured the poetry and virtuosity of this *Fantaisie*, Mr.
> Gaston Crunelle proved himself to be the most accomplished of all and de-
> served the *prix d'excellence*.[54]

Crunelle was now ready to embark upon a career as a professional flutist.

3

Between Wars

Music in Paris

The year 1920 was a propitious time for a flutist bearing a first prize from the Conservatory to launch a career. For centuries, France had been the world's most centralized nation, with most of its cultural and economic resources in Paris. Between the two world wars, the city, whose population was second only to London in Europe, was a musical capital with a bewildering variety of offerings, rivaled only by Berlin.

At the center of musical life was opera, and the city hosted two major opera houses, both receiving substantial government support. The Paris Opéra, or Théâtre national de l'opéra, was founded by Louis XIV in 1669 and was the more prestigious, performing opera and ballet at the sumptuous Palais Garnier, which opened in 1875. The Théâtre national de l'opéra-comique, founded in 1714, performed in the smaller but lovely Salle Favart, which opened in 1898 and is a short walk from the Garnier.[1] The name of this latter company is misleading, as comic opera was only part of its repertoire, which overlapped that of the Paris Opéra. As a genre, *opéra-comique* simply means opera in French with spoken dialog, but the Opéra-Comique was not limited to this genre. Upon entering the Salle Favart, one is greeted by statues of Carmen and Manon, and these, along with a handful of other operas, were the bread and butter that attracted a loyal audience.[2] The Comique was also known for its ambitious programming and many world premieres, as opposed to the staid Opéra. Both houses presented several different operas each week from September through May. Other theaters, including the Gaîté-Lyrique and the Trianon-Lyrique, also presented opera and operettas. Ballet was well represented in Paris, with the Ballets russes, the Ballets suédois, the Ballets Ida Rubenstein, and the Opéra's own productions.

Paris hosted four major orchestras, each with roots in the nineteenth century, and each presented weekly concerts on Saturday and Sunday from September through May. The most respected was the Orchestre de la société des concerts du conservatoire, established in 1828.[3] The others, the Concerts Colonne, Concerts Pasdeloup, and the Orchestre Lamoureux, were named

Gaston Crunelle and Flute Playing in Twentieth-Century France. Leonard Garrison, Oxford University Press.
© Oxford University Press 2024. DOI: 10.1093/9780197778579.003.0003

for their founders. There were many shorter-lived orchestras, including the Concerts Koussevitsky (1921–28), the Orchestre des concerts Straram (1925–33), the Concerts Poulet (1926–32), the Orchestre symphonique de Paris (1928–39), and the Concerts Siohan (1929–36). The orchestras had to balance the popularity of the standard repertoire with the critics' insistence upon adventurous programming. The most popular composers, in order, were Wagner, Beethoven, Debussy, Mozart, and Ravel.[4]

Parisians were passionate about chamber music, and the most established series was the Société nationale de musique (SN), founded by Camille Saint-Saëns and others in 1871 with the goal of presenting French music; it existed until 1939 and was revived after World War II. In 1910, Gabriel Fauré, Maurice Ravel, and Charles Koechlin broke away from the SN to form the Société musicale indépendante, which regularly presented newer works by an international array of composers until 1935. With similar goals, La Sérénade was established in 1931 and Le Triton in 1932. In 1934, pianist and composer Pierre d'Arquennes (1907–2001) founded Le Triptyque with the support of Ravel, Dukas, and Roussel; this series aimed to promote young composers and performers, and presented 1,474 concerts through 2001. In addition, there were numerous independent chamber music concerts. Each of these societies typically presented programs with a great diversity of music, juxtaposing art songs, string quartets, instrumental solos, and even choral and orchestral music in various styles.

Some of the great French composers were active between the wars, including Vincent d'Indy (1851–1931), André Jolivet, Charles Koechlin (1867–1950), Olivier Messiaen (1908–1992), Gabriel Pierné (1863–1937), Maurice Ravel (1875–1937), Albert Roussel (1869–1937), and the group Les Six—Georges Auric (1899–1963), Louis Durey (1888–1979), Arthur Honegger (1892–1965), Darius Milhaud (1892–1974), Francis Poulenc (1899–1963), and Germaine Tailleferre (1892–1983). There was no common-practice style; new music could range from Neoclassical to Futurist.

Paris was also a magnet for composers from around the world: from America, George Antheil (1900–1959), Elliott Carter (1908–2012), Aaron Copland (1900–1990), George Gershwin (1898–1937), Roy Harris (1898–1979), Walter Piston (1894–1976), Roger Sessions (1896–1985), and Virgil Thompson (1896–1989); from England, Frederick Delius (1862–1934); from Brazil, Heitor Villa-Lobos (1887–1959); from Spain, Manuel de Falla (1876–1946), who was in Paris from 1907 until 1914; from Russia, Sergei Prokofiev (1891–1953), Sergei Rachmaninoff (1873–1943), Igor Stravinsky

(1882–1971), and Alexander Tcherepnin (1899–1977); from Czechoslovakia, Bohuslav Martinů (1890–1959)—and from Romania, George Enescu (known in France as Georges Enesco); not to mention francophone composers from Belgium and Switzerland. The city was also a haven for Black Americans, who had established a lively jazz scene during World War I.

There were many excellent concert halls of various sizes, including the Salle de l'ancien conservatoire at the original location of the Conservatory on rue Bergère, the Salle Berlioz at the newer Conservatory on rue de Madrid, the Théâtre du Châtelet, the Théâtre des Champs-Élysées, the Salle Pleyel (with its smaller halls, the Salle Chopin and the Salle Debussy), the Salle Gaveau, the Salle Cortot at the École normale de musique, the Salle Érard, the Salle des agriculteurs, and the Théâtre Mogador.

The city had been a center of early music since the nineteenth century. Fauré's *alma mater,* the École Niedermeyer, founded in 1853 as a revival of Choron's short-lived École de musique classique et religieuse (1818), based its curriculum on Gregorian chant and the choral music of Palestrina, Bach, and Victoria.[5] Vincent d'Indy established the Schola Cantorum of Paris in 1896 with the goal of reviving Gregorian chant and the polyphony of Palestrina. The Chanteurs de Saint Gervais performed sacred music from the Renaissance to the cantatas of Johann Sebastian Bach. In 1905, composer, conductor, and organist Gustave Bret (1875–1958) created the Bach Society of Paris (Société de J.-S. Bach) with the goal of performing the composer's complete works.[6] The society was based on others that existed in Germany and England, and co-founders included Bret's teacher Charles-Marie Widor (1844–1937), Alsatian musicologist, organist, philosopher, and humanitarian Albert Schweitzer (1875–1965), composer Paul Dukas (1865–1935), organist and composer Alexandre Guilmant (1837–1911), and Vincent d'Indy. Crunelle would be a frequent soloist with the Société de J.-S. Bach. Although she was Polish, Wanda Landowska (1879–1959), the main figure in the revival of the harpsichord, spent most of her career in France. In 1925, she founded the École de musique ancienne in Saint-Leu-la-Forêt in the northwestern suburbs of Paris and performed and taught there until 1940, when she moved to America to escape the Nazis.

Parisian churches have enjoyed an unrivaled tradition of great organists since the time of Louis Couperin (c.1626–1661) and François Couperin (1668–1733) at St. Gervais. Between the wars, organists included Widor and Marcel Dupré (1886–1971), who succeeded him at St. Sulpice, Charles Tournemire (1870–1939) and his assistant Jean Langlais (1907–1991) at

Ste. Clotilde, Louis Vierne (1870–1937) at Notre-Dame, Maurice Duruflé (1902–1986) at St. Étienne du Mont, Albert Alain (1880–1971) and his son Jehan Alain (1911–1940), who served as his assistant at St. Germain-en-Laye, Joseph Bonnet (1884–1944) at St. Eustache, Charles Quef (1873–1931) and Olivier Messiaen at La Trinité, and Henri Dallier (1849–1934) at La Madeleine.

There were regular radio broadcasts of operas and classical music concerts, and various newspapers announced their programs. Radio presented new opportunities for performing musicians but was blamed for the drop-off in attendance at live operas and concerts during the 1920s and 1930s.[7] Radio Tour Eiffel started broadcasting in 1921. Radiola started in 1922, becoming Radio-Paris in 1924, and Radio PTT (Les Postes, Télégraphes et Téléphones) was on the air between 1923 and 1940. In 1934, the Orchestre national de la radiodiffusion française was established. This would become a leading orchestra and since 1974 has been known as the Orchestre national de France. In 1937, PTT created the Orchestre radio-symphonique, which became the Orchestre philharmonique de Radio France in 1964.

Paris was also the home of many distinguished music publishers, including Billaudot, Choudens, Costallat, Durand, Eschig, Heugel, Leduc, Lemoine, Salabert, and Senart.

The general press covered musical events, but there were also twenty-nine music journals in 1917.[8] The weekly Guide du concert announced upcoming concerts and operas and offered a listeners' guide to some of them. Le Ménestrel, L'Art musical, and Le Monde musical were also weeklies with feature articles, concert reviews, and performance listings. Other widely read journals were Le Courrier musical and La Revue musicale. Comœdia was a daily newspaper focusing on the arts until the Occupation, when it appeared weekly. An impressive publication, the Annuaire des artistes et de l'enseignement dramatique et musical is witness to the plethora of musical activity in Paris and elsewhere in France. Running over a thousand pages and published from 1894 through 1929, it lists theaters with seating capacities, musical organizations and their personnel, music publishers, instrument makers, and even the addresses of musicians.

Paris was brimming with excellent flutists; the Annuaire listed 311 of them in 1926. Gaubert was becoming less active as a flutist because of his conducting and composing, but his students dominated the professional world. Moyse was principal flutist of the Orchestre de la société des concerts from 1919 to 1938, when Lucien Lavaillote (1898–1968), who had won a first prize in 1923, succeeded him; Lavaillote later served as principal flutist in the Opéra (1955–63). Crunelle's classmate Robert Hériché (1906–91) received a first prize in 1921 and became a flutist in the Paris Opéra. Fernand Caratgé (1902–91), first prize in 1924, was a flutist in the Opéra-Comique and Concerts Lamoureux. Fernand Dufrêne (1911–2000), first prize in 1927, was principal flutist in the Orchestre national de France. René Le Roy, who had earned a first prize in 1918 as a student of Lafleurance and had also studied with Hennebains and Gaubert, became active in chamber music. The older generation included Lafleurance, who played piccolo in the Opéra until 1947; Gaston Blanquart (1877–1962), first prize in 1898 with Taffanel and principal flutist of both the Opéra and Concerts Colonne; and Louis Fleury (1878–1926), first prize in 1900 under Taffanel and the dedicatee and first performer of Debussy's *Syrinx* for solo flute (1913).

Silent Films and Casinos

Crunelle's first professional experience was playing in orchestras in Parisian silent-movie houses,[9] which were considered "refuges of Conservatory first-prize winners."[10] He later told students that "the silent movie era represented a fortune, a financial golden age for musicians, because they played three times a day at the movie houses."[11] There were almost 200 Parisian cinemas listed in the *Annuaire*. The larger cinemas had house orchestras, and some of the orchestra directors were well known. Most orchestras had a collection of music appropriate for certain types of scenes, and the conductors provided "cue sheets" for each film.[12]

In 1920, the composer Louis Ganne heard Crunelle play principal flute in his operetta *Les Saltimbanques* ("The Acrobats"), which had been performed hundreds of times since its premiere on December 30, 1899.[13] Ganne hired him on the spot for his orchestra in Monte Carlo, and the young flutist then moved to Beausoleil, a less expensive community just outside Monaco. His monthly salary was 3,000 francs rather than the 820 francs he had received from the cinema.[14] The archives of the Orchestre philharmonique de Monte Carlo confirm that Crunelle played in the Concerts Louis Ganne from December 21, 1920 through April 15, 1921. He was often a soloist in such works as Ganne's *Andante et Scherzo*, Chaminade's Concertino, Godard's Suite, op. 116, Mouquet's *La Flûte de Pan*, and Widor's Suite, op. 34.

Crunelle's work in Monte Carlo gained him entry into lucrative performances at casinos and resorts, a main feature of his subsequent career.
In the *belle époque*, the period between the Franco-Prussian War and World
War I, these resorts built lavish theaters and concerts halls. Through the
1960s, they recruited the best musicians from all over France to perform
operas, orchestral concerts, and chamber music during the summer season
from May through September. The schedule was busy, and young musicians
learned a great deal of repertoire playing for European and American high
society.

The most prestigious summer employment for musicians was in Vichy,
which had hosted an orchestra since 1865.[15] Flutists who had played there
included piccolo virtuoso Eugène Damaré (1840–1919); composer of
Variations on the "Carnival of Venice," Paul-Agricole Génin (1832–1903);
principal flutist of the Boston Symphony, Charles Molé (1857–1905); and
later occupant of the same chair in Boston, Georges Laurent (1886–1964).
Crunelle was second solo flutist with the Orchestra of the Grand Casino
in Vichy from June 1 through September 30 in the 1921, 1922, and 1923
seasons. For these years, he earned 7,846, 7,408, and 7,983.50 francs, re-
spectively, almost $8,000 in today's dollars each summer.[16] The principal
flutist was René Bergeon (b. 1887), who had earned a first prize at the
Paris Conservatory under Paul Taffanel in 1906, the same year as Marcel
Moyse. During the winter season, Bergeon played at the Grand Théâtre in
Bordeaux.[17] At Vichy, each day there was an orchestra concert, a chamber
concert, and an opera, and the repertoire prepared Crunelle for his later
positions with the Orchestre Pasdeloup and the Opéra-Comique. The director of the opera orchestra was Paul Bastide (1879–1962), a composer
who also conducted the opera in Strasbourg, and the conductor of the orchestra concerts was Pierre Sechiari (1877–1932), a violinist in the Concerts
Lamoureux who had founded the Sechiari String Quartet and conducted
his own series of concerts in Paris.

Unique among second wind players, Crunelle appeared as a soloist in
Vichy on the following occasions:[18]

June 30, 1921: Chaminade's Concertino and one movement from Godard's
    Suite, Op. 116
July 18, 1921: First movement of Mozart's Concerto No. 1 in G Major
July 29, 1921: Gaubert's *Trois Aquarelles*

August 12, 1921: Berlioz's "Trio of the Young Israelites" from *L'Enfance du Christ*

August 23, 1921: Fantasy on Meyerbeer's *Étoile du nord*

September 30, 1921: Berlioz's "Trio of the Young Israelites" from *L'Enfance du Christ*

June 28, 1922: Berlioz's "Trio of the Young Israelites" from *L'Enfance du Christ*

July 20, 1922: Fantasy on Meyerbeer's *Étoile du nord*

August 23, 1922: "Idylle" and "Allegretto" from Godard's Suite, Op. 116

Le Figaro reported that Crunelle performed chamber music for the Concerts Louis Ganne at the Monte Carlo Casino on January 12 and March 5, 1923,[19] and he was a soloist at the casino in Dieppe in September 1924.[20] Forging what was to become his most important artistic partnership, Crunelle was co-soloist with harpist Pierre Jamet (1893–1991) in Mozart's Concerto for Flute and Harp, K. 299, with Walther Straram[21] conducting at the Évian-les-Bains Casino in August 1926.[22] In August and September of 1930, he was a flute soloist with the orchestra at the Bellevue Casino in Biarritz.[23] In 1934, Opéra-Comique director Pierre-Barthélemy Guesi, in a letter to his supervisor, expressed dismay that Crunelle had not returned from the summer season at the casinos for the beginning of the opera season in Paris.[24]

Meanwhile, back in Paris in May 1922, Crunelle had auditioned for the position of principal flutist in the Paris Opéra; the other candidates included familiar names: André Delaître (first prize from the Paris Conservatory, 1918), Jean Boulze (1890–1969), Marcel Moyse, Bernard Depannemacker, Pierre or André Castel, Gaston Blanquart, Edmond Blanchard, and René Grisard. Moyse won the audition but decided to remain principal flutist in the Opéra-Comique, so the Opéra position was given to Jean Boulze, who had earned a first prize at the Conservatory in 1910 as a student of Hennebains.[25]

At that time, Crunelle lived at 3bis rue Bleue in the ninth arrondissement of Paris, and on June 24, the twenty-three-year-old married Raymonde Jeanne, née Martinet at the *Mairie* (town hall) of the Sixth Arrondissement.[26] They may have met at the Conservatory. Raymonde was Parisian and had received a second prize in the viola *concours* on June 21. Two years later in 1924, she received a first prize as a student of Maurice Vieux (1884–1951). In 1925, she gave birth to their only child, Éliane.[27] She was to play in the Orchestre Pasdeloup with Gaston.

Concerts Pasdeloup

Pianist and conductor Jules Pasdeloup (1819–1887), who had been an assistant conductor at the Opéra-Comique, founded the Concerts populaires in 1861. At the time, the Orchestre de la société des concerts du conservatoire, the main orchestra in Paris, brought symphonic music to a relatively small audience, as its hall, the Salle du conservatoire, seated just under a thousand. Pasdeloup's goal was to introduce orchestral music to a larger public, so the orchestra initially played in the Cirque d'hiver, a circus arena seating five thousand. The concerts quickly became a staple of Parisian life. The orchestra ceased performances in 1884, and film producer Serge Sandberg (1879–1981) revived the series in 1919 with Rhené-Baton (1879–1940) as music director. In January 1921, the organization become the Association des concerts Pasdeloup, giving the musicians control of artistic and administrative decisions.[28]

On October 16, 1924, the orchestra held an audition for principal flute, which Crunelle, then aged twenty-six, won with a unanimous vote (see Figure 3). The other candidates were Léon Blanc, Georges Boo, Pierre Castel, André Delaître, Robert Hériché, Alphonse Kenvyn, Jean Rambeaud, and Paul Samson. Through most of Crunelle's years, André Castel played second flute and Oscar Delettre played piccolo. By the 1940s the piccolo player was Georges Kenvyn. Until he left in 1945, Crunelle was a star of the orchestra, frequently singled out by critics and often appearing as soloist. The orchestra performed world premieres of many works, hosted world-class soloists, and made numerous recordings. Crunelle played under two music directors, Rhené-Baton, who served from 1919 through 1933, and Albert Wolf (1884–1970), who served from 1933 through 1970. He also played under many guest conductors, including Eugène Bozza, Gustave Bret, André Caplet, Gustave Cloëz, Piero Coppola, Claude Delvincourt, Massimo Freccia, Philippe Gaubert, Vladimir Golschmann, Reynaldo Hahn, Désiré-Émile Inghelbrecht, Fausto Magnani, Henri Rabaud, Manuel Rosenthal, and Robert Siohan. The orchestra's main halls were the Théâtre Mogador (1924–28), the Théâtre des Champs-Élysées (1928–34), the Salle Pleyel (1934–40), and the Salle Gaveau after 1940. Robert Hériché related that Crunelle was a member of the orchestra's board.[29]

The weekly concerts of the 1924–25 season started on October 26 with a program featuring the Overture to *Benvenuto Cellini* by Berlioz, *The Sorcerer's Apprentice* by Dukas, the Symphony in D Minor by Franck, and the world premiere of the *Concerto Franco-Américain* by Jean Wiéner (1896–1982), a mélange of jazz, blues, ragtime, waltzes, polkas, and Bach-inspired counterpoint. On November 28 and December 27, Crunelle was soloist in Debussy's *Prelude to the Afternoon of a Faun*, and in *Le Ménestrel*, Jean Lobrot wrote that he "achieved personal success."[30] He would perform the *Faun* at least a dozen times with the Pasdeloup Orchestra.

The orchestra also played the Suite No. 2 from Ravel's *Daphnis et Chloë* with its extended flute solo more than a dozen times during Crunelle's tenure.[31] René Brancour wrote of the 1931 performance, "Let us praise Mr. Crunelle, whose agile and limpid flute sang so agreeably."[32]

Crunelle was a frequent soloist in Bach's works. On January 10–11, 1925, he performed the Orchestral Suite No. 2 in B Minor, BWV 1067, in a concert conducted by Rhené-Baton. Jean Lobrot wrote in *Le Ménestrel*, "Mr. Crunelle played the flute solo part in a remarkable way. Incidentally, it seemed rather difficult, which excuses certain badly placed breaths."[33] Maurice Boucher reported in *Le Monde musical*, "Mr. Crunelle, who had left his flute chair to offer us the exquisite gifts of the Suite in B Minor more directly, fervently dispensed this eternal richness."[34] He was again a soloist in Bach's Suite on January 29, 1927, when Jean Lobrot praised him: "Bach's Suite in B minor, with flute solo, found in Mr. Crunelle a very skillful interpreter endowed with a fine quality of sound, which earned him a very lively personal success."[35] The piece was repeated on February 16, 1936, November 29, 1936, January 12, 1941, and May 18, 1941. He also played the Bach Suite at an independent concert called "Strings and Winds" on April 26, 1926.[36] Crunelle often appeared as a soloist in Bach's Brandenburg Concertos Nos. 2, 4, and 5[37] and the Concerto in F Major, BWV 1057, the composer's own arrangement of his Brandenburg Concerto No. 4 for two flutes, keyboard, and orchestra, which the Pasdeloup performed on October 30, 1938:

> The Concerto in F major—properly delicious in the classical sense—was heavenly. Albert Lévêque, on the keyboard, competes in grace and purity with the flutes of Crunelle and [André] Castel, in arabesques and divine curves."[38]

Crunelle would record the Concerto in F Major with Jean-Pierre Rampal and pianist Céliny Chailley-Richez in 1953 (see Appendix 1). *Comœdia* noted Crunelle's obbligato solos in Bach's B Minor Mass on December 14, 1930.[39] He established an artistic relationship with Bach specialist Gustave Bret, who conducted the Pasdeloup on December 31, 1932, when Crunelle was a soloist for the Brandenburg Concerto No. 5. Crunelle performed as a soloist with Bret's Société J.-S. Bach in performances of the B Minor Mass on December 3, 1937 and the *Magnificat* on November 13, 1936 and December 17, 1937 at the Église Étoile.[40] With Bret, he recorded Bach's "Peasant Cantata" No. 212, *Mer hahn en neue Oberkeet*, in 1934 (see Appendix 1). Another Bach recording was the aria "Esurientes, implevit bonis" from the *Magnificat* in 1938. Maurice Imbert wrote that "Mr. Crunelle was highly appreciated" in his performance of the flute obbligato in "Frohe Hirten" from Bach's *Christmas Oratorio* with the Pasdeloup on December 19, 1938.[41]

Mendelssohn's Scherzo from *A Midsummer's Night's Dream* became a signature work in Crunelle's repertoire. René Brancour wrote of his performance on October 10, 1925, "The adorable 'Scherzo' of *A Midsummer Night's Dream* was struck up with all the indispensable lightness and suppleness, and Mr. Crunelle's flute inserted his notes of crystalline purity in the most agreeable way."[42] The orchestra repeated the piece on November 22 and on Christmas Day as an encore.[43] On December 3, 1927, Jean Loriot noted, "The aerial 'Scherzo' from Mendelssohn's *A Midsummer Night's Dream* was perfectly executed as far as the woodwinds (and especially Mr. Crunelle) were concerned."[44] The piece was performed again on February 5, 1933.

Audiences were enthusiastic about Crunelle as a soloist in Rimsky-Korsakov's *Flight of the Bumblebee*.[45] After a 1930 concert, which featured the first public appearance of the *ondes Martenot,* a new electronic instrument, *Le Ménestrel* reported:

> The *Overture on Greek Themes* by Glazunov, the *Unfinished Symphony* by Borodin, the *Flight of the Bumblebee* by Rimsky-Korsakov (which the public demanded as an encore, and which earned the solo flutist, Mr. Crunelle, a great personal success), and sections from the *Coq d'Or* had preceded the performance by the *ondes.*[46]

Given Crunelle's success with the solo, he is probably the soloist on the orchestra's 1928 Pathé recording, although the Pathé catalogs for 1929 and 1933 do not credit him (see Appendix 1).

In at least one Pasdeloup concert, on March 21, 1937, Crunelle, along with second flutist André Castel and harpist Pierre Jamet, performed the "Trio of the Young Israelites" from Berlioz's *Enfance du Christ* "to ravishing delight"[47] He had performed this several times in Vichy.

During Crunelle's years, the Orchestre Pasdeloup presented many premieres, including the following:

Maurice Ravel, *Le Tombeau de Couperin* (1929)
Désiré-Émile Inghelbrecht, *Sinfonia breve da camera* (1930)
Darius Milhaud, Piano Concerto No. 1 (1931)
Albert Roussel, Symphony No. 4 (1935)
Marcel Landowski, *Rhythmes du monde* (1941)
Marcel Landowski, Piano Concerto No. 1 (1942)
Jean Martinon, Symphony No. 2 (1944)

The Pasdeloup recorded only one of those works, Inghelbrecht's *Sinfonia breve da camera*. The orchestra made many recordings with Inghelbrecht (1880–1965) and Piero Coppola (1888–1971), and those with prominent flute solos are listed in Appendix 1. Inghelbrecht also recorded a series of works with an unidentified orchestra, and his recording of the Entr'acte to Act II of *Carmen* identifies Crunelle as the soloist. *Le Temps* remarked, "The performance of the *Carmen* interlude, with its famous flute solo, well executed here by Mr. Crunelle, is to be praised."[48]

The Concerts Pasdeloup occasionally featured chamber music, and Michel-Léon Hirsch wrote of their concert on March 4, 1939, "Messieurs Crunelle, Debondue,[49] Vacellier,[50] Plessis[51] [*sic*], and Richard,[52] the valiant soloists of the orchestra, presented themselves as infallible jousters, with Jacques Ibert's *Trois Pièces brèves.*"[53]

Chamber Music

Alongside his orchestral duties, chamber music became increasingly important to Crunelle's career, culminating in his performances with the Quintette Pierre Jamet (QPJ) after 1940. In the interwar period, he collaborated with leading Parisian musicians, appearing on programs for the major music societies and in other concerts. On January 20, 1926, in the Salle Pleyel, he and violist Étienne Ginot (1901–1978), who had recently married Crunelle's sister Suzanne and was to become Crunelle's colleague in the QPJ, played with harpist Suzanne Stell on her recital featuring Debussy's Sonata for Flute, Viola, and Harp (1915), the first time he performed this piece in public. Also on the program was Handel's Sonata in B Minor arranged for flute and harp.[54]

Crunelle, Ginot, and Stell were co-soloists for a concert broadcast by Radio Tour Eiffel on February 9, 1927, presumably performing the same Debussy Sonata.[55]

With soprano Marthe Brega[56] on January 11, 1927, in the Salle Pleyel, Crunelle played in one of the earliest performances of Ravel's *Chansons madécasses* (1925–26). Paul Bertrand wrote,

> We must praise the talent as an accompanist of Mr. Maurice Jaubert and also of Mr. Marcel Delannoy and pay tribute to the high value of Mr. Crunelle and Gaston Marchesini,[57] who shone in the accompaniment of the *Chansons madécasses*.[58]

In March of the same year, he performed Ravel's *Introduction and Allegro* (1905) with harpist Micheline Kahn (1889–1987), clarinetist Louis Cahuzac,[59] and the Krettly Quartet.[60] Kahn, professor of harp at the École normale de musique, had played the premiere of Ravel's work in 1907.

On April 3, 1930, a festival of music by Heitor Villa-Lobos in the Salle Gaveau included the world premieres of the difficult *Quintette en forme de chôros,* W. 231 (1928) and the *Quarteto simbolico,* W. 181 (1921) for flute, alto saxophone, celeste, and female voices:

> A *Quintet* for flute, oboe, English horn, clarinet, and bassoon, performed by Messieurs Crunelle, Mercier,[61] Brun,[62] Cahuzac, and Lenom,[63] produced an effect of somewhat disconcerting harshness, perhaps because the rhythmic element ceased to be so clearly delineated. On the other hand, a Quartet for harp, celesta, flute, saxophone, and female voices, performed for the first time, again testified to a great rhythmic richness, an extreme variety of impressions, without, moreover, focusing on musical structure. The sound balance is remarkable, and the beginning of the second piece, in particular, gives an extraordinary impression of fullness. It was performed by Mesdames Micheline Kahn and Denise Cools, Messieurs Crunelle, Mule,[64] and the Nivard Chorale.[65]

For the Société nationale (SN), Crunelle played in the first performance of Piero Coppola's *Cinq Chansons françaises des xi et xvii siècles* for flute, clarinet, trumpet, string quartet, and piano on February 25, 1933, in the Salle Chopin.[66] On May 7, 1934, he played a trio for flute, cello, and piano on a concert of works by Belgian composer Armand Merck (1883–1962).[67] Then, on

June 8, he played the Nonet by Hungarian composer Tibor Harsanyi (1898–1954) at a concert of Le Triton at the École normale.[68] Crunelle was listed as a soloist in a "Festival Saint-Saëns" featuring the *Carnival of the Animals* on December 14, 1935 in the Salle d'Iéna.[69]

In 1936, Crunelle performed several chamber music concerts in the Salle Chopin. On January 11, he made another appearance at the SN, performing the *Rhapsodie,* op. 70 (1922) by Belgian composer Joseph Jongen (1873–1953) with Roland Lamorlette,[70] oboe, Auguste Périer,[71] clarinet, Gustave Dhérin,[72] bassoon, Jean Devémy,[73] horn, and Marie-Antoinette Pradier, piano. They repeated this performance for the Société Claude de France in Avignon a week later.[74] The Quatuor français Maurice Blondel presented a concert on March 19, collaborating with Crunelle in the Beethoven Serenade, op. 25 for flute, violin, and viola and a Mozart flute quartet.[75] There were two concerts that year with the theme, "Paysages et musique," each devoted to composers from a region of France. Normandy came first on March 25, with Crunelle performing Duruflé's *Prélude, récitatif et variations,* op. 3 with pianist Hélène Pignari-Salles[76] and violist Pierre Pasquier.[77] At the December 10 concert, "Paysages et musique" was dedicated to the music of two composers from the southwest, Fauré and Gaubert, and the latter was

> welcomed with warm applause. The subsequent musical part assembled a host of renowned artists . . . The flutist Mr. G. Crunelle who, with the talented collaboration of the remarkable pianist Mille. Irène Aïtoff,[78] showcased the First Sonata.[79]

The "renowned artists" also included soprano Lisa Daniels and the Trio Pasquier.[80]

On March 8, 1937, Le Triton presented a program featuring the *Sept Haï-kaïs* (1924) by Maurice Delage (1879–1961). Conducted by Louis Aubert,[81] the performers were soprano Madeleine Grey,[82] Crunelle, oboist Roland Lamorlette, clarinetist André Vacellier, and the Quatuor Calvet.[83] In his review, Henry Barraud praised the wind players, "the top of the Parisian orchestras,"[84] an indication of Crunelle's esteem at the time. On March 28, 1938, Crunelle played Pierné's *Sonata da camera* with cellist Charles Bartsch[85] and pianist Giuseppe Benvenuti[86] for Le Triton at the École normale de musique "to great success."[87]

In 1939, Crunelle was busy with chamber music. In a precursor of his work for the QPJ, he gave the premiere of *Marionettes,* op. 26 (1937) by

Laszlo Lajtha (1892–1963) on March 20 for Le Triton at the École normale de musique. His collaborating artists were violinist Janine Andrade,[88] violist Alice Merckel,[89] cellist Charles Bartsch, and harpist Micheline Kahn. Florent Schmitt wrote in *Le Temps*, "The interpreters were able to render all the flavor wonderfully."[90] Lajtha was a Hungarian composer, conductor, and ethnomusicologist who studied with Zoltán Kodály in Budapest and then in Paris with Vincent d'Indy. He was active in Paris from 1932 to 1939 and a member of Le Triton's board; he would write two pieces for the QPJ. His music shows the influence of Bartók. On the same program, Crunelle performed Albert Roussel's Trio for flute, viola, and cello with Merckel and Bartsch. The Institut international de coopération intellectuelle presented a concert, "International Friendships" ("Amitiés internationales"), on April 27, and Crunelle performed *Three Pieces* by Dutch composer Rosy Wertheim (1888–1949) with Dutch Jewish pianist Iskar Aribo (1908–1999).[91] On May 3, he played a *Suite en forme de trio* by André Lermyte (1882–1963) with oboist Roland Larmorlette and Pierre Jamet at the SN. The same performers were scheduled to give the premiere of a trio by Pierre Vellones[92] for the Cercle musical de Paris on May 17 at the Salle Debussy, but "as an accident happened to Jamet's harp, we were deprived of the pleasure of hearing the Trio."[93] Subsequently, Vellones became ill, and they played the piece for him on his sickbed before he died on July 17.[94] A dance recital on June 13 featured Crunelle in Debussy's *Syrinx* and—no surprise—the *Flight of the Bumblebee*. With pianist Cécile Cormier, he played a sonata by Haydn.[95]

In sum, Crunelle in the interwar years often played with the most prestigious chamber musicians in Paris in a great span of repertoire.

The Opéra-Comique

Marcel Moyse resigned as principal flutist of the Opéra-Comique in 1933. Crunelle won the audition as his replacement and was hired on July 1.[96] He served in this position until 1964. Hériché relates that Crunelle also served as president of the Social Insurance for Artists Committee at the Opéra-Comique.[97] At first, the flute section consisted of Crunelle, Eugène Portré, who had often substituted when Moyse was away, and Albert Manouvrier (b. 1896), who received his first prize with Hennebains in 1915. In 1939, Fernand Caratgé replaced Portré, and then in 1951, the section expanded to include Jean Chefnay, who won his first prize the same year as Crunelle, in 1920.

Crunelle played under music directors Paul Bastide (1932–36), Eugène Bigot (1936–44), and André Cluytens (1947–53), and many guest conductors. He performed the most popular operas, especially *Carmen* and *Manon*, hundreds of times. During these years, the Opéra-Comique presented premieres of works by Milhaud, Ibert, Roussel, Barraud, André Bloch, and others, many forgotten today.

Crunelle's first season opened on October 15, 1933, with three Rossini operas: *The Barber of Seville, Cinderella*, and *The Italian Girl in Algiers*, all conducted by Tullio Serafin (1878–1968) with singers from La Scala including mezzo-soprano Conchita Supervía (1895–1936), contralto Ebe Ticozzi (1896–1977), tenors Dino Borgioli (1891–1960) and Nino Ederle (1892–1951), baritones Ernesto Badini (1876–1937) and Riccardo Stracciari (1875–1955), and basses Vincenzo Bettoni (1881–1954) and Carlo Scattola (1878–1947).[98] Throughout Crunelle's tenure, the schedule averaged thirty services a month, and there were seldom rehearsals for standard repertoire, only for premieres.[99] He later told his students:

> Quite often I encountered a score I had never seen, and that taught me a lot about my job, to build up a whole bunch of reflexes but also to find fingering systems that make note sequences easier.[100]

During the next three decades, the Opéra-Comique saw much change and instability. Both opera houses had financial difficulties in the 1930s due to the Great Depression,[101] waning ticket sales, and insufficient government support. There was a general strike at the Opéra-Comique in 1936, and in 1939, the financing and direction of the Opéra-Comique and the Paris Opéra were merged into the Réunion des théâtres lyriques nationaux, with Jacques Rouché (1862–1957), previously director of the Opéra, in charge.

Radio Broadcasts

Radio broadcasts of classical music grew throughout the 1920s and 1930s and regularly featured the Pasdeloup Orchestra. As a soloist or chamber musician, Crunelle performed several times on radio during this period. *Le Temps* announced a concert on Radio Tour Eiffel on May 2, 1923, featuring "Mme. Bertelli de l'Opéra," Gaston and Suzanne Crunelle, flute, Louis Gromer,[102] oboe, and Mme Gromer, piano. Tour Eiffel again broadcast

Crunelle on January 9, 1935, playing a concert of the Société Claude de France. The program included the *Tarantella* for flute, clarinet, and piano by Saint-Saëns. Other musicians included pianist Marie-Antoinette Pradier, oboist Roland Lamorlette, clarinetist Auguste Périer, and hornist Jean Devémy.[103] The same Société broadcast a concert on July 15, 1936 on the radio station Poste Parisienne, when Crunelle played with a similar group including Pradier, Lamorlette, and Devémy, but now with clarinetist Ulysse Delécluse[104] and bassoonist Gustave Dhérin.[105] On October 2, he performed Duruflé's *Prélude, récitatif, et variations,* op. 3 with violist Pierre Pasquier and pianist Hélène Pignari-Salles on Radio Tour Eiffel.[106] On February 27, 1937, Crunelle was a soloist in Gluck's *Dance of the Blessed Spirits* for a concert organized by the Association des journalistes parlementaires and conducted by Robert Krettly, also broadcast on Radio Tour Eiffel.[107] A program called "A Half-Hour of Composers," broadcast on Paris PTT on April 5, 1937, featured works by Hector Fraggi (1882–1944). Crunelle and the composer performed a Nocturne; also featured were harpsichordist Corradina Mola (1896–1948), soprano Germaine Corney (1901–2001), and tenor Jean Planel (1903–1986).[108]

Recordings and Crunelle's Style

Between 1924 and the outbreak of World War II, Crunelle made twelve recordings of solo and chamber music on 78 rpm (see Appendix 1). As a principal flutist in a major orchestra, he had already built a reputation, and his first recordings identify him as soloist of the Concerts Pasdeloup. His solo repertoire was typical of the lighter music favored by flutists of the era, including transcriptions of Chopin and Gluck, starting with Taffanel's arrangement of the Sicilienne from Gluck's opera *Armide,* which Hennebains had recorded in 1908. Crunelle's brilliant recording of Taffanel's arrangement of Chopin's "Minute Waltz" is like Hennebains', with a full and penetrating low register but without such an extreme *rubato*. Showcasing his lightening technique, Crunelle made two recordings of the *Badinerie* by Pierre Camus[109] in 1928 and 1933, the only ones from the 78-rpm era. A rarity is his performance of the *Vision* by Hedwige Chrétien (1859–1944), a pianist and composer who taught solfège at the Paris Conservatory and composed 250 works. Évette & Schaeffer published *Vision* in 1920, but it is out of print today, and her music is mostly forgotten. The piece is charming *salon* music. Its main theme begins with an ascending octave, exactly anticipating the warm-up that Crunelle advocated in later years, connecting his rich low register to upper notes spinning with vibrato. He continued to perform the piece for at least the next two decades (see Chapter 5).

Crunelle recorded the "Idylle" from Godard's *Suite de trois morceaux*, op. 116 in 1933; Moyse had recorded it in 1929. Whereas Crunelle's tone is alluring, Moyse's sound has theatrical urgency and never relaxes. Crunelle's *rubato* is understated—he takes time at phrase endings and at harmonic turns, but Moyse pushes forward, even losing his pianist at several points.

One of Crunelle's best recordings of this period was of the "*Scène des Champs-Elysées*," or "Dance of the Blessed Spirits" from Gluck's opera, *Orpheus and Eurydice*. The record was made in 1933–34 with Gustave Cloëz (1890–1970) conducting an orchestra identified only as the "Paris Philharmonic." Cloëz frequently conducted both opera and ballet at the Opéra-Comique from 1922 through the 1940s and made numerous recordings of orchestral and operatic repertoire. He guest-conducted all four major Parisian orchestras. Crunelle's playing shows mastery of shapely phrasing and expressive nuances.

Already admired for his performances of Bach's music, Crunelle made important connections to the early music movement during the 1930s. Fleeing the Nazis, the eminent Jewish musicologist Curt Sachs (1881–1959) left Germany and moved to Paris in 1933, founding the *Anthologie sonore* series of recordings, bringing to light music from the Middle Ages through the eighteenth century. The recordings were issued in France until the mid-1950s, and Crunelle played in five of these releases, beginning with a set of medieval dances on flute and piccolo in 1935 and Johann Christian Bach's Quintet in D Major, W.B. 75 in 1937. The modern approach to early music based on resurrection of historical performance practices had not yet affected French performers, and Crunelle's style, with its intense vibrato, seems Romantic to twenty-first-century ears.

Crunelle's interpretation was always unaffected, an approach that respects "the honesty of the text in relation to what the composer wrote."[110] His straightforward approach recalls Louis Fleury's description of Taffanel's playing:

> Taffanel's artistry was essentially refined, supple and sensitive, and his prodigious virtuosity was made as little apparent as possible. He hated ostentation, followed the printed text with absolute respect, and the fluid flexibility

of his playing concealed an absolute rigor in the observance of tempo and rhythm.[111]

Crunelle's student Jean Étienne, who would become professor of flute at the Rouens Conservatory, admired his "extraordinary musicality."[112] Maxence Larrieu commented,

> I think that he had certain elegance in interpretation while being faithful to the text. And I think that what was very important, what he made us understand, is to let the music have its own personality.[113]

Jean-Pierre Rampal also mentioned Crunelle's elegance while comparing him to his colleague in the Opéra-Comique, Fernand Caratgé:

> Caratgé and Crunelle formed a perfectly complementary pair of influences on my musical progress. They both played beautifully, but completely differently. Caratgé had an integrity of style and a seriousness in total contrast to Crunelle's more elegant, poetic playing, which had both an allure and a chicness that was exciting."[114]

Crunelle's tone was clear and captivating. He encouraged his students to play with intensity, which was an attribute of his own playing. Typical of the early twentieth century, he employed a fast vibrato, but it is less prominent than in Moyse's playing. Unlike Moyse, who often played very sharp, Crunelle performed with accurate intonation, although at times slightly flat.[115] His sound was smaller than that of modern players, with the embouchure hole more covered, because the halls were smaller and because he played chamber music, whereas later soloists like Rampal and Galway often played concertos with orchestra.[116] According to Michel Debost, "His way of playing was rather tight, very delicate, very spinning in the high register and a little punchy in the low register,"[117] and Edward Beckett described Crunelle's tone as "brilliant" and "thin, very sweet, the result of a very tight embouchure."[118] Despite its apparent thinness, his sound carried easily: "Up close, there was a lot of air, and a few meters away it was superb, very tense, very alive."[119]

Early in his career, Crunelle, like virtually all professional flutists of his era in France, probably played a Louis Lot flute. At some point, he started using a silver-plated, closed-hole flute with raised keys and an offset G, C foot, and C-sharp trill key by Couesnon, for which he was an official artist, and encouraged his students to play the same instrument. Marcel Moyse designed this model in the 1930s. More resonant and technically superior American and Japanese flutes were not yet available, and the older flutes were more difficult to play in tune.

Crunelle's life would change dramatically in the 1940s, but before we explore his later career, we need to trace the history of the Quintette instrumental de Paris.

4

The Quintette instrumental de Paris

From the 1920s through the midsixties, the Quintette instrumental de Paris (QIP), consisting of flute, violin, viola, cello, and harp, was one of the most prominent chamber groups in France. The Quintette dominated the Parisian chamber music series, performing 1,800 concerts in Paris and on tour in France, Belgium, Czechoslovakia, England, Germany, Holland, Italy, Poland, Spain, Switzerland, Yugoslavia, northern Africa, the United States, and Canada. The QIP also appeared on national broadcasts, recorded 78-rpm and LP records, and commissioned around fifty works, bequeathing a sumptuous repertoire (see Appendix 2). In addition to the individual members' excellent musicianship, the ensemble's success was assured by its impresario, Madeleine de Valmalète (1899–1999), a well-connected pianist.[1] Saint-Saëns praised her, she played concertos under the direction of Gabriel Pierné, Wilhelm Furtwängler, and Arturo Toscanini, and she taught at the École normale de musique in Paris. Her brother, Marcel de Valmalète, founded the Bureau de Concerts Valmalète in 1924, and it was the largest management agency for classical musicians in Europe, eventually launching the career of Jean-Pierre Rampal.

Over time, there were several iterations of the QIP; Table 4.1 lists the musicians and their years of service. All of these musicians held first prizes from the Paris Conservatory. René Bas (b. 1894) and Pierre Grout (b. 1892) were members of the Orchestre de la société des concerts du conservatoire, and Bas was also in the Opéra-Comique. Roger Boulmé (1899–1942) was principal cellist of the Concerts Colonne. Marcel Grandjany (1891–1975) was professor of harp at the Fontainebleau Summer School and later at the Montreal Conservatory and at the Juilliard School.

René Le Roy

Flutist René Le Roy founded the QIP in 1922. He already had a track record as a soloist and chamber musician with the Société nationale de musique

Gaston Crunelle and Flute Playing in Twentieth-Century France. Leonard Garrison, Oxford University Press.
© Oxford University Press 2024. DOI: 10.1093/9780197778579.003.0004

Table 4.1 Musicians of the Quintette instrumental de Paris

Flute	Violin	Viola	Cello	Harp
René Le Roy (1922–40)	René Bas (1922–65)	Pierre Grout (1922–40)	Roger Boulmé (1922–40)	Marcel Grandjany (1922–24)
				Pierre Jamet (1924–58)
Gaston Crunelle (1940–65)		Étienne Ginot (1940–45)	Marcel Frècheville (1940–45)	
		Georges Blanpain (1945–58)	Robert Krabansky (1945–63)	
		Pierre Ladhuie (1959–65)	Michel Tournus (1965)	Bernard Galais (1959–65)

(SN) and the Société musicale indépendante (SMI) and was a successor to Paul Taffanel in the wind quintet he founded. Many solo works were dedicated to him, including Arthur Honegger's *Danse de la chèvre* (1921) and Jean Rivier's *Oiseaux tendres* (1935), and he recorded widely. He became an influential teacher, publishing the *Traité de la flûte, historique, technique et pédagogique* (1966). Among his students were Geoffrey Gilbert (1914–1989), who brought the French style of playing to the United Kingdom and the United States, and Claude Dorgeuille (1929–2009), a psychoanalyst and amateur flutist whose book *The French Flute School* portrays Le Roy as the true heir of Taffanel, Gaubert, and Moyse.

Debussy as Inspiration

The timbral possibilities of flute, viola, and harp in Debussy's Sonata (1915) inspired Le Roy to establish the QIP. Debussy was not the first composer to explore this instrumentation—Théodore Dubois wrote a brief *Terzetto* for the same instruments in 1905—but Debussy used the instrumental colors in novel ways. He briefly considered combining flute, oboe, and harp as an homage to the French Baroque trio sonata, replacing the harpsichord with harp, but later changed the oboe to a viola.[2] Early performances are detailed in Table 4.2.

It may seem curious that the world premiere took place in America, but the Boston Symphony at that time was dominated by French musicians,

Table 4.2 Early performances of Debussy's Sonata for Flute, Viola, and Harp

Date	Location	Musicians
November 7, 1916 (world premiere)	Longy Club, Jordan Hall, Boston	Arthur Brooke, flute; Florian Robert Wittmann, viola; and Theodore Cella, harp[a]
December 10, 1916	Private performance at the home of Debussy's publisher Jacques Durand	Albert Manouvrier, flute; Darius Milhaud, viola; and Jeanne Dalliès, harp
February 2, 1917	Aeolian Hall, London	Albert Fransella, flute; H. Waldo Warner, viola; and Miriam Timothy, harp[b]
March 9, 1917 (first public performance in France)[c]	Salle (à manger) Laurent, Paris	Albert Manouvrier, flute; Sigismond Jarecki, viola; and Pierre Jamet, harp
April 21, 1917	Salle des agriculteurs, Société musicale independent (SMI)	Albert Manouvrier, flute; Sigismond Jarecki, viola; and Jeanne Dalliès, harp[d]
November 22, 1921	Salle Érard	René Le Roy, flute; Robert Siohan, viola; and Marcel Grandjany, harp
December 15, 1922	Salle Érard	René Le Roy, flute; Robert Siohan, viola; and Marcel Grandjany, harp
December 1923	Strasbourg	René Le Roy, flute; Pierre Grout, viola; and Pierre Jamet, harp

[a] François Lesure, *Claude Debussy* (Paris: Fayard, 2003), p. 564. English-born Arthur Brooke (1866–1950) was the Assistant Principal Flute of the Boston Symphony Orchestra from 1909 to 1923. He wrote the popular *Modern Method for Flute* (Boston: Cundy-Bettoney, 1912). Born in Austria, Florian Robert Wittmann (1877–1941) played viola in the Boston Symphony from 1913 to 1920. Theodore Cella (1896–1960) was the harpist of the Boston Symphony from 1915 to 1920.

[b] Kenneth Thompson, "First Performance?" *The Musical Times* 109 (October 1968): p. 914. Fransella (1865–1935) was a flutist in various Dutch and British orchestras, prominent recording artist, and Professor of Flute at the Guildhall School of Music in London.

[c] François Lesure, *Catalogue de l'œuvre de Claude Debussy* (Geneva: Éditions Minkoff, 1977), p. 145.

[d] Lesure, *Catalogue de l'œuvre de Claude Debussy*, p. 145. That spring, there was also a private performance at the home of the Marquise de Clermont-Tonnerre in Passy, but the performers are not known. Debussy declined to attend. François Lesure, *Claude Debussy: A Critical Biography*, tr. Marie Rolf (Rochester, NY: University of Rochester Press, 2019), p. 334.

including Georges Longy (1868–1930), its principal oboist from 1898 to 1925. Longy's name endures in the Longy School of Music, which he established in Cambridge, Massachusetts, in 1915. He had earned a first prize at the Paris Conservatory and founded the Longy Club (1900–17), which presented chamber music performances in Boston. Longy would visit Paris each summer to look for new music, and in 1916 he secured Debussy's newly published Sonata.

Regarding the private performance in December 1916, Debussy wrote:

Despite the weather yesterday, which was the sort for staying at home in [sic], I went to Jacques Durand's house to hear a performance of the sonata for flute, viola, and harp. The harp part was taken by a young lady who looked like one of those priestess musicians you see on Egyptian tombs—nothing but profile! She's just come back from Munich, which she had a job to get away from; she spent a little time in prison and eventually left without her harp . . . worse than losing a leg. Even though it was chromatic (not her leg, the harp she played on yesterday), which distorts the sonority rather, it didn't sound bad, all things, considered. It's not for me to say anything about the music . . . Although I could do so without blushing, because it's by a Debussy I no longer know! . . . It's terribly sad and I don't know whether one ought to laugh at it or cry? Perhaps both.[3]

Ann McCutchan's statement seems to refer incorrectly to this performance: "Moyse played in one of the earliest performances of the Sonata possibly at the home of Debussy's publisher, Jacques Durand, with a woman harpist who had just escaped from Munich after spending time in prison."[4] Moyse was not the flutist who played for Debussy—Manouvrier was. Milhaud described his experience playing the Sonata:

I came to play Debussy's Sonata for viola, flute, and harp, with Manouvrier and Jeanne Dalliez [sic]. When Durand heard about this, he asked us to give the first performance at his house. During one of the rehearsals he sent me to Debussy's house to ask for advice on one or two points. This was the first and only opportunity I ever had of meeting him."[5]

Dalliès played the chromatic harp, and Debussy was not happy with the instrument. "I want to hear my Sonate played on something other than that horrible instrument! I want to hear it on an Érand."[6] Pierre Jamet played an Érard pedal harp, and with Manouvrier and Jarecki, he went to Debussy's apartment to play for the composer. The composer coached them on how he wanted the Sonata to be played, and then, pleased with their progress, invited them to perform on a benefit concert he was organizing for the Vêtement du blessé ("clothe the wounded") organization; the program also included soprano Rose Féart[7] and pianist Walter Rummel.[8] The concert was held in the "Salle à manger" (dining room) of the Restaurant Laurent, which still exists at 41 avenue Gabriel in the eighth arrondissement, near the Palais de l'Élysée.

To sum up, Le Roy, Grout, Grandjany, and Jamet had each performed the Debussy Sonata by 1922, and Le Roy then expanded the sonority of the trio by adding violin and cello to create a new ensemble. The unprecedented instrumentation allowed a colorful mix of music from the Baroque to the present with duos, trios, quartets, and the full ensemble.

Performances and Commissions before World War II

Although the idea for the quintet came to Le Roy in 1922, the ensemble did not perform until May 24, 1924. In *Le Monde musical*, Edmond Delage described the evening in the Salle des agriculteurs as a "very pretty concert,"[9] featuring the premiere of their first commission, *Concert à cinq* by Joseph Jongen, an organist and the leading Belgian composer of his generation, who wrote several works with flute. The concert established a common format, combining the premiere with a sonata by Alessandro Scarlatti arranged by Germaine Tailleferre, a divertimento by Mozart for string trio, the Suite for Flute, Violin, and Harp (1915) by British composer Eugene Goosens (1893–1962), and Ravel's Sonata for Violin and Cello (1920–22)—in other words, a variety of styles and textures.

In 1929, the ensemble would record Tailleferre's arrangement of Scarlatti's Sonata in D Major, originally one of six sonatas for *flauto* (probably recorder), two violins, and basso continuo, so in the QIP recording, the viola plays the second violin part, and the harp plays a realization of the continuo. There are five short movements for a total duration of ten minutes.

After that first concert in 1924, Pierre Jamet replaced Marcel Grandjany, who left for America. Jamet had been only thirteen when he entered the Paris Conservatory in 1906, when there were two harp classes, one for chromatic harp with Marie Tassu-Spencer and the other for pedal harp with Alphonse Hasselmans (1845–1912). Jamet started in Tassu-Spencer's class but transferred to Hasselmans' class in 1909. He won a first prize in 1912 and became harpist in the Concerts Lamoureux in 1920, then in the Paris Opéra from 1936 to 1959, the Orchestre Pasdeloup from 1936 to 1938, and the Concerts Colonne from 1938 to 1948. He was professor at the Paris Conservatory from 1948 to 1963, taught at the Fontainebleau Summer School, and established the Association internationale des harpistes et amis de la harpe in 1962. Although Le Roy spearheaded the QIP and was responsible for many of its commissions,[10] Jamet became the quintet's artistic focus, and later, when Le Roy left the group, it would become the Quintette Pierre Jamet. After Jamet joined the ensemble, the QIP embarked on an extraordinary period of commissioning and concertizing. *Le Guide du concert* remarked on October 25, 1925:

> More than a year ago, we pointed out in this space the originality of this instrumental grouping, then new, its undeniable usefulness for bringing to light works from the past that are charming and almost unknown, the possibilities that it offered modern composers, and the prominent place it would occupy in musical activity. Our predictions have now become reality. The Paris instrumental Quintet, made up of justly renowned artists: René Le Roy (flute), Pierre Jamet (harp), René Bas (violin), Pierre Grout (viola), Roger Boulmé (cello), will have to satisfy very many engagements which will hardly leave time for them to appear in Paris: Luxembourg, Belgium, and provinces of the East (in November), tour in Burgundy, in Normandy and in Switzerland (in February), the Côte d'Azur, the Midi and Spain (in March), etc....
>
> Its repertoire has grown significantly. Modern works have been written especially for it. It has just played the premiere of the Roussel's *Sérénade* at the SMI and has added to its programs *Les Chansons de Bilitis* by G. Dequin, the *Trio* by Swan Hennessy, etc.[11]

Although unpublished, Dequin's work has historical interest. Georges Dequin was the Director of the Caen Conservatory from 1927 through 1951. The *Chansons de Bilitis* are a collection of erotic lesbian poems (1894) by Pierre Louÿs (1870–1925), which Debussy set to music in 1897–98; subsequently, many composers also wrote settings, including Dequin's purely instrumental version. The QIP first performed *Chansons de Bilitis* for the SN on May 16, 1925, in the Salle Gaveau.

The *Sérénade* (1925) by Albert Roussel is the first masterwork written for this ensemble, a mainstay of the quintet's repertoire, and a lasting legacy of the QIP, which gave the premiere in the Salle Gaveau on October 15, 1925, for the SMI. One of the major figures of French music in the interwar period, Roussel trained for a career in the French Navy, from which he resigned in 1889 to become a composer. He studied at the Schola Cantorum of Paris and subsequently taught there. He again served in the navy during World

War I. As a composer, he retained an individual voice and refused to join any group. The poetic heart of his *Sérénade* is its *Andante*, where expressive melodies sing in counterpoint.

As the article in *Le Guide du concert* noted, the quintet also commissioned works for a subset of the ensemble, including the *Petit Trio celtique*, op. 52 for violin, viola, and cello by Swan Hennessy (1866–1929), an Irish American composer who lived in Paris from 1903 until his death. Other works included the *Suite brève* (1923) for flute, viola, and harp by Ladislas de Rohozinski (1886–1938) and the Trio for violin, cello, and harp (1944) by Jacques Ibert (1890–1962).

A concert of the SN in the Salle Érard on January 9, 1926, featured the first performance of Rohozinski's *Suite brève* and two colorful premieres for the quintet, Charlotte Sohy's *Triptyque champêtre*, op. 21 (1925) and Jacques Pillois' *Cinq Haïkaï: Épigrammes lyriques du Japon* (1926). Sohy (1887–1955), one of five women to write for the quintet, was a cousin of *Les Six* composer Louis Durey and was married to Marcel Labey (1875–1968), who also wrote for the QIP. She studied with Vincent d'Indy at the Schola Cantorum and wrote an opera and works for chorus, orchestra, piano, and chamber ensembles. Her scores were signed "Ch. Sohy," giving the impression that they were composed by a Charles Sohy. After the SN premiere, *Le Ménestrel* reported:

> The *Triptyque champêtre*, by Ch. Sohy (the works written under this pseudonym reveal the charming sensitivity of a woman) breathes, as its title indicates, the perfume of the countryside: it has freshness, joyful clarity: it is a "land of pleasure," and the morning enchantment is that which depicts, not the dawn when, on the still gray roads, the peasants, half awake, drag their clogs, on their way to their arduous work of harvest, but the picture of the garden all dapper with wisteria and nasturtiums. The shutters slam along the wall; at the window appears a young woman; she smiles at the birds chirping in the nearby poplar; her eyes blink in the rays of the already rising sun. Although not harsh, the piece is nonetheless very lively and very true.[12]

A student of Widor, Jacques Pillois (1877–1935) taught at the American School at Fontainebleau from 1920 to 1928 and was a professor of harmony at Smith College. The *Cinq Haïkaï*, which he transcribed from his version for piano, reflects the tradition of *japonisme*, or French fascination with Japanese art in the nineteenth and twentieth centuries.

The year 1928 was a fruitful one for the QIP, with four world premieres. On May 19, they performed Henry (Henri) Woollett's *Nocturne, Sérénade* in the Salle Gaveau for the SN. A French composer with English parents, Woollett (1864–1936) studied piano with Raoul Pugno and composition with Jules Massenet. A prolific composer, Woollett taught piano in Le Havre; among his students were André Caplet, Arthur Honegger, and Raymond Loucheur.

The ensemble also gave the first performance of Marcel Tournier's *Suite*, op. 34 on May 28, 1928, in the Salle Érard. Tournier (1879–1951) and Pierre Jamet both studied harp with Alphonse Hasselmans, and Tournier was professor of harp at the Paris Conservatory (1912–48) between Hasselmans and Jamet. His works for solo harp are frequently played. The *Suite* is a four-movement work in a Debussyist style.

On November 24, the QIP presented two premieres at the Salle Érard, including *Prélude, Marine et Chansons* (1928) by Guy Ropartz (1864–1955), who studied composition with Théodore Dubois and Jules Massenet and organ with César Franck at the Paris Conservatory. He was the director of conservatories in Nancy and Strasbourg. His youth in Brittany and the sea inspired his music, and he published poems in Breton. The *Chansons* movement surrounds a Breton noel, "Peh trouz zo ar en douar" ("What is that noise on the ground?"), with two original folklike themes.[13]

The other premiere at this concert was *Rapsodie arabesque* (1926) by Cyril Scott (1879–1979), a prolific English writer, poet, and composer who wrote operas, ballets, orchestral music, choral music, chamber music, and works for solo piano. He had many interests outside music, including the occult, health food, and alternative medicine.

A first performance that in hindsight shows unfulfilled promise was Léo Smit's *Quintette* (1928), which the quintet presented for the SMI on April 20, 1929, in the Salle de la société des concerts du conservatoire. Smit (1900–1943) was a Dutch composer and pianist of Jewish heritage. A graduate of the Amsterdam Conservatory, he lived in Paris from 1927 through 1936, an experience which imbued his music with Gallic influences, especially Milhaud, an acquaintance. He had previously written a trio for flute, viola, and harp. He perished in the Nazi extermination camp at Sobibor, Poland.

The 1930s were the richest decade for commissions written for the quintet, starting with the four-movement *Quintette* (1928) by Jean Cras (1879–1932), which the QIP first performed on May 17, 1930, for the SN at the École normale de musique. Cras combined careers as an officer in the

French Navy—he was a professor at the Naval Academy—and as a composer. He befriended Henri Duparc (1848–1933), who became his only composition teacher. The attractive quintet by Cras continues to be performed and recorded.

One of the major figures of early twentieth-century French music, Vincent d'Indy, composed the *Suite en parties*, op. 91 (1927) for the QIP, and the piece became a pillar of their repertoire. D'Indy was one of the founders of the Schola Cantorum of Paris. A student of Franck, he admired German music in an era of French nationalism. The *Suite* refers to older styles and forms: a sonata-form first movement, a second movement marked "*air désuet*" (*désuet* means old-fashioned), a *Sarabande*, and a *Farandole* (a Provençale dance, familiar through Bizet's *Farandole* from *L'Arlésienne*). The first of many performances by the quintet was at the École normale de musique for the SN on May 17, 1930. After d'Indy died on December 2, 1931, the SN devoted an entire concert (on May 7, 1932) to his music, including the *Suite en parties*. The QIP recorded the work in 1933, and their performance is sensitive to the shifting balances of the work, with each solo dominating the texture. Le Triptyque also devoted a program to d'Indy on March 16, 1937, at which the QIP reprised the *Suite en parties*.

On February 28, 1931, the ensemble presented the first performance of the Quintet, op. 10 (1927) by Robert Casadesus (1899–1972) for the SMI at the École normale de musique. Many members of the Casadesus family were musicians; Robert was a legendary pianist and composer. He taught at and became director of the American Conservatory at Fontainebleau. His quintet is a French re-interpretation of Italian forms.

Gabriel Pierné was a major figure of French music—composer, conductor, pianist, and organist. At the Conservatory, where his composition teacher was Jules Massenet, he won first prizes in solfège, piano, organ, counterpoint, and fugue and then won the Prix de Rome. He wrote two exquisite works for the quintet, the *Variations libres et final*, op. 51 (1933) and the *Voyage au pays du Tendre* (1935). The QIP gave the premiere of the *Variations* for the SN at the École normale de musique on April 1, 1933, and recorded it that December. Georges Masson writes,

> Mastering chamber writing, he [Pierné] gives the flute, the violin, the viola, the violin, and the harp, which have many affinities even if they are not all from the same family, a more independent role. The virtuosity of dense and uncompromising melodic writing, close counterpoint, and a

light and translucent instrumental texture give the *Variations* a character that is both Rousselian and Ravelian, refashioned in the composer's personal voice.

In the Lydian mode, the finale, agile and rhythmic, presents the soloists with an instrumental game full of truculence and petulance, in the style of a divertimento. Almost Iberian, it ends, after many detours, with a reprise, in unison, followed by a recitative-like reminder of the initial theme.[14]

Another premiere in 1933 was of the *Poème: Le Pavillon sur l'eau* (1925) by Timothy Mather Spelman (1891–1970), an American composer who lived in Florence from 1918 to 1935 and from 1947 to 1970. Many of his scores are kept at Johns Hopkins University.[15]

The QIP first appeared in New York on March 1, 1934, and Olin Downes wrote in *The New York Times*:

> The Paris Instrumental Quintet, an admirable organization, made its first New York appearance in the Town Hall. The repertory of the organization is unusual. It explores old and new music and offers a refreshing variety and novelty of material. The gentlemen of the Paris Instrumental Quintet have exceptional musicianship, taste, devotion to their task. They forget individual achievement in the quality of the ensemble and with high interpretive purpose in view. Each one is an accomplished instrumentalist and an artist with the most scrupulous concern for the execution of this task.
>
> There is a typical French precision, sensitiveness, zeal in the performances, which are those of jewelers of tone, acutely aware of every beauty that they must set and unfold, and wholly absorbed in the purpose of revealing beauty. This is accomplished with an art and in a spirit immediately felt by the listener. The large audience showed its delight in the exceptional nature and the fine tone qualities of the interpretations.[16]

Back in Paris, the quintet played two premieres for a SN concert at the École normale de musique on April 28, 1934, the *Suite de danses* by Yvonne Desportes (1907–1993) and the *Suite mythologique* by Jules Maugüé (1869–1953). A composer and painter, Desportes won a Prix de Rome and taught solfège, fugue, counterpoint, and composition at the Paris Conservatory. Joseph Baruzi called Desportes's *Suite* "lively . . . with very personal approaches to colors and rhythms."[17] A student of Dubois and Widor at the Paris Conservatory, Maugüé was director of the Cambrai Conservatory and violinist in the Lamoureux Orchestra and the Paris Opéra. He wrote several *morceaux de concours* for the Paris Conservatory, although none for flute. Joseph Baruzi called his Suite "A musical triptych of sudden lights and subtle shadows."[18] The score describes each movement:

> <u>Napaeans</u> (nymphs). On the slopes of the wooded hillside the Napaeans fearfully remain hidden, as Pan, guided by Cupid, explores the plain. <u>Aegipans</u> (Pan-like beings). Among the reeds and the white lotuses of the golden lake, the Aegipans come and go maliciously amused by the fright of the Dryads. <u>Bacchae</u>. Wild valley; naked, seductive, magic forms; orgiastic dances in front of the unknown sacrificial victim.[19]

The ensemble led an extensive tour of the United States from January through March 1935, visiting both coasts and many cities in between. At the Toledo Museum of Art, they performed the first half of a concert whose second half featured Igor Stravinsky and violinist Samuel Dushkin[20] performing the composer's own works. After the quintet's New York performance, *The New York Times* reported: "Something for the musical epicure. An ensemble of suavity and charm. A jewel-cut and perfectly balanced performance."[21]

The last concert of Le Triton's season at the École normale de musique on May 24, 1935, featured premieres of pieces by Jean Françaix, Gian Francesco Malipiero, and Florent Schmitt written for the QIP. The *Quintette* (1933) by Françaix is an early work in his long and productive career. He was a child prodigy and had a first prize in piano from the Paris Conservatory by the time he was eighteen. The humor of the second and fourth movements and the lyricism of the first and third movements are typical of his writing. Gian Francesco Malipiero wrote some 200 works, including seventeen symphonies and forty operas and was the editor of the complete works of Monteverdi and Vivaldi. His Neoclassical *Sonata a cinque* (1934) is in several sections performed without break.

The concert for Le Triton also featured the *Suite en rocaille*, op. 84 (1934) by Florent Schmitt, a leading composer in the interwar period. Having studied with Fauré, Massenet, Dubois, and Lavignac, he won the Prix de Rome in 1900. With Ravel, he was a member of *Les Apaches*, a group of composers named after Parisian street gangs and formed to discuss and support new currents in music. As Schmitt was a collaborationist and antisemitic during the Occupation, his music became controversial in France afterwards.

En rocaille literally means rock garden and refers to rococo art of the mid-eighteenth century. He wrote the following regarding this suite:

> Short suite worth less than four *sous* . . . The first movement is built on two themes tinged with archaism. The second takes the form of a scherzo with two themes as well. The third is unique in that it can be played in two tempos: moderate or slow. The composer chose the first. This movement has two themes. Finally, the fourth movement is a kind of rondo with refrains, in homage to Haydn. It is very facile.[22]

Throughout, the harmony is conservative, avoiding any sharp dissonance. The 5/8 second movement is rhythmically complex. The third movement, a minuet, could have written by Ravel. In its recording of *Suite en rocaille* from February 1936, the quintet emphasizes breakneck tempos, and the ensemble almost disintegrates in the last movement. The piece continues to be performed widely.

The SN concert on February 22, 1936, in the Salle Chopin showcased premieres for the quintet by Paul Pierné and Marcelle de Manziarly. Paul Pierné, a cousin of Gabriel Pierné and a Prix de Rome winner, was organist at the Église Saint-Paul-Saint-Louis in Paris. The QIP returned to his *Variations au clair de lune* (1935) often, recording it during World War II. Although Manziarly's *Quintette* is still unpublished, *Le Ménestrel* found it the most promising work on the program:

> M. de Manziarly's *Quintet* for flute, violin, viola, cello, and harp appeared to be the most remarkable of the various works presented for the first time at this performance of the National. The distinguishing feature of her inspiration and of her writing is elegance, an elegance, constantly sustained, always pleasant and melodious, enhanced in the last two movements by a vivacity whose momentum signifies the author's gifts most favorably.[23]

Radio PTT featured the ensemble in a concert on April 1, 1936, and the program included Jean Françaix's Quintet and Cyril Scott's *Rapsodie arabesque*.[24]

The quintet first performed the most charming work in their repertoire, Gabriel Pierné's *Voyage au pays du Tendre* (1935), on French National Radio on May 8, 1936. This piece is inspired by the *Carte de Tendre* or *Map of Tendre*, originally conceived as a social game by Madeleine de Scudéry

(1607–1701) in 1653 and published as an engraving in the first part of her ten-volume roman à clef, *Clélie* (1654–61). Tendre is an imaginary land, and the voyage to it is an allegory for love with its trials and tribulations. As Table 4.3 illustrates, Pierné's orchestration is ingenious; many of the work's episodes feature a subset of the ensemble, providing a variety of textures and timbres that underline dramatic contrasts.

Table 4.3 Structure of Gabriel Pierné's *Voyage au pays du Tendre*

Section	Instrumentation	Tempo and Meter	Key
L'Embarquement (Boarding)	harp solo (with cello)	*Quasi Andantino*, 4/4 (quarter = 50)	C major
Fleuve: Inclination (River: Inclination)	flute solo (with violin, viola, and cello)	*Quasi Andantino*, 4/4 (quarter = 63)	C major
[reprise of *L'Embarquement*]	harp solo (with cello)	*Quasi Andantino*, 4/4 (quarter = 50)	C major
Villages: Petits soins (Villages: Pampering):	flute solo (with viola and cello)	*Allegretto*, 2/4 (quarter = 92)	E-flat major
Tendresse (Tenderness)	violin solo (with flute, viola, and cello, occasionally harp)	*Poco meno*, 2/4 (quarter = 69)	D-flat major
[transition]	flute, violin, viola, and cello	*Animato un poco*, 2/4 (quarter = 96)	[chromatic]
Empressement (Eagerness)	all five instruments	*Animato un poco*, 2/4 (quarter = 96)	A major
Confiante Amitié (Trusting Friendship)	viola solo (with violin, cello, and harp)	*Lento moderato*, 6/8 (dotted quarter = 44)	F-sharp major
Perfidie-Méchanceté (Betrayal-Malice)	all five instruments	*Allegro vivo*, 3/4 (quarter = 126–132)	A minor
Mer d'inimitié (Sea of Enmity)	all five instruments	*Allegro vivo*, 3/4 (quarter = 126–132)	A minor
Soumission (Obedience)	cello solo (with harp)	*Lent, Quasi recitativo*, 3/4 (quarter = 63)	B-flat major
Billets galants (Flirtatious Messages)	flute, violin, viola, cello	*Vif*, 2/4 (quarter = 92)	D major
Jolis Vers (Gracious Poetry)	violin solo with viola and cello	*Vif*, 5/8 (eighth = 184)	G major
Billets-doux (Affectionate Notes)	all five instruments	*Vif et léger*, 3/8 (eighth = 184)	E-flat major
Retour par Tendre sur Inclination (Return by way of *Tendre sur Inclination*)	flute solo (with violin, viola, and cello)	*Quasi Andantino*, 4/4 (quarter = 63)	C major
[reprise of *L'Embarquement*]	harp solo (with violin, viola, and cello)	*Quasi Andantino*, 4/4 (quarter = 50)	C major

The quintet subsequently performed the work at the SN on May 25, 1938[25] and recorded it in 1942 with their new personnel—Crunelle, Jamet, Bas, Ginot, and Frècheville. It was a staple of their repertoire through the early 1960s.

On May 6, 1937, the QIP played the premiere of *Cinq Moudras sur un rubayat à sept notes* by Marius-François Gaillard (1900–1973) in the Salle Chopin. Dumesnil included Gaillard in his list of notable young French composers,[26] but he has since been forgotten. He was the first to perform the complete piano works of Debussy over three recitals (in 1920) and recorded most of them for Odéon between 1928 and 1930. He established a concert series in which he conducted the premiere of the revised version of Varèse's *Intégrales* in 1929. As a composer, he wrote film scores, songs, piano works, and chamber and orchestral music. The title of Caroline Rae's article about him sums up his stylistic tendencies: "Debussyist, Modernist, Exoticist," and Rae characterizes his works of the 1930s as "eclectic, primitivist modernism."[27] Mudras are ritual gestures in Hinduism, Jainism, and Buddhism, and rubayat refers to collections of Persian poetry.

Le Triton remained on the cutting edge of presenting new music, and at its concert on May 9, 1938, at the École normale de musique, the QIP introduced two new works, the *Petite Suite de printemps* by Henri Tomasi (1901–1971) and the *Sérénade* by Laszlo Lajtha.[28] Tomasi was a composer and conductor and would become music director of the Orchestre national de France during World War II. His music shows the influence of Bartók. In a review of the concert, Michel-Léon Hirsch wrote:

> Mr. Lajtha's *Sérénade* surprises with a more robust accent, a frank and somewhat coarse decisiveness, in tempo and manner; there is even in the first part an impatient and sometimes angry expressiveness, which one would often like to find in such a mixed ensemble; the conclusion carries the work away in a mocking petulance that is not new, but whose effect remains sure.[29]

At its concert on March 20, 1939, in the École normale de musique, Le Triton presented another premiere of a work for the same instrumentation by Lajtha, his *Marionettes*, op. 26 (1937). Although the piece is dedicated to the QIP, the performers were Crunelle, Andrade, Merckel, Bartsch, and Kahn, as discussed in Chapter 3. Crunelle's appearance presages his joining of the QIP a year later. *Marionettes* illustrates a puppet show, from the *pantins* (jumping-jacks) of the first movement to the *chamailleries* (quarrels) of the fourth movement.

The repertoire created by the QIP is especially rich in works by well-known French composers–d'Indy, Françaix, Jolivet, Koechlin, Gabriel and Paul Pierné, Roussel, and Schmitt––and features a few pieces by women—including the three listed above—and non-French composers. Reflecting a conservative bent, most of the commissioned composers had studied at the Schola Cantorum. Notable is the absence of major composers of the period, signaling either a lost opportunity or a narrow outlook; Claude Dorgeuille asked Le Roy:

CD: Why didn't you ask Gabriel Fauré for anything?

RLR: I was too young.

CD: Maurice Ravel?

RLR: He was too original.

CD: Igor Stravinsky?

RLR: He would have written me something pointillist, and when you ask a composer for a work you cannot then refuse to play it.

CD: Béla Bartók?

RLR: I didn't think of it.[30]

5

Paris During the Occupation

The Nazi Occupation of Paris from June 1940 through August 1944 was one of the most painful periods of French history, whose effects are still present. One can hardly walk a few feet in the city without seeing some remnant: bullet holes in walls, a plaque memorializing the roundup of a Jewish family, or a metro station named for a murdered resister. Life became increasingly difficult: food was rationed, and its scarcity led to widespread hunger; the Vichy government and German occupying authorities arrested Jewish people, Freemasons, communists, resisters, and others and sent them to death camps; and later in the Occupation, the Allies bombed parts of the Paris region. French people faced difficult choices. Those who cooperated with the Nazis were collaborationists, those who actively worked to undermine the occupiers were resisters, and in between were the *attentistes*, those who took a "wait and see" attitude.

In the late 1930s, France was confident that it could repel an invasion from Germany, as it had built the "Maginot Line" of defenses along most of its eastern frontier. On September 3, 1939, France and Britain declared war on Germany, and troops were mobilized, but nothing happened for eight months, a period known as the *drôle de guerre* (phony war). Crunelle himself served in the Reserves from February 9, 1940, until June 25 of that year. In a surprise move, German troops pushed through the weakest part of France's defenses, the hilly and forested Ardennes region, and quickly overwhelmed the French and British, entering Paris on June 14.

The Occupation impacted the music world along with everyday life. Many musicians had left Paris. The audiences for concerts and operas included German military personnel. Programming had to consider German censorship, which forbade music by Jewish composers and encouraged more representation of German music. Numerous music journals were gone, including *Le Courrier musical* (1900–35), *Le Ménestrel* (1833–1940), and *Le Monde musical* (1889–1940), but a new publication, *L'Information musicale* (1940–44), covered music under the Occupation. Despite challenges, this was the busiest period of Crunelle's career (see Figure 4 for a photo of Crunelle

Gaston Crunelle and Flute Playing in Twentieth-Century France. Leonard Garrison, Oxford University Press.
© Oxford University Press 2024. DOI: 10.1093/9780197778579.003.0005

taken during this mid-career period). He taught at the Conservatory, played in the Opéra-Comique, the Pasdeloup Orchestra, the Quintette Pierre Jamet, the Association des concerts de chambre de Paris, and other chamber music, and he appeared on radio and recordings.

The Paris Conservatory

Many Parisians left ahead of the invasion, clogging roads and railroads leading west and south.[1] The director of the Conservatory, Henri Rabaud, and its flute professor, Marcel Moyse, were among them. Although Moyse was not Jewish, his name means "Moses," so he feared that the Nazis would arrest him. He stayed in Saint-Amour, his birthplace near the Swiss border, throughout the Occupation.

The German military governed Paris, northern France, and the Atlantic coast and established a so-called Unoccupied Zone in central and southern France with a new government in Vichy, the spa town where Crunelle had previously played. Marshal Philippe Pétain (1856–1951), a hero from World War I, led this collaborationist regime. Its laws supposedly had jurisdiction over all of France despite Nazi control of the north. As Robert Paxton has demonstrated, its increasingly authoritarian and antisemitic policies often anticipated those of the Nazis.[2]

The Conservatory closed on June 8 and delayed its end-of-year *concours*. On June 18, in the precarious atmosphere of a Paris with "shutters closed," a few faculty performed a concert at the Conservatory in support of students.[3] After newspapers published a public notice ordering government ministries to re-open, a faculty meeting was held at the Conservatory on June 20, and ten attended.[4] An announcement in *Paris-Soir* on June 23 urged faculty and students to return to the Conservatory, which reopened the following day, the functions of the director executed by a committee of faculty members.

Rabaud was back in Paris on July 20 and ordered all professors, including Moyse, to return. He wrote to Moyse saying that the flute *concours* was scheduled for October 1, and he expected him to be there.[5] Moyse asked for leave, but on October 14, Rabaud denied the leave, pointing out that all the other faculty had returned, that his salary for October would not be paid, and that if he did not return by November 1, he would be considered as having resigned.[6]

It is not known whether the flute class met that fall. An interesting, un-
dated letter to an unnamed prospective student stated

Sir,

In response to your letter, I have the honor to inform you that it is not currently possible to specify the number of places available for the flute class.
We do not know if by the date of the entrance *concours* the students currently
mobilized or still residing in the free zone will have resumed their classes.
Their possible replacement can thus can hardly be determined at this date.

Applicants will have to perform a piece of their choice and sight-read a piece.

Please accept, Sir, the assurance of my distinguished sentiments.

DEPUTY CHIEF OF THE SECRETARIAT, A. BLIN[7]

On December 26, Rabaud wrote to Georges Ripert, the Secretary of State
for Public Instruction and Youth, that he had hired two new professors to start
in January. Replacing André Bloch as professor of harmony, who had been
discharged because of his Jewish heritage, was "Mlle. Pelliot,"[8] and replacing
Moyse was Jean Boulze, principal flutist in both the Concerts Lamoureux and
the Paris Opéra. Boulze taught for a very short time if at all, as Rabaud again
wrote Ripert on March 26, 1941, saying that Boulze had become ill, and that
the Conservatory had hired Gaston Crunelle, now forty-two years old, as flute
professor. Another letter dated May 5, 1941, from the Secretary General of
the Conservatory (Jacques Chailley) to Crunelle confirms that his appointment as temporary flute professor had been officially approved as of April
15, adding that only temporary appointments were possible "until the end
of hostilities."[9] The end-of-year *concours* was held June 12, and Crunelle was
listed as the professor. The photographer André Zucca documented classes
at the Conservatory in July 1941, including three photos of Crunelle's class.[10]
During the war, *L'Information musicale* occasionally published a list of
music teachers in Paris, and in 1941 Crunelle lived at 129 rue Lamarck in the
eighteenth arrondissement, just north of the Montmartre Cemetery and a
short commute from the Conservatory.[11] He quickly made an impact, as the
following year, Arthur Honegger wrote in *Comœdia*:

Indeed, at the latest *concours* twelve out of thirteen [flute] students were
rewarded. Congratulations are due to the new professor of the class,

Gaston Crunelle, who continues in the fine traditions of Paul Taffanel and Philippe Gaubert.[12]

The Effect of Antisemitic Policies at the Conservatory

The Holocaust was devastating in France. In 1940, 340,000 Jewish people lived in metropolitan France, of whom 75,000 were sent to concentration camps and 72,500 were murdered. These included French citizens and Jews who had recently immigrated. As director, Henri Rabaud complied with and even anticipated the increasingly restrictive policies regarding Jews promulgated by the Vichy government and the occupying authorities.[13] In late September and October 1940, he carried out a survey of staff, faculty, and students to determine who was Jewish, defined at that time as "persons of Jewish religion who have more than two Jewish grandparents." Three faculty were dismissed because of their Jewish heritage: Lazare Lévy (1882–1964), professor of piano, Maurice Franck (1897–1983), professor of harmony and solfège, and André Bloch. Between twenty and twenty-four students were determined to be Jewish and about fifteen "half-Jewish," and in February 1941, Rabaud declared that they could no longer participate in exams and the end-of-year *concours*.

That spring, Rabaud reached retirement age, and Claude Delvincourt, an admired pianist and composer, replaced him on April 15. Delvincourt was wounded in World War I and was originally a member of the right-wing political associations Action française and Croix-de-feu; nevertheless, he became an active resister, doing what he could to protect students and faculty. He was told not to admit any more Jewish students and to dismiss those who were still there. For instance, his letter to Odette Gartenlaub, who later became a successful composer, reads:

Ministry of Public Instruction and Fine Arts
National Conservatory of Music and Dramatic Art
Paris, September 20, 1942
Director of the National Conservatory of Music and Dramatic Art

To Mademoiselle Gartenlaub:
I have the honor of bringing to your attention that in a letter of September 21, 1942, the Minister of Education informed me that from now on, "It is acknowledged that the Conservatory shall retain or admit no Jewish students."

In applying these instructions, I am obliged to consider you removed from the rosters starting next October 1.

With my strong regrets, Mademoiselle, please know I regard you with distinction.

The Director of the Conservatory, Claude Delvincourt[14]

According to law, Jewish people had to wear a yellow star and could not perform in public. Crunelle's student Jean Étienne recalls that, when Henri Dutilleux's *Sonatine* was the required work for the 1943 end-of-year *concours*,

> We had rehearsed the *Sonatine* with an accompanist who, being Jewish, wore the yellow star; as she was forbidden from entering concert halls and coming to hear us, another pianist accompanied us the day of the *concours*.[15]

Some faculty displayed courage in the face of these horrible events. Jules Boucherit (1877–1962), professor of violin, hid his Jewish students at the Paris home of Brazilian pianist Magda Tagliaferro (1893–1986), who was away in the United States. Among them was the child prodigy Serge Blanc (1929–2013), who would lead a successful career as a violin soloist. There is a remarkable short film showing Blanc playing in Boucherit's class in 1942.[16]

The Front national des musiciens and the Orchestre des cadets du conservatoire

Delvincourt was an efficient and visionary administrator who brought many changes to the Conservatory. He initiated new programs of study—for example hiring Marcel Mule as the first professor of saxophone since Adolphe Sax. He had the composers of the *morceaux de concours* sit on performance juries, and he hired new talented faculty, including cellists Pierre Fournier (1906–1986) and André Navarra (1911–1988), and composer Olivier Messiaen (1908–1992). In 1946, he established a separate Conservatoire national supérieur d'art dramatique, and the dramatic arts moved to the original location of the Conservatory at the corner of rue Bergère and rue du Conservatoire.

Clandestinely, Delvincourt joined the Front national des musiciens, an arm of the French communist party formed in August 1940 by Elsa Barraine (1910–1991), a composer; Roger Désormière, originally a flutist but now a leading conductor; and Louis Durey, one of the composers of *Les Six*. Other members included composers Georges Auric, Henri Dutilleux, Arthur Honegger, Francis Poulenc, and Alexis Roland-Manuel (1891–1966), musicologist Jacques Chailley (1910–1999), organist Marie-Louise Gigout-Boëllmann (1891–1977), and soprano Irène Joachim (1913–2001). Their goals included preserving French music, resisting collaboration with the Nazis and the Vichy government, and protecting Jewish musicians.

On June 22, 1942, the Vichy government passed a law encouraging French people to work in German factories supporting the Nazi war effort, but due to a low rate of volunteerism and pressure from the Germans to send more, a new law of February 16, 1943 established the Service du travail obligatoire (STO), which required all able-bodied young men and some single women to work in Germany. As a clever ruse to save Conservatory students from the STO, Delvincourt and Boëllmann established the Orchestre des cadets du conservatoire, a group of about eighty student musicians, which also included a chorale.[17] Ostensibly, the orchestra provided services to the state, performing at ceremonies and civic events. The conductor was Roger Désormière, who at the time was professor of conducting at the Conservatory. The orchestra played its first concert on December 12, 1943, and continued to perform until 1954.

Likewise, with Delvincourt's support, bassoonist Fernand Oubradous established a new class in chamber music for wind instruments in 1942 and led the class until 1970. Students who won a first prize on their instruments sometimes stayed an extra year to obtain a prize in chamber music and thus avoided the STO. As Delvincourt wrote, "Mr. Oubradous prevented several young musicians from leaving for Germany and hid French people wanted by the Gestapo."[18]

Jean-Pierre Rampal began his studies at the Paris Conservatory through a similar evasion. After obtaining his *baccalauréat* at the Lycée Thiers in Marseille and having studied flute with his father, Joseph Rampal,[19] he enrolled in medical school. But in April 1943, he was obliged to serve in the Chantiers de la jeunesse, work camps for youth that the Vichy regime established after the Armistice in 1940. With military discipline, the young worked on civic projects such as building roads. Rampal left the camp in

October to audition for the Paris Conservatory, then, according to Denis Verroust,

> At the end of the audition, Jean-Pierre Rampal came to say hello to Gaston Crunelle, while explaining to him that it will be difficult for him to take his place in the class, being obliged to return to the *Chantiers*. But Crunelle, like many other professors, knew that the Conservatory was still likely to serve as a perfect escape from the Service du travail obligatoire (STO) for many young musicians. The director Claude Delvincourt was actively involved in this. Knowing that the situation was likely to worsen, the *maître* recommended that his student take a leave of absence rather than resign from the start. Who knows what the future will hold . . . ? Precious advice, the wisdom of which Jean-Pierre Rampal was soon to appreciate.[20]

Upon returning to the work camp, Rampal heard that everyone there was likely to be called up to the STO, and so, he escaped. He also found that staying in Marseille was dangerous and that he could more easily evade capture in Paris. Thus, he joined the flute class in late January or early February 1944, moving to a different address every so often. Although Delvincourt obtained a card exempting him from the STO, Rampal could not participate in the Orchestre des cadets for fear of being exposed. He subsequently earned his first prize at the *concours* on May 23, two weeks before the D-Day landings in Normandy. The *concours* was interrupted several times by air-raid alarms.[21]

The Opéra-Comique and the Revival of Debussy's *Pelléas et Mélisande*

Crunelle continued to play in the Opéra-Comique through the war. Edward Beckett remembers his story about a performance that illustrated the tense atmosphere during the Occupation:

> Crunelle turned up late, and they had dimmed all the lights in the auditorium because it was going to start, and then they said, "We can't start when our flute's not there." So, they all sat in the dark, and apparently there was Göring or one of the Nazi bigwigs, and they thought this was going to be an assassination attempt. It was really secured, people running around with

guns. And he said that after the performance, he was summoned up before the Nazis and given a real talking to.[22]

The Opéra-Comique was the scene of one of the most dramatic musical events of the Occupation, the revival and subsequent recording of Debussy's *Pelléas et Mélisande*. Upon occupying Paris, German authorities wanted cultural life to resume as soon as possible. "The occupant, while initially banning German opera out of concern for French public opinion as well as fear of a poor performance, desired above all to maintain a sense of normalcy and thus keep the French public calm."[23] Besides, attending performances and visiting museums was a perk for German military personnel. Jacques Rouché, the head of the Réunion des théâtres nationaux, opened the season at the Opéra on August 24 with *Le Damnation de Faust*, a safe choice, since it had recently been in the repertoire and since it is a French opera based on a German play, Goethe's *Faust*.

The Comique opened on August 22 with *Carmen*, which had been performed thousands of times. Previously, the programs were printed only in French, but now they were in French and German.[24] Notably, Debussy's *Pelléas et Mélisande* was revived on September 12, its 266th performance at the Opéra-Comique but the first featuring Roger Désormière, the house's chief conductor since 1937, and a new, young cast:

Pelléas: Jacques Jansen (1913–2002)
Mélisande: Irène Joachim
Golaud: Henri Etcheverry (1900–1960)
Geneviève: Germaine Cernay (1900–1943)
Arkel: Paul Cabanel (1891–1958)
Yniold: Leïla Ben Sedira (1903–1982)

Pelléas et Mélisande originated in 1893 as a play by Belgian writer Maurice Maeterlinck (1862–1949) and became the basis for Debussy's opera, first performed in 1902 at the Opéra-Comique with André Messager (1853–1929) conducting.

The start of the 1940 season was a tentative time, when the Vichy regime had not yet shown the extent it would collaborate with the Germans, the resistance had not yet gained traction, and the Nazis had not demonstrated the full extent of their brutality. The mounting of Debussy's masterwork was a daring act, reaffirming the strength of French music in an era of German hegemony, and Désormière, as we have seen, was an early resister, cofounding the Front national des musiciens that August. Henri Dutilleux described the opening night of *Pelléas*:

> The picture of that evening of September 12 at the Opéra-Comique, where a truly extraordinary audience packed the house: in the ranks of the parterre, there are all those important to Paris in the world of theatre, literature, and music—and then there are the others . . . the officers in uniform, who by chance this evening sit next to those who will soon form the "National Front," as Désormière himself is on the podium . . . The room is vibrant with an emotion that continues to grow, from the performers to the public, throughout the work whose spirit and mystery have never, it seems, been more faithfully translated . . . the electricity that one always feels at any moment has never been so intense as on that evening of September 1940 in an occupied Paris.[25]

The Opéra-Comique presented forty-one performances of *Pelléas et Mélisande* between 1940 and 1944.[26] During this run, Désormière made the first complete recording of the opera with the same cast on twenty 78-rpm discs (forty sides) with a deluxe booklet. In an era of deprivation, extraordinary resources were lavished on this project. The best musicians were hired from both opera houses, all four major orchestras, and acclaimed chamber groups. The wind playing is particularly alluring. The flute section was from the Opéra-Comique: Crunelle, principal, Albert Manouvrier, second, and Fernand Caratgé, third and piccolo, and the other principal winds were oboist Roland Lamorlette from the Opéra-Comique, clarinetist François Étienne (1901–1970), principal clarinetist of the Opéra and the Orchestre de la société des concerts du conservatoire, and bassoonist Gustave Dhérin from the Opéra-Comique. There were twenty-three recording sessions in the Salle du conservatoire between April and November 1941, and the recording was released in February 1942.[27] It is still the gold standard of *Pelléas* recordings and has been rereleased many times on LP and CD and is now streaming.

Pasdeloup Orchestra

During World War II, all major Parisian orchestras received support from the Vichy government. The Orchestre national moved to Rennes from

October 1939 until June 1940, then was re-formed in Marseille in March 1941—without Jewish musicians—and performed on Radiodiffusion nationale. It returned to Paris in March 1943. The Concerts Colonne was renamed the Concerts Pierné because its founder, Édouard Colonne (1838–1910), was Jewish. After the Armistice in June 1940, the Pasdeloup regrouped with eighty-five musicians for a successful twelve-concert season beginning in October. The orchestra depended on many substitutes to replace regular musicians who had fled Paris. As Music Director Albert Wolff went to Argentina for the course of the Occupation, Philippe Gaubert was director for a short time until his death on July 8, 1941, then Gustave Cloëz and Maurice-Paul Guillot shared duties as temporary music directors.[28] The Pasdeloup played regular seasons throughout the war, often featuring Debussy's *Faune* and Ravel's *Daphnis*. Hervé Le Boterf relates that the hall was full at each of their Sunday concerts.[29]

The orchestra played a curious non-subscription concert of new works in the Salle Gaveau on July 7, 1943, conducted by Henri Forterre (1882–1958) with Crunelle and cellist Gaston Marchesini listed as soloists.[30] Forterre was a film composer, and the program included his *Trois Poèmes* for soloists and orchestra, *Trois Spirituals* by Paul Boisselet (1917–1972), *Rapsodie en forme de valse* by Louiguy, and *Capriccio espagnol* by Rimsky-Korsakov. Boisselet and Louiguy were also film composers, and the latter, whose given name was Louis Gugliemi (1916–1991), wrote the melody for Edith Piaf's *La Vie en rose*.

It is not known why Crunelle stopped playing with the Pasdeloup Orchestra. In musicians' sign-in sheets, or *feuilles de présence*, his name last appears on January 21, 1945.[31]

The Quintette Pierre Jamet

In 1940, René Le Roy moved to New York, and Gaston Crunelle become the quintet's flutist. Cellist Roger Boulmé died serving in the war, and Marcel Frècheville (1902–1968), a cellist in the Concerts Lamoureux and the Orchestre de la société des concerts du conservatoire, replaced him. Violist Pierre Grout left the group and was replaced by Étienne Ginot, professor at the Conservatory and principal violist of the Opéra-Comique and the Concerts Lamoureux. Ginot had been Crunelle's brother-in-law when he was married to Suzanne Crunelle from 1925 until they divorced in 1932. From 1940 through 1958, the group was known as the Quintette instrumental

Pierre Jamet or simply the Quintette Pierre Jamet (QPJ) (see Figure 5). Crunelle and Jamet developed a close working relationship. Pierre Jamet's daughter, Marie-Claire (b. 1933), herself a renowned harpist who played in the Orchestre national and the Ensemble intercontemporain, said, "I know that Gaston Crunelle was my father's favorite. And he was really a friend."[32]

A survey of *L'Information musicale* shows that the ensemble performed at least eight concerts between 1941 and 1944, including one for Le Triptyque, which remained active during the Occupation and introduced many young composers, including Pierre Boulez (1925–2016), to Parisian audiences. Other new series that featured the QPJ included the Association de musique contemporaine, which was not limited to contemporary music, and the Groupement des compositeurs de Paris.

The concert for Le Triptyque, held in the Hostel de Sagonne on March 9, 1941, featured music exclusively by women composers. The personnel were slightly different from the QPJ's normal lineup, with Gaston Crunelle, flute, Pierre Jamet, harp, Jean Pasquier, violin, Pierre Pasquier, viola, and Nelly Gauthier, cello.[33] They premiered *En regardant Watteau* (1928) by Marguerite Béclard d'Harcourt (1884–1964), who studied at the Schola Cantorum of Paris with Vincent d'Indy and Maurice Emmanuel and was an expert on the music of Peru. Her music employs a modal language. This work is inspired by paintings of Antoine Watteau (1684–1721) depicting charming rustic scenes. The QPJ reprised the work on May 26, 1942.

Although it was dedicated to the QPJ, Marcel Labey's *Quintette* received its first performance on June 5, 1942, with André Prieur, flute, Th. Raabe, violin; Gisèle Weber-Labey, viola; Edwige Bergeron,[34] cello; and Bernard Galais (1921–2009), harp, in the Salle Gaveau for the École César Franck where the composer was director. The QPJ subsequently performed Labey's work on Radio-Paris on December 12, 1943. A student of Vincent d'Indy, Labey was a French conductor, composer, and professor of piano at the Schola Cantorum of Paris. Labey was married to Charlotte Sohy, who had composed her *Triptyque champêtre*, op. 21 for the QIP in 1925 (see Chapter 3).

In another performance for Le Triptyque at the École normale de musique on December 22, 1942, the QPJ premiered the *Variations, Interlude et Tarantelle sur un thème populaire corse* by Suzanne Demarquez (1891–1965), a composer and critic who published monographs on Purcell, Jolivet, de Falla, and Berlioz.

On March 14, 1944, the QPJ presented the world premiere of the *Primavera Quintet*, op. 156 (1936), by Charles Koechlin for Le Groupement des compositeurs de Paris at the École normale de musique. The QPJ had given a private performance on June 10, 1943, at the home of a Mme Amos. The composer described the inspiration for the piece: "Like the *Septuor* [op. 165] it is a work in which there are *no shadows*. I wrote it to celebrate the 'Return of Spring' in 1936, when the weather was wonderful, as it has been these past few days."[35] France-Yvonne Bril wrote in *L'Information musicale*:

> Ch. Koechlin's work, *Primavera*, which had its first performance, dominated the program: the youthfulness, the freshness of spring, the spidery sonorities of the Pierre Jamet Instrumental Quintet, the grace with which it unfolds, all compete to make this delicate score a true masterpiece.[36]

One of the most original and prolific composers of the twentieth century, Koechlin studied at the Paris Conservatory with Gabriel Fauré, André Gedalge (1856–1926), and Jules Massenet. He wrote a comprehensive treatise on orchestration and was inventive in crafting instrumental colors; he was also a master of counterpoint.

During the Occupation and afterward, the QPJ often performed with singers. For instance, on October 18, 1941, the ensemble joined Algerian soprano Leïla Ben Sedira in a program at the Salle Gaveau that included Debussy's Sonata for Flute, Viola, and Harp, Ravel's *Shéhérazade* for soprano, flute, and piano, and Ravel's *Introduction and Allegro*. Pierre Capdevielle wrote, "It would take the language of the poet to describe this concert."[37] Ben Sedira was celebrated for her roles at the Opéra-Comique as Rosina in *The Barber of Seville*, the title character in *Lakmé*, and Yniold in *Pelléas et Mélisande*. She recorded several works with members of the QPJ on January 12, 1942: Ravel's *Shéhérazade*, two arias by Boiledieu, "Rossignols amoureux" from Rameau's *Hippolyte et Aricie*, and de Falla's *Psyché* (see Appendices 1 and 3), and these recordings were subsequently broadcast on French radio.

The conception of Manuel de Falla's five-minute *Psyché* for voice, flute, harp, and string trio predates the founding of the Quintette Instrumental de Paris, although it became a mainstay of their repertoire. It is a setting of a poem by music and literary critic Georges Jean-Aubry (1882–1950), the composer's longtime friend. Aubry presented the poem in 1917 to de Falla, who signed a contract for the work on December 19, 1919, but did not complete it until September 1924 in Granada.[38] *Psyché* may have been first performed in Barcelona with Spanish soprano Conceptió (Conchita)

Badía (1897–1975) in December 1924,[39] but other sources give the premiere at the Palau de la Musíca Catalana in Barcelona on February 9, 1925.[40] The performers in Barcelona were soprano María Josepa Regnard, harpist Raquel Martí, flutist Miguel Pérez, violinist Fermín Pérez, violist Fernando Romero, and cellist Segismundo Romero.[41] De Falla dedicated the piece to Swedish soprano Louise Alvar, who had been his host in London in 1919 and 1921. She performed the Paris premiere at the Salle Érard for the Société musicale indépendante (SMI) on December 2, 1925, and the performers included flutist Louis Fleury and harpist Lily Laskine (1893–1988).[42] De Falla's reverence for Debussy's Sonata for Flute, Viola, and Harp is reflected in the instrumentation, harmony, melody, and delicate texture of *Psyché*. In the poem, Psyché, lover of Eros (known as Cupid to the Romans), awakens to a spring day resplendent with nature's charms. It has four stanzas, which de Falla surrounds with a short instrumental introduction, interludes, and a postlude.

The QPJ presented a second concert with Ben Sedira on June 1, 1943, in the Salle Gaveau in memory of their former cellist Roger Boulmé. The quintet again played Debussy's Sonata and works by Pierné, Ravel, Roussel, and Schmitt, and joined Ben Sedira in the following works for soprano and quintet:[43]

Pierre de Bréville (1861–1949), *Bernadette* (arranged by the composer)
Pierre Capdevielle (1906–1969), *Doux fut le trait* (poem by Ronsard)
Manuel de Falla, *Psyché*
Arthur Honegger, *Céline*, H. 168 (arranged by the composer)
Henri Sauguet (1901–1989), *Madrigal sur un poème de Jean-Aubry* (1942)

Besides the two concerts with Leïla Ben Sedira, Crunelle performed Debussy's Sonata with Étienne Ginot and Pierre Jamet on the following occasions:

December 2, 1940: Association de musique contemporaine, Salle Chopin
March 11, 1942: QPJ
May 26, 1942: Le Diapason, Théatre du Vieux-Colombier
March 31, 1943: "Dernières œuvres de Debussy"

The QPJ made recordings of Paul Pierné's *Variations au clair de lune* and Marius-François Gaillard's *Cinq Moudras sur un rubayat à sept notes* on 78 rpm for the Association française d'action artistique (French Association for Artistic Action [AFAA]). The AFAA, an organ of the Vichy government, produced forty-two discs, all recorded between November 1, 1942, and November 10, 1943, and shipped them to embassies throughout the world to propagate knowledge of French culture.[44] The QPJ had performed Gaillard's work on Radio-Paris on July 21, 1943.

Other Solo and Chamber Music

The Association de musique contemporaine presented a concert in the Salle des agriculteurs on March 22, 1941, featuring Crunelle in two works: Roussel's Trio, op. 40 with violist Pierre Pasquier and cellist Charles Bartsch, and Duruflé's *Prélude, récitatif, et variations* with Pasquier and pianist Jean Doyen.[45] Crunelle played Pierre Capdevielle's *Sonata pastorale* for flute and viola with Étienne Ginot for Le Triptyque on November 23, 1944, and Lionel de Pachmann wrote, "Mr. Gaston Crunelle and Mr. Étienne Ginot marvelously combined their fine talents, bringing out all the charm and all the freshness of this little first-class work."[46]

Crunelle played the public premiere of Dutilleux's Sonatina with pianist Geneviève Joy (1919–2009) in a concert honoring Prix de Rome winners Dutilleux and Raymond Gallois-Montbrun at the Salle des agriculteurs on January 7, 1944. Joy was a leading interpreter of Dutilleux's works and married him on September 17, 1946. Suzanne Demarquez wrote that the Sonatina, written for the end-of-year *concours* at the Conservatory the previous year, "is charmingly imaginative; it was very popular."[47] As mentioned in Chapter 2, Crunelle and Joy also performed the Sonatina in 1951 in Douai.

In 1940, bassoonist and conductor Fernand Oubradous revived the Société des instruments à vent founded by Paul Taffanel in 1879 and rechristened it the Association des concerts de chambre de Paris, then the Concerts symphoniques de chambre de Paris; it was known informally as the Concerts Oubradous. The first concert was in the Salle du Conservatoire on October 12, 1941, and the *flûtiste titulaire* (resident flutist) was Lucien Lavaillote. Crunelle was a frequent soloist with the ensemble; he first performed on January 23, 1943, in a concert featuring Roussel's Divertissement, op. 6 for wind quintet and piano, Ravel's *Introduction and Allegro* for flute, harp, and string quartet, and the *Tombeau de Couperin*. He performed at least twenty-three concerts between 1943 and 1946 in repertoire ranging from Bach to premieres of works by Daniel Lesur and Henri Martelli.[48] Regarding the Oubradous orchestra, Henri Martelli reported in 1944:

> His chamber orchestra, a magnificent group where the greatest wind instrumentalists in France have been gathered for three years now: Crunelle, Morel,[49] Lefebvre,[50] Devémy, Allard,[51] Greffin, Foveau,[52] Alviset,[53] Billard, Mule, Chevert.[54]

Crunelle's work with the ensemble included a 1943 recording of Taffanel's wind quintet and Pierné's *Pastorale*, op. 14, with oboist Myrtil Morel, clarinetist Pierre Lefebvre, hornist Jean Devémy, and bassoonist Fernand Oubradous. Pierné's piece is his own transcription of the first of a set of six pieces for solo piano, the *Album pour mes petits amis*, op. 14 (1887). Crunelle was also soloist in Bach's Brandenburg Concertos Nos. 2 and 5 for a "Festival Bach-Beethoven" with Oubradous conducting at the Théâtre du casino de Vichy on May 15, 1943, a benefit for the Red Cross and prisoners of war. Crunelle was still on the roster for the Concerts Oubradous in 1954, but after Rampal played his first concerto with the organization on March 2, 1947, the younger flutist appeared much more often than Crunelle.

Continuing his association with the *Anthologie sonore* series, Crunelle recorded Louis-Nicolas Clérambaut's cantata *Léandra et Héro* in 1941 with Martha Angelici (1907–1973), a soprano at the Opéra-Comique, Jean Fournier, violin, Victor Clerget,[55] viola da gamba, and Pauline Aubert,[56] harpsichord. In 1943, he recorded again with Clerget and Aubert, performing three movements from François Couperin's *Les Goûts réunis*, Concert No. 9 in E Major, *Il Ritratto dell'amore*.

Radio Broadcasts

When the Germans invaded France, they took control of radio in the Occupied Zone. The Nazi *Propaganda Abteilung* started a new station and gave it the same name as one that existed previously, Radio-Paris. It was the largest and most popular station, heard throughout metropolitan France.[57] The content was designed to appeal to the French: a mixture of entertainment—with stars such as Maurice Chevalier—along with classical music, Sunday masses, and news. The station had a policy of limiting

German music to 35 percent of content, with 65 percent French or foreign music. Julien Jackson writes:

> Radio-Paris contained subtle propaganda for the new Europe, virulent anti-Semitism, irreverent mockery of Vichy conservatism, and after June 1941, anti-Bolshevism. On the day the Germans invaded Russia, Radio-Paris applauded this "liberating" conflict to rid Europe of "the Bolshevik nightmare which has haunted it for twenty years."[58]

Karine Le Bail states that French musicians were initially hesitant to perform on Radio-Paris, but after the Germans hired a French production team, this hesitancy evaporated.[59] In its journal *Musiciens d'aujourd'hui*, the Front national de la musique discouraged musicians from performing for Radio-Paris, but most French musicians ignored this advice.[60] Burrin coined a new term, "accommodation," for those who mingled with the Germans without political intent, actions resulting from "a partially confused image of the occupier, an opaque future, disagreement as to the correct definition of the national interest."[61]

The *Propaganda Abteilung* published *Les Ondes*, a weekly guide to programs on five stations: (1) Radio-Paris; (2) Radiodiffusion nationale, a network of stations in the Unoccupied Zone controlled by the Vichy government, which had a weak signal in the north of France; (3) Rennes-Bretagne; (4) Radiodiffusion allemande; and (5) La voix du Reich. Jacques Tilley featured the QPJ in an article in the January 23, 1944, issue, and Jan Mara's caricature of Crunelle appeared in the October 17, 1943, issue (see Figure 6).

Gaston Crunelle was frequently a flute soloist and chamber musician on Radio-Paris and occasionally on Radiodiffusion nationale. He performed often with pianist Marthe Pellas-Lenom[62] and once with Marguerite André-Chastel.[63] Notably, his performance of Dutilleux's Sonatina with Marthe Pellas-Lenom was broadcast on January 28, 1944, just half a year after the piece had been played at the Conservatory *concours* and three weeks after he had played it at the Salle des agriculteurs. *Les Ondes* documents the following repertoire for flute and piano that Crunelle performed on Radio-Paris:

Johann Sebastian Bach, Sonata in C Major
Marc Berthomieu,[64] *Suite romantique*
Pierre Camus, *Chanson et Badinerie*
Cécile Chaminade, Concertino

Hedwige Chrétien, *Vision*
Franz Doppler, *Hungarian Pastoral Fantasy*
Henri Dutilleux, Sonatina
Gabriel Fauré, *Fantaisie*
Philippe Gaubert, *Deux Esquisses*
Philippe Gaubert, *Nocturne and Allegro Scherzando*
Philippe Gaubert, Sonata
Georges Hüe, *Fantaisie*
Benedetto Marcello, Sonata in G Minor
Jules Mouquet, *La Flûte de Pan*
Louis Moyse, *Danse sacrée* and *Burlesque*
André Prieur, *Ballade*
Albert Roussel, *Joueurs de flûte*
Gustave Samazeuilh,[65] *Luciole*
N. Siloiroc,[66] *Humoresque*
Charles-Marie Widor, "Romance" from Suite, op. 34

Les Ondes seldom specified whether a program was live or a broadcast of recordings, but the only piece from this list he had recorded was the *Vision* by Chrétien (1933), and recording quality had advanced since then. Thus, all his solo appearances were probably live.

Crunelle played a variety of chamber music, most of it with the QPJ:

Marc Berthomieu, *Arcadie* for flute quartet
Jean Cras, Quintet for flute, harp, and string trio
Manuel de Falla, *Psyché* for soprano, flute, harp, and string trio
Vincent d'Indy, *Suite en parties* for flute, harp, and string trio
Marius-François Gaillard, *Cinq Moudras* for flute, harp, and string trio
Louis-Gabriel Guillemain (1705–1770), *Conversation galante* transcribed
    for flute, violin, cello, and harp[67]
Georges Hüe, *Soir paën* for flute, voice, and piano
Marcel Labey, Quintet for flute, harp, and string trio
Pierre Lentier,[68] *Petite Suite* for flute quartet
Lœillet, Sonata No. 5 in C Minor for flute and harp
Gian Francesco Malipiero, *Concerto a cinque* for flute, harp, and string trio
Wolfgang Amadeus Mozart, Quartet for flute and strings
Gabriel Pierné, *Voyage au pays du tendre* for flute, harp, and string trio
Paul Pierné, *Variations on "Clair de lune"* for flute, harp, and string trio

Jean-Philippe Rameau, excerpt from *Hippolyte et Aricie* for soprano, flute, and harp

Jean-Philippe Rameau, *Pièces en concert* for flute, cello, and harp

Maurice Ravel, "La flûte enchantée" from *Shéhérazade*

Maurice Ravel, *Introduction and Allegro* for flute, clarinet, harp, and string quartet

Guy Ropartz, *Prélude, Marine et Chansons* for flute, harp, and string trio

Albert Roussel, Trio for flute, viola, and cello

Marcel Tournier, Suite for flute, harp, and string trio

These chamber works, aside from those with the QPJ, had not been recorded, so they were live broadcasts. Those with the quintet were probably a mixture of recordings and live broadcasts. For d'Indy's *Suite en parties*, the stations could have broadcast the recording made by the QIP with Le Roy as flutist in 1933, and the broadcasts of the excerpt from Rameau's *Hippolyte et Aricie*, Ravel's *Introduction and Allegro*, and works by de Falla, Gabriel Pierné, and Paul Pierné could draw from the recordings made by the QPJ in 1942–43.

Radio-Paris also had a resident orchestra, and Crunelle performed as soloist on July 19, 1941, in the *Tarantella* by Saint-Saëns with clarinetist André Vacellier as co-soloist and German conductor Anton Dewanger (1905–1974). Then, on March 29, 1944, he performed Mozart's Concerto for Flute and Harp with Pierre Jamet as co-soloist for the Association des concerts Marius-François Gaillard.

Crunelle's name appeared often on the pages on *Les Ondes*, and he would have reaped significant income from the Nazis for these performances. On August 15, 1944, however, soon after the liberation of Paris, Radio-Paris was shut down.

In addition to performances on Radio-Paris, *Les Ondes* lists the following on Radiodiffusion nationale:

February 2, 1942, at 11:15 a.m. (*Concert des disques*): Vincent d'Indy, *Suite en parties*, QIP (with René Le Roy)

June 4, 1943, at 11:30 a.m.: Joseph Haydn, Trio in D Major, Gaston Crunelle, flute; Auguste Cruque,[69] cello; André Collard,[70] piano

June 7, 1943, at 5 p.m.: Hour-long program of chamber music including *Variations sur "Clair de lune"* by Paul Pierné, QPJ (the ensemble had just recorded this piece in 1942)

October 4, 1943, at 3:15 p.m.: repertoire not specified, Gaston Crunelle, flute; Auguste Cruque, cello; André Collard, piano

November 9, 1943, at 3:20 p.m.: *Musique de chambre* (repertoire not specified), Leïla Ben Sedira, soprano, and the QPJ

December 8, 1943, at 6 p.m.: repertoire not specified, Marguerite Pifteau, soprano with the QPJ

April 17, 1944, at 10:25 p.m.: Carl Maria von Weber, Trio, Gaston Crunelle, flute; Auguste Cruque, cello; and André Collard, piano

July 5, 1944, at 10:58 p.m.: Vincent d'Indy, *Suite en parties*, QPJ

Travel from Paris to the Unoccupied Zone was difficult, even after the Germans assumed direct control of the whole country on November 11, 1942, so it is doubtful that the musicians crossed to the southern zone to perform. The broadcast on February 2, 1942, is the only specific mention of recordings, and the QIP had recorded the d'Indy in 1933 with René Le Roy as the flutist. On November 9, 1943, the performance with Leïla Ben Sedira could have been a broadcast of the recordings made in January 1942. It is curious that the listing from July 5, 1944, specifically mentions the personnel as Pierre Jamet, Gaston Crunelle, René Bas, Étienne Ginot, and Marcel Frècheville; thus the 1933 recording could not have been used. No recordings exist of the other performances, so they were probably live, possibly from a studio in Paris.

Épuration

The period immediately following the liberation of Paris in August 1944 was called the *épuration* or purge. Before a new judicial system could be established, many people were accused of collaborating with the Nazis and were either publicly humiliated or killed. Legal hearings continued until 1949, and some were punished, depending on the scope of collaboration, with death, imprisonment, or "national degradation," (loss of civil rights). Musicians were also censured. For playing on Radio-Paris, the *Comité national d'épuration des artistes dramatiques, lyriques et des musiciens exécutants* banned musicians from performing for a period based on the committee's assessment of their infractions.[71] About a dozen musicians, including Gaston Crunelle and Pierre Jamet, were called to the committee's hearing on October 30, 1944. On November 5, these musicians and others sent a letter to the

Direction générale des beaux arts protesting their treatment. The signatories included some of the leading chamber ensembles in France: The QPJ, the Trio Pasquier, the Trio d'anches de Paris, the Quatuor Loewenguth,[72] and the Quintette à vent de Paris.[73] Their main defense was the following:

> The undersigned artists believed it was their duty to maintain the reputation of French Music during the occupation. What would have happened if there were only German or pro-German artists on the Parisian stages and on the Radio (the only one in Paris)?[74]

The Archives nationales de France (ANF) contains a list of suspensions ranging from three months to one year, dated January 9, 1945.[75] Cellist Pierre Fournier was forbidden from playing for a year because of his recitals in Germany in addition to eighty-three broadcasts for Radio-Paris. Crunelle was censured for three months for playing 107 broadcasts, and Pierre Jamet also for three months for ninety broadcasts. On October 31, 1944, Claude Delvincourt reported to the Minister of National Education that he had surveyed the Conservatory faculty to determine the extent of their collaboration.[76] Fifty-three had no record of collaboration, twenty-six admitted to some—mostly performances on Radio-Paris—and fourteen did not respond. Delvincourt indicated as a mitigating circumstance that Crunelle had served on a committee for the Front national des musiciens at the Opéra-Comique. As a result of his greater collaboration, Pierre Fournier was put on leave without pay for sixteen months.

In her discussion of Marcel Dupré's German-sponsored recitals, Lynn Cavanagh concludes, "Generally speaking, sanctions and punishments of French musicians following the Liberation did not affect their careers or posthumous reputations very much at all."[77] The damage to their careers depended on the extent of their collaboration. Crunelle and Jamet did not suffer greatly, but soprano Germaine Lubin was imprisoned for three years, and Pierre Fournier's career also languished for several years.

Moyse and Crunelle

Marcel Moyse returned to Paris in the fall of 1944 and demanded that his 1940 "resignation" by default and Crunelle's subsequent hiring be revoked. In various government ministries, post-liberation committees of reintegration considered such requests. Letters from Claude Delvincourt to the Ministries of National Education and Fine Arts reaffirmed Rabaud's decision to hire Crunelle but called for Moyse's reinstatement. His solution was the creation of two flute classes and the doubling of the number of flute students. His letter of November 15, 1944, to the General Director of Fine Arts reads:

> You have kindly forwarded to me a letter from Mr. MOYSE, former professor at the Conservatory, requesting his reinstatement by cancelling of the decree of December 27, 1940 declaring him to have resigned by default.

> In returning this document to you, I am honored to inform you of the following:

> The measure taken in 1940 against Mr. MOYSE was not motivated by personal, racial, political, or other reasons, but by the refusal of the person concerned to return to his post as directed by my predecessor: Mr. MOYSE had to choose between his teaching and his activity on the radio, which was then moved to Marseille. For material reasons, he preferred the latter solution, and my predecessor only followed the consequences. If one keeps to the strict administrative point of view, it does not seem that Mr. MOYSE's request is admissible.

> On the other hand, it is undeniable that Mr. MOYSE is an artist and a very valuable professor and that his teaching can only honor the prestige of the French school. I can therefore only consider the eventual return of Mr. MOYSE, if it should one day take place, with pleasure.

> However, we should not lose sight of the fact that his successor, Mr. CRUNELLE, was appointed through regular processes and that he has been providing impeccable teaching for the past four years. I cannot therefore see his rights being violated without protest.

> In my opinion, the solution lies in the fact that the appointment of Mr. CRUNELLE was made on a temporary basis and that at the expiration of the time limit implied by this clause, a time limit which will undoubtedly be fixed later by ministerial decision, the question can again be raised before the competent authority which can make a fair decision.[78]

Delvincourt's letters to Moyse each begin, "Cher ami," (Dear Friend), a strikingly personal address. In the meantime, René Le Roy also applied for the position of flute professor, to which Delvincourt replied, "I regret to inform you that there are currently no prospective vacancies for this class."[79] After months and much correspondence, Delvincourt was finally able to establish separate flute classes for Moyse and Crunelle starting in the fall of 1946. The roster for each class was determined at the entry *concours* in October. Three students—Aurèle Nicolet, Raymond Guiot, and Jean Droussard—transferred from Crunelle's class to Moyse's, which began with thirteen students. Moyse was unhappy with the situation[80] and in January 1949 left for South America and eventually Vermont, where he was co-founder of the Marlboro Music Festival. Roger Cortet, a former student of Gaubert and Moyse, took over his class and stayed on a temporary appointment until spring 1953. Cortet had recorded Bach's Brandenburg Concerto No. 5 with violinist Jacques Thibault (1880–1953) and pianist Alfred Cortot (1877–1962) and was also a painter. After 1953, there was only one flute class.

Crunelle did not seem to harbor any resentment toward Moyse. As Pierre-Yves Artaud related, "When Crunelle spoke of Marcel Moyse, he obviously had a great affection and admiration for him that was not really shared."[81]

6

Postwar performances

Les Trente glorieuses

After the liberation of Paris, fighting in France dragged on for months until the Germans surrendered on May 9, 1945. The privations under the Occupation continued for months, even years, as food and other necessities were scarce. But despite the challenges of the 1945–6 war in Vietnam, the 1954–62 Algerian War, and the massive protests of May 1968, France embarked on a period of unprecedented prosperity, a rising standard of living, and economic expansion known as the *trente glorieuses*, or thirty glorious years, from 1945 through 1975. Charles de Gaulle (1890–1970), who during the Occupation had led the Free French in exile from London, dominated French politics through most of this period and served as President from 1958 through 1969.

World War II represented a rupture from the past, and Paris was no longer the unsurpassed cultural center that it had been. Television and radio cut into the audience for live music. The two opera companies, managed under one umbrella, continued to struggle financially until finally the Opéra-Comique disbanded in 1972, to re-emerge as an independent organization in 2005. The Orchestre de la société des concerts du conservatoire ceased in 1967 and was replaced by the new Orchestre de Paris. The Pasdeloup Orchestra, the Lamoureux Orchestra, and the Concerts Colonne were still in existence but less active than in previous years. According to *Le Guide du concert*, the number of symphonic concerts in the 1951–52 season was 210, down from 282 in 1937–38, and the total number of concerts of any kind was down to 739 from 993.[1]

But there were also exciting new beginnings; Henri Dutilleux called the postwar years a *jaillissement de musique* or outpouring of music.[2] Composers wrote everything from electronic music to serial music. Young composers flocked to study analysis with Olivier Messiaen, first in his apartment and then at the Conservatory. His acolytes included Pierre Boulez, who founded the Domaine musical (1954–1973), presenting avant-garde music. Boulez came to dominate French music for the rest of his life. In 1959, the French

Gaston Crunelle and Flute Playing in Twentieth-Century France. Leonard Garrison, Oxford University Press.
© Oxford University Press 2024. DOI: 10.1093/9780197778579.003.0006

government created a new ministry of culture under André Malraux (1901–1976), and public spending on the arts increased dramatically. Eventually, government support resulted in such large projects as IRCAM, the *Institut de recherche et coordination acoustique/musique* founded by Pierre Boulez in 1977; the new Opéra Bastille (1989); and an impressive complex of buildings in the nineteenth arrondissement including the new Conservatory (1990), the Cité de la musique (1995)—containing a musical instrument museum, rehearsal rooms, offices, a medium-sized concert hall—and the Philharmonie de Paris concert hall (2015).

Although he no longer performed in the Pasdeloup Orchestra, Crunelle appeared on French radio as a chamber musician in at least thirty broadcasts between 1947 and 1965 (see Appendices 1 and 3). He was still principal flutist with the Opéra-Comique and flutist in the Quintette Pierre Jamet, and made some of his best recordings after the war. Alongside the meteoric rise of Jean-Pierre Rampal in the late 1940s and 1950s, Crunelle was a prominent flutist until his retirement from playing in 1965.

Crunelle's Apartment

The combined income from teaching at the Conservatory and private lessons, performing in the Opéra-Comique, chamber music concerts, resorts, and on the radio was substantial, and Raymonde Crunelle also had an active career playing viola in the Orchestre Pasdeloup and later the orchestra at the Cannes casino. Sometime between 1942 and 1946, the family could afford to move into a comfortable apartment on the fifth floor of 12 rue Raynouard in the sixteenth arrondissement. The 1946 census shows four people in the household, Gaston and Raymonde Crunelle, their daughter Éliane, and a maid, Cécile Gommercy (b. 1921).[3] The route of rue Raynouard dates from the Gallo-Roman era, and in the village of Passy, it was called the Haute Rue and then Grande Rue.[4] After the area was annexed into Paris in 1860, the street was named for the dramatist and linguist François Raynouard (1761–1836) in 1867. Jean-Jacques Rousseau and Benjamin Franklin had lived on the same street, and Honoré de Balzac's house was at no. 47, now a museum. Today, the area is exclusive, but in the first half of the twentieth century,

The neighborhood presents a picture, not really of a rich area, but rather of the residence of a population of intellectuals, artists, executives, and members of the *professions libérales* [independent professionals such as doctors and lawyers] ... In 1931, teachers were limited to music, but there are still a dozen, ranging from flute to organ![5]

Former students described the apartment as "*de grande classe*" (high-class), "*grand*" (big), "*beau*" (beautiful), "*bourgeois*" (upper-middle class), "*luxueux*" (luxurious), "*très chic*" (very stylish), and "*superbe*" (superb). When they took lessons there, Crunelle's flute was always on the piano. Each year after the June *concours*, he would invite his students to a celebration at his apartment.[6]

A windfall from playing in a film enabled Crunelle to buy his first Citroën.[7] He enjoyed driving to work and first owned a Citroën Traction Avant, and later, a Citroën ID, and then a Citroën BX. Parking and traffic were less problematic during his lifetime than now.

The family also owned a villa called "Syrinx" in Théoule-sur-mer, southwest of Cannes, with a view of the Mediterranean. His ties to the region date from his days with the orchestra in Monte Carlo in the 1920s. The villa "was a building from the 1870s. In the heart of a pine forest, it was very beautiful; I especially remember its terrace."[8] Crunelle loved to go there whenever his busy schedule allowed, and students sometimes visited. Since then, the area has become the exclusive retreat of celebrities.

The Opéra-Comique

Despite its financial challenges, the Opéra-Comique gave important premieres in the postwar years. Two works to remain in the repertoire were Poulenc's *Les Mamelles de Tirésias* (*The Breasts of Tiresias*) in 1947 and *La Voix humaine* (*The Human Voice*) in 1959.[9] The company recorded both operas shortly after their opening performances (see Appendix 1). The Opéra-Comique often presented French premieres of works, including Britten's *The Rape of Lucretia* in 1948 and Stravinsky's *The Rake's Progress* in 1952.

For Crunelle, a highlight of these years was the recording, first released in 1961 and conducted by Pierre Cruchon (1908–1973), of *Les Noces de Jeannette* (*Jeannette's Wedding*) by Victor Massé (1822–1884). The virtuoso interaction between voice and flute in the "Air du rossignol" is like the more famous "Il dolce suono" ("Mad Scene") from Donizetti's *Lucia di Lammermoor*, and the performance by soprano Liliane Berton[10] and Crunelle is a tour de force.

By the early 1960s, Manouvrier had retired and was replaced by Rémy Cotton, who had obtained a first prize at the Conservatory with Crunelle in 1941, so the flute section was Crunelle, Caratgé, Chefnay, and Cotton. Crunelle retired in 1964, and his name last appears on the sign-in sheets or *feuilles de présence* for the Opéra-Comique on March 25 of that year.[11] His former student Maxence Larrieu replaced him as principal flute.

Recordings

Crunelle's recording career reached a pinnacle in the decade after World War II. Two of his most famous recordings, first on 78 rpm in 1946 and then on LP in 1954, were of Mozart's Concerto in C Major for Flute and Harp with Pierre Jamet (see Appendix 1). These performances showcase a perfect partnership, and their give and take seems like chamber music. The two soloists had performed the Mozart with Walther Straram conducting at the Évian-les-Bains Casino in August 1926,[12] with Fernand Lubricous conducting at the Paris Conservatory on March 19, 1944, and with Marius-François Gaillard conducting on Radio-Paris on March 29 that same year; they would also perform the concerto with Fernand Oubradous conducting the Orchestre symphonique de chambre de Paris on March 24, 1946, and April 10, 1949. Their first recording was with Gustave Cloëz conducting; he had previously led the orchestra in Crunelle's 1933 recording of Gluck's "Dance of the Blessed Spirits" (see Chapter 3). Their second recording was with Bernhard Paumgartner (1887–1971) conducting the Orchestre de la Camerata Academica du Mozarteum de Salzbourg. Paumgartner, also a composer and musicologist, was the director of the Mozarteum from 1917 to 1938 and 1945 to 1953 and director of the Salzburg Festival from 1960 to 1971. He was the teacher of Herbert von Karajan (1908–1989).

The two Mozart recordings are similar, with subtle differences. The sound in the 78 is more intimate, whereas on the LP it has the effect of listening at a distance in a large hall with reverberant acoustics. The 78 features virtuosic, extensive cadenzas by Reynaldo Hahn (1874–1947), but the shorter cadenzas on the LP have not been identified. The tempos in the fast movements are more spirited in the earlier recording; despite a longer cadenza, the first movement takes almost a minute less to play on the 78 than on the LP. In each recording, their slow movement is simple and elegant without the excessive rubato that is often employed. Crunelle's sound is lovely throughout both recordings, but his intonation shows slight deficiencies on the LP.

The Crunelle–Jamet collaboration stands up well next to other French soloists of the era. In her long career, the harpist Lily Laskine recorded Mozart's Concerto for Flute and Harp with at least four flutists: Moyse in 1931, Le Roy in 1947, Roger Bourdin[13] in 1955, and Rampal in 1958 and 1963. Moyse makes no differentiation between solo and accompanying passages, and his incessant intensity inappropriately eclipses intricate harp passagework. Perhaps because of distant microphone placement or other conditions, Le Roy's sound lacks the warmth of Crunelle's, and he is sharp in the high register and flat in the low register. Rampal's recordings are among the best-selling Classical records in history, and for good reason: they exude an atmosphere of joviality and effortless musicianship.

Debussy's Sonata for Flute, Viola, and Harp had been important to Crunelle's career from his first performance of the piece in 1926 through many concerts in the 1940s. Just before he recorded it with violist Georges Blanpain and harpist Pierre Jamet on July 1, 1948, the trio had played it as part of a day-long Debussy celebration at the composer's house at 80 avenue du Bois-de-Boulogne (now avenue Foch) on March 26.[14] The recording, certainly one of the best of this work, captures its mystery and freedom, as a review in *Disques* remarked:

> The sonata for three, of which there were formerly two very good recordings no longer available, appears in a version full of finesse by the excellent artists Crunelle, Blanpain and Jamet. These three performers, however, seem to be among the Debussyists whom I would gladly call "more Debussyist than Debussy." So much has been said and written—that Debussy was the master of the reaction against Wagner, against Gluck, against "Germanism," against Romanticism, finally, the champion of a certain French music synonymous with "grace," "elegance," and lightness—that his true message, passionate, painful, and delirious by turns, like that of any great artist, is in great danger of being, in certain circles, totally misunderstood. Having said that, I am truly pleased with the release of these records of a very high musical level, and with a recording technique, in all its subtlety, corresponds perfectly to the intentions of the performers.[15]

The two previous recordings cited in the *Disques* review were probably those by Marcel Moyse, one with violist Étienne Ginot and harpist Lily

Laskine in 1927–8 and the second with violist Alice Merckel and Laskine in 1938.[16] As mentioned in Chapter 4, Pierre Jamet had worked on the Sonata with the composer, and the Crunelle–Blanpain–Jamet interpretation is extraordinarily detailed: they capture every dynamic nuance, every indication of balance—Debussy often marks *en dehors* to indicate that one instrument should dominate the texture—every articulation, and every tempo change. Debussy was particularly interested in a transparent sonority, as Jamet recollects:

> The artistic collaboration with Debussy was a great experience for me. His awareness of sound and his sensitivity were extraordinary. His piano playing was not the least bit heavy, as if he were not even touching the keys . . . From him, I learned how to play a true *pianissimo*.[17]

A common gesture in Debussy's music is a crescendo followed by a *subito piano*, and this effect emerges beautifully in the 1948 recording. Crunelle employs a great range of timbres, especially when delicacy is required, and achieves a perfect blend between flute and viola. On the other hand, Moyse's sound on both of his recordings is invariably intense and penetrating, even where the flute is marked *mélancoliquement*, *leggierissimo*, or *pp*, or is an accompaniment to the harp, and he ignores the *subito piano* markings. Jamet's touch is dulcet, except in the stormy last movement, where Debussy wanted the sound of a raucous *tambourin*, a tenor drum with a snare (*une chanterelle*) from Provence.[18] Another detail reflected in this recording is the tempo of the second movement. Debussy told Jamet that the words *grave et lent* should be added to the marking *Tempo di Minuetto*,[19] and their pacing is appropriately solemn.

Under the direction of Fernand Oubradous, Crunelle recorded a musical curiosity, Mozart's Adagio and Rondo, K. 617, originally for glass harmonica and quartet. This performance featured Crunelle with Yvette Grimaud,[20] celeste; Pierre Pierlot,[21] oboe; Pierre Ladhuie, viola; and Étienne Pasquier, cello. *Disques* magazine commented,

> This is Yvette Grimaud's first appearance on record in the perilous solo part; she reveals herself as an accomplished Mozartian, and we look forward to applauding her in other works from the "Divine Master," whose style she seems to sense perfectly. Her collaborators, renowned and justly appreciated soloists, chisel this delicate masterpiece with emotion and joy.[22]

Crunelle continued his association with Baroque music in three releases. He recorded Bach's Partita in A Minor, BWV 1013, in 1950, the same year as Jean-Pierre Rampal and Gustav Scheck (1901–1984), and theirs are among the earliest complete recordings of this piece. The Partita did not yet have a long performing tradition and was not included in the first complete Bach edition, the *Bach-Gesellschaft-Ausgabe*, published between 1851 and 1900. Discovered by German musicologist Karl Straube in 1917, the Partita became part of René Le Roy's repertoire in 1919,[23] and he recorded it in 1938 on Musicraft, an American label; Durand published his edition in 1932.[24] Marcel Moyse recorded just the *Sarabande* in 1935.

Table 6.1 compares the timings of the three recordings made in 1950.

The constraints of record formats might have influenced these flutists' decisions regarding tempos and repeats. In Crunelle's case, all four movements plus spoken commentary needed to fit on two ten-inch discs, each restricted to a little over three minutes of material per side. He skips all repeats except in the first parts of the Sarabande and Bourrée anglaise, and his tempos are brisk, with brilliant technique in the Corrente and Bourrée anglaise. Rampal, whose recording is on a single twelve-inch disc, which could contain at least four to five minutes per side, does no repeats. Throughout his career, he favored brisk tempos, which are like Crunelle's in this instance. Deutsche Grammophone Gesellschaft released Scheck's recording, and their variable microwave technology permitted well over six minutes per side. Scheck does all the first repeats, and his tempos are more leisurely.

Crunelle tackles the greatest challenge of the work—keeping the forward momentum despite the need to breathe. His articulation in the Allemande is heavy, whereas Rampal's is lighter, and Scheck adds many slurs. Crunelle's Sarabande is probably the fastest on record, in contrast to the stately pace of Moyse. Crunelle undoubtedly played from the 1939 Leduc edition edited by Moyse, as he closely matches the articulations, dynamics, accents, breaths, and several wrong notes in Moyse's edition. According to Moyse, this edition

Table 6.1 Timings of 1950 recordings of Bach's Partita

Flutist	Allemande	Corrente	Sarabande	Bourrée anglaise	Total
Crunelle	2:11	1:41	2:58	1:29	8:19
Rampal	1:56	1:47	2:47	1:18	7:48
Scheck	3:18	2:20	3:58	1:54	11:30

reflects the ideas of Hennebains: "I did nothing. I just printed everything I learned from Hennebains."[25] *Disques* magazine compared the Crunelle and Rampal recordings:

> Crunelle's flute is stronger, dare I say more human? The instrumentalist seems to be more present: we think we hear him, we hear him catch his breath. J.-P. Rampal's instrument is lighter, more ethereal, more immaterial.[26]

Crunelle had already recorded twice with harpsichordist Pauline Aubert (1894–1978)[27] before releasing a fetching collection, *Au Jardin de la flûte de France*, in 1950. This was the first recording of these selections from sonatas by Michel Blavet, Jacques-Christophe Naudot (ca. 1690–1762), Joseph Bodin de Boismortier (1689–1755), and François Danican Philidor (1689–1717). His tone is resonant in the slow movements, and his fast movements are sprightly. *Disques* wrote:

> Mr. Gaston Crunelle plays delightfully, and we feel he does it with pleasure. Too bad this garden is quite small, since it fits in a single disc. But we can certainly admire the collection.[28]

Crunelle and Rampal are well matched in their 1953 recording of Bach's Concerto in F, BWV 1057 (based on the Brandenburg Concerto No. 4), with pianist Céliny Chailley-Richez[29] and conductor George Enescu, although the approach sounds heavy to modern ears. The recording is part of a series of LPs with Chailley-Richez as soloist in nearly all of Bach's keyboard concertos.

The Quintette Pierre Jamet

After the war, the quintet regrouped. In 1945, Georges Blanpain (1907–1986), violist in the Opéra-Comique and the Concerts Lamoureux, replaced Étienne Ginot, and Robert Krabansky, cellist in the Opéra-Comique, replaced Marcel Frécheville. Benefitting from the musical effervescence of postwar Europe, the QPJ performed an average of fourteen concerts each year from 1945 through 1958, with the high point of twenty-three concerts in 1949 and tapering off in the next decade.[30] The quintet continued to tour France and elsewhere in Europe and was broadcast twelve times between

1948 and 1958 on French radio. They collaborated in concert with sopranos Leïla Ben Sedira, Noémie Pérugia,[31] Geneviève Touraine,[32] and Mado Robin.[33] The format of the concerts was familiar from earlier years—a mixture of solos, duets, trios, quartets, and quintets.

One of their most important premieres was of the *Chant de Linos* (1944) by André Jolivet. The composer took counterpoint lessons with Paul Le Flem (1881–1984), professor at the Schola Cantorum, then founded the group La Jeune France with Yves Baudrier (1906–1988), Daniel-Lesur (1908–2002), and Olivier Messiaen. He transcribed *Chant de Linos*—originally written for flute and piano for the 1944 *concours*—for quintet, and Pierre Jamet made suggestions to the composer regarding the harp part. Jolivet dedicated the quintet version to Crunelle and the Quintette Pierre Jamet. The demanding flute part is the same in both versions. According to the composer's note in the score, "The CHANT de LINOS was, in Greek antiquity, a sort of threnody: a funeral lament, a lament interspersed with cries and dances."[34] The quintet version was performed by the QIP in the Salle du Conservatoire on June 1, 1945, in a program that also included music by Guillemain, Honegger, Malipiero, Ravel, and Roussel.[35]

On March 17, 1946, the quintet presented the first performance of the *Petite Suite dominicale* by André Bloch. A student of André Messager, Bloch won the Prix de Rome in 1893. *Le Guide du concert* reported:

> The composer wrote this work during the occupation, at the request of the Quintette Pierre Jamet to whom it is dedicated. The title indicates the religious character of the *Suite*. The first piece, *À l'Église*, exposes and develops the Kyrie theme from one of Dumont's *Royal Masses*.[36] No. 2 is a short light interlude on the name of the dedicatee J.A.M.E.T which in music is written *do, la, mi, fa.* No. 3, *Angelus*, is a prayer with the sounds of two bells. The fourth movement is simply titled [as No. 4]."[37]

The four-hundredth concert of Le Triptyque on May 21, 1947, at the École normale de musique featured premieres by Henri Sauguet and Paul Boisselet. The QPJ played four works, including the *Suite en rocaille* by Florent Schmitt and premieres of the *Quintette en mi* by Robert Bernard (1900–1971), the *Aubade*, op. 62, by Yvonne Desportes, and the *Suite médiévale* by Daniel-Lesur. Bernard was a French composer, pianist, musicologist, and music critic of Swiss origin. He was the editor of *La Revue musicale*. The *Aubade* was the second work Desportes wrote for the quintet. Lesur taught at the Schola Cantorum of Paris and then became its director. He was in the group La Jeune France with Baudrier, Jolivet, and Messiaen. After the war, he became an administrator for French radio and television and the Ministry for Culture. His *Suite* is based on Medieval modes. The second movement is inspired by the famous "Smiling Angel" statue on the facade of the Reims Cathedral.

The quintet gave three premieres in 1950. The group had presented a private performance of André Amellér's *Suite française dans le goût romantique*, Op. 33 (1947), on November 20, 1948, in the salon of a Madame Rossignol in Neuilly, but the public premiere was on March 26, 1950, in the Salle du Conservatoire. With several first prizes from the Paris Conservatory, Amellér (1912–1990) was a contrabassist at the Paris Opéra (1937–54), composer, conductor, and director of the Dijon Conservatory. On May 20 at 28 rue Marbeau[38] in the sixteenth arrondissement of Paris, the QPJ premiered the *Prélude, danse, air et finale* (1942) by Max Lang (1917–1987), a Swiss composer and trumpeter who studied composition with Arthur Honegger. Then, in June at a concert of the SN in the École normale de musique, the quintet gave the first performance of Marcel Orban's *Trois Danses* (1948). Orban (1884–1958) was a Belgian composer and critic who studied with d'Indy and Roussel at the Schola Cantorum of Paris, and his lyrical, contrapuntal, and modal writing remained faithful to the precepts of the Schola.

Performing for Les Amis de la musique de chambre, the QIP premiered Henri Martelli's *Quintette*, op. 73 (1951), at 24 place Malesherbes[39] in Paris. A prolific French composer, Martelli (1895–1980) was born in Argentina and studied at the Paris Conservatory. He wrote operas, ballets, orchestral music, and chamber music.

At a concert honoring Charles Koechlin in the Salle du Conservatoire on October 21, 1952, and broadcast on Radiodiffusion française, the ensemble gave the first performance of one of the last works of the composer's long career, the *Quintet No. 2*, op. 223 (1949). In his review, Paul Le Flem observes that Koechlin's late works strike a balance between polyphony and lyricism:

The *Second Quintet*, written for harp, flute, violin, viola, cello—which the Quintette instrumental Pierre Jamet performed with understated brilliance and a fine sense of balance—expresses, through its four movements, the same polyphonic suppleness as well as an intimate range of feeling.[40]

The first movement is pastoral in character with imitative entrances of the melody. The third movement, subtitled "Morning Sun" ("*Soleil au matin*"), is in ternary form, the outer sections calm with a faster middle section. The finale consists of many contrasting episodes building to an outpouring of counterpoint followed by a placid conclusion.

There were two premieres in 1953, starting in Paris on May 3 with Jean Absil's *Concert à cinq*, op. 38 (1939). Absil (1893–1974) was a Belgian composer, a graduate of the Royal Conservatory of Brussels, winner of the Belgian Prix de Rome, and professor at the Music Academy of Etterbeek for four decades. His work begins with a dramatic and stormy first movement in a chromatic idiom. The second movement includes a short cadenza for flute, followed by a spirited finale. On December 15, the QIP performed Charles Brown's *Concert en l'honneur de la nativité* at the Schola de Saint-Étienne in Bourges. Brown (1898–1988) was a French violinist and composer who studied violin with Lucien Capet (1873–1928) and composition with Guy de Lioncourt (1885–1961). He was director of the Bourges Conservatory.

The QIP gave the first performance of Raymond Loucheur's *Quatre Pièces en quintette* (1953) on February 21, 1958, for the SN at the École normale de musique. Loucheur (1899–1979) won the Prix de Rome in 1928 and was director of the Paris Conservatory from 1956 to 1962. He wrote vocal music, orchestral music, and chamber music.

The last work written for the ensemble was the *Quintette* by Alain Margoni (b. 1934), premiered on June 4, 1961, at the Festival des nuits de Sceaux and broadcast on June 8. The festival is still held in the Orangerie of the Château de Sceaux in the southern suburbs of Paris and is focused on new music. Margoni's piece is a complex modernist work in eight movements, unlike any other work in the quintet's repertoire. Margoni, a student of Schmitt, Aubin, and Messiaen, had just won the Prix de Rome in 1959. An early work, the piece has since been withdrawn from the composer's catalog.

The QPJ probably gave the premieres of five additional works, but the performance dates have not been identified. These works are Hendrik Andriessen's *Variations sur un thème de Couperin*, Pierre de Bréville's *Trois Pièces*, the *Quintette*, op. 2 (1947) by Jean-Michel Damase (1928–2013), and Christian Manen's *Quintette*, op. 33 (1958). Andriessen (1892–1981) was a Dutch composer, brother of pianist and composer Willem Andriessen (1887–1964) and father of composers Jurriaan Andriessen (1925–1996) and Louis Andriessen (1939–2021). He was a graduate of the Royal Conservatory of The Hague, where he was also a professor. Pierre de Bréville (1861–1949) studied composition with Théodore Dubois and César Franck and taught at the Schola Cantorum of Paris and the Paris Conservatory. Damase's mother was harpist Micheline Kahn, and he wrote many works for harp. He won the Prix de Rome in 1947 and the same year earned a first prize in composition from the Conservatory with the *Quintette*, dedicated to his composition teacher, Henri Büsser. There is no record of the premiere of this piece, but the QIP's recording was released in 1962. Manen (1934–2020) was a Prix de Rome winner and taught at the Conservatory of Asnières from 1954 to 1999 and at the Paris Conservatory from 1965 to 1999.

Between 1946 and 1951, the quintet performed around thirty concerts for Jeunesses musicales de France, an international organization with chapters in many countries, founded in Belgium in 1940. Its mission is to bring live music to young people, particularly in remote or disadvantaged regions.[41]

The 78-rpm record was giving way to the LP, and the quintet made two last recordings on the old format: Albert Roussel's *Sérénade* in 1946 and Jean Françaix's *Quintette* in 1950 (see Appendix 3). Both pieces had long been staples of the quintet's repertoire. *Disques* magazine wrote of Françaix's work,

> This Quintet can claim the title of Entertainment. If the first andante has charm where the flute of Gaston Crunelle sings in a vaguely Debussyish atmosphere, the second is not so characteristic. It is in the Scherzo (No. 2), and the Rondo (No. 4), that we find the personality full of amiability and rhythmic charms of Jean Françaix . . . The artists of the ensemble Pierre Jamet, Gaston Crunelle, René Bas, Georges Blanpain and Robert Krabansky, of course, are excellent, as usual.[42]

The QIP made two more recordings on LP in 1956: the *Prélude, Marine et Chansons* by Guy Ropartz and, with soprano Pierrette Alarie,[43] *Psyché* by de Falla. The group had recorded *Psyché* with Leïla Ben Sedira on 78 rpm in 1942; the sound on the LP is much clearer, and Alarie's interpretation has more dramatic range than Ben Sedira's.

When Pierre Jamet retired from the ensemble in 1959, Bernard Galais joined the group. A harp student of Marcel Tournier at the Conservatory, Galais won a first prize in 1939 and became a harpist in the Paris Opéra, the Orchestra de la société des concerts du conservatoire, the Concerts Colonne, and the Garde républicaine. He also wrote compositions and transcriptions for solo harp. At the same time, violist Pierre Ladhuie replaced Blanpain. Ladhuie, a violist in the Paris Opéra, had recorded Mozart's Adagio and

Rondo, K. 617 with Crunelle in 1949, Fauré's first piano quartet in 1956 with pianist Claude Helffer, violinist Georges Tessier, and cellist Roger Albin, and Debussy's Sonata with flutist Lucien Lavaillote and harpist Bernard Galais in 1957. In its new configuration, the quintet reverted to its original name, the QIP, made one recording, and performed eight concerts and broadcasts. The recording, released in 1962, featured Jean-Michel Damase's *Quintette*, op. 2, Jean Françaix's *Quintette*, and Daniel-Lesur's *Suite médiévale*. For this LP, Pierre Coddée, a cellist in the Paris Opéra, substituted for Robert Krabansky. Despite the three new members of the group, there are no substantial differences between the recordings made of Françaix's *Quintette* in 1950 and 1960.

   Their final eight concerts were all broadcast on French radio and are accessible at the Inathèque, the library of the Institut National de l'Audiovisuel (INA) in the Bibliothèque national de France (BNF, see Appendix 3). The programs included works already in the QIP repertoire, along with the premiere of Alain Margoni's *Quintette*. Krabansky played on some of these performances, and Pierre Coddée and Michel Tournus[44] also substituted as cellists. Although Crunelle had retired from the Opéra-Comique in 1964, his playing in 1965 was still excellent, at age sixty-six.

Legacy of the QIP

A few ensembles with the same instrumentation have been formed, and they continue to perform, record, and expand the repertoire created by the QIP. René Le Roy himself, when he returned in France in 1950, tried to create a rival quintet with harpist Odette Le Dentu,[45] violinist Marie-Ange Henry, violist Henri Benoît, and cellist Jacques Heuclin, but the group never got off the ground.[46] The Quintette instrumental de l'Orchestre national de France existed at the same time as the QIP and played some of the same repertoire, but they also commissioned a *Quintette instrumental* (1957) by Heitor Villa-Lobos. From 1959 to 1971, Marie-Claire Jamet performed in the Quintette instrumental Marie-Claire Jamet with her husband, flutist Christian Lardé, a Crunelle student; José Sanchez, violin; Colette Lequien, viola; and Pierre Degenne, cello. Other ensembles with the same instrumentation include:

   Ensemble Arpæ: Aldo Baerten, flute; Gudrun Vercampt, violin; Diederik Suys, viola; Marie Hallynck, cello; Sophie Hallynck, harp

Ensemble Lumaka: Jana Machalett, flute; Saskia Viersen, violin; Martina Forni, viola; Charles Watt, violoncello; Miriam Overlach, harp

Instrumental Quintet of London: Susan Milan, flute; Nicholas Ward, violin; Matthew Jones, viola; Sebastian Comberti, cello; Gabriella Dall'Olio, harp

Mirage Quintet: Robert Aitken, flute; Jacques Israelievitch, violin; Teng Li, viola; Winona Zelenka, cello; Erica Goodman, harp

Oxalys Ensemble: Ton Fret, flute; Shirly Laub, violin; Elisabeth Smalt, viola; Martijn Vink, cello; Annie Lavoisier, harp

Montreal Chamber Players: Timothy Hutchins, flute; Neal Jonathan Crow and Marianne Dugal, violin; Gripp, viola; Brian Manker, cello; Jennifer Swartz, harp

Linos Harp Quintet: Gaby Pas-VanRiet, flute; Annette Schäfer, violin; Gunter Teuffel, viola; Jan Pas, cello; Sophie Hallynck, harp

Anne Ricquebourg, harp, and the Quatuor Hélios: Christel Rayneau, flute; Nathanaëlle Marie, violin; Isabelle Lequien, viola, and Christoph Beau, cello

Of the forty-nine pieces written for the QIP, twenty-eight have been published, and hopefully more will be rediscovered and printed. Works by Cras, d'Indy, Françaix, Jolivet, Koechlin, Malipiero, Pierné, Roussel, and Tournier have a firm foothold in the repertoire.

7

Crunelle's Teaching

Sir James Galway's unflattering portrait of Crunelle has been widely read and has damaged his reputation:

> It was when the classes began that my disappointment set in . . . Gaston Crunelle explained very little, although when he did say something, he made a real difference . . . Five or six of us sat there, and, one by one each of us stood up and played his piece—each of us playing the same piece, and each trying to outdo the one before him. Dear old Crunelle, meanwhile, sat there reading his newspaper and smoking one Gauloise after another— although if you made a mistake or played a wrong note, he immediately brought it to your attention. All in all, I would say the standard of playing in that class under his leadership was the best I had ever encountered."[1]

Galway goes on to relate that because of his frustration, he left the flute class in 1961 to the dismay of the Conservatory administrators, who exclaimed, "People don't walk out on scholarships."[2]

During interviews with twenty-two of Crunelle's former students, I asked them about Galway's depiction of the class. None characterized their teacher as distant or unobservant. Michel Debost explains Crunelle's singular behavior with Galway:

> I read James Galway's book, in which he acknowledges that he did not stay very long at the Paris Conservatory and that he did not learn anything from Gaston Crunelle, who read his *Figaro* while smoking his *blue unfiltered Gitanes*. Crunelle, who thought Galway was terrific and recognized his talents, told me later that he felt he had things to say to him, but that his pupil preferred to stick to his own, otherwise very respectable ideas. Since *Jimmy* (James Galway) was a free spirit, and did not take any advice from the master, whom he even argued with, the latter ostensibly read his newspaper for this reason. Mr. Crunelle had instinctively found the only thing that could annoy the future Sir James: not to listen to him. His departure

Gaston Crunelle and Flute Playing in Twentieth-Century France. Leonard Garrison, Oxford University Press.
© Oxford University Press 2024. DOI: 10.1093/9780197778579.003.0007

from the Conservatory was not due to a theatrical resignation, but to an understandable failure in the solfège exam that had to be passed to enter the final competition. To be honest, the French-style solfège courses were a problem for the young English-speaking musician.[3]

Galway's scathing comments notwithstanding, Crunelle's students describe an extremely dedicated teacher (see Figure 7 for a photo of Crunelle with his flute class in 1953). From a modern viewpoint, his pedagogy seems limited—practical rather than artistic—but in the context of his era, his methods were logical, appropriate, and effective, with his students' best interests in mind. Whereas in American schools of music, the capstone project is a degree-required recital, at the Paris Conservatory during his tenure, there was no recital, but rather the end-of-year *concours*. Crunelle's goal was to prepare each student to earn a first prize at the *concours*.[4] As Michel Debost relates, "His stated ambition was to bring his students to their best for the *concours*. Many obtained their prizes thanks to him because he pumped them up."[5] Isabelle Chapuis adds, "It's like training a racehorse to do one thing, we were racehorses."[6] In France at the time, a musician lacking a first prize had limited career options.

The entrance audition had not changed much from Crunelle's own time at the Conservatory, still with juries chaired by the director; the professor had no vote. Edward Beckett described his experience in 1961:

> There were two pieces. One was the *Nocturne and Allegro Scherzando* by Gaubert, and the other was the Enesco *Cantabile and Presto*. You were called in, and there were two cards on the table face down, and you turned one of the cards over, A or B, and depending on the card, that was the piece you were going to play. So, you never knew until the last minute.[7]

Some entrants passed onto a second round, for which there was a different *morceau de concours*. One had three weeks to prepare, and those who passed this round were admitted and started right away.

With Crunelle's consent, any student, regardless of how long they had been in the flute class, could participate in the end-of-year *concours*. The event was held in June in the Salle Berlioz at the Conservatory and open to the public, and each student performed a new *morceau imposé* (required piece) by memory and a *déchiffrage* (sight-reading piece). Both pieces were for flute and piano and commissioned by the director of the Conservatory. Most *morceaux* were between six and nine minutes long and designed as contest pieces; thus, they featured both lyrical and technical material. The new *mor-ceau* was published and available for sale about a month before the *concours*. Isabelle Chapuis remembers flute students waiting at the music store around the corner from the Conservatory, before it opened on the day the *morceau de concours* was available.[8] The *déchiffrages* were one to two minutes long, mostly written in a conservative style but including challenges such as meter changes, polyrhythms, or extreme dynamics; students had one minute to look them over.[9] The Conservatory director chaired the jury, which included distinguished guests. For instance, the jury on June 6, 1964, was:

Raymond Gallois-Montbrun, director
Tony Aubin, composer of the *morceau imposé*
Jean Chefnay, flutist in the Opéra-Comique
Michel Debost, second flutist, Orchestre de la société des concerts du conservatoire
Jean-Pierre Eustache (1930–2014), principal flutist, Opéra
Henri Lebon (1911–1996), principal flutist, Société des concerts du conservatoire
Jean-Pierre Rampal, recording artist[10]

With success at the *concours* the objective, Crunelle's pedagogy focused on the following: (1) stellar technique and beautiful tone; (2) sight-reading; (3) memorizing; (4) performing in front of others; and (5) principles of in-terpretation of *morceaux de concours*. Other issues, such as solo repertoire in a variety of styles or orchestral excerpts, were addressed less often, as they distracted from preparation for the *concours*.

The regular flute class met for twelve hours each week, on Tuesdays, Thursdays, and Saturdays for four hours each; there were no private lessons. All students studied the same exercises, études, and pieces, and devoted a month to each solo. "Each student had fifteen to twenty minutes of individual instruction time on Saturday, which was technique day, and about thirty minutes on Tuesday or Thursday, the etude-solo days."[11] Every class started with scales from the Taffanel–Gaubert method: "There was something ritu-alistic in the way we began our scales."[12] Playing in front of peers motivated students to prepare thoroughly and gave them constant experience with high-pressure situations. Attendance was obligatory on technique day and one of the other days. There were twelve students, later increased to sixteen, most of whom were French, although there were several foreign students. In addition, from 1947 through 1970, there was a *section spéciale des étrangers*, a class for foreigners, who paid tuition and took private lessons at Crunelle's apartment.[13] They could attend the regular class at the Conservatory.

Fernand Caratgé sometimes taught for Crunelle when he was away.[14] Occasionally other flutists visited the class, including Crunelle's longtime friend Robert Hériché and Crunelle's former student Jacques Castagner, flutist of the Quintette à vent de Paris and in Boulez's Domaine musical.[15]

Besides the flute class, students took solfège—including dictation. Passing the successive levels of solfège, which foreign students in the regular flute class found challenging, was required before participating in the end-of-year *concours*. They also took orchestra, music theory, music history, and chamber music for winds with Fernand Oubradous or René Le Roy—the latter taught this class from 1955 to 1969.

In the postwar years, the Conservatory's home on the rue de Madrid was showing its age: George Waln reported in 1957,

> The physical plant at the Conservatory because of its age falls short of the comforts and luxury of most of our modern American music schools. The rooms are gray and plain. Benches are common.[16]

Isabelle Chapuis describes the room where the flute class met: "We were in the old dark part, wood floor, big somber painting on the wall."[17]

Crunelle's personality contrasted with this gloomy atmosphere; former students describe him as positive, endearing, kind, gentle, sweet, warm, generous, and possessing a heart of gold. Jean-Pierre Rampal said, "He was the most affectionate man one could imagine,"[18] and Jean-Louis Beaumadier recalls, "He was extremely benevolent and had a great musical and human experience of life, with a paternal kindness . . . he was always very positive and very friendly."[19] Brigitte Buxtorf related, "He was always there when we needed him, even on the phone."[20] Pierre-Yves Artaud added, "Very fatherly with his students, his personality pleased me a lot, and I felt good in his class."[21] Marie-Claire Jamet, who was married to Christian Lardé, related,

> Christian adored Mr. Crunelle because he had lost his father when he was nine. And later, he caught polio. He had begun to learn to play the violin, but when he heard a concert with Fernand Dufrêne on the radio he said, "I want to play the flute." He went straight to see Mr. Crunelle, who told him he was gifted. He practiced the flute sitting in his bed, and Mr. Crunelle

came to give him lessons, both of them sitting on his bed in his apartment, a sixth-floor walkup in the suburbs. Mr. Crunelle came to give him lessons until he could manage to walk again, and Christian never forgot that. He was for him a second father.[22]

Crunelle demonstrated extreme generosity at other times, too. After Jean-Claude Dhinaut's wedding, the Crunelles offered the young couple their car so they could enjoy a honeymoon. He would sometimes put students up in his apartment, and he found concerts for students to play to earn a little money.[23] Gérard Jemain took lessons with Crunelle before applying to the Conservatory. He asked how much he should pay, and the *maître* responded, "Oh, I don't think you have any money, so it doesn't matter. Don't pay me, I'm happy to be with you."[24]

Despite the intense competition, he encouraged a friendly and supportive atmosphere:

> It was very cordial, and Gaston Crunelle made sure that a friendship existed among the students and that there was no negativity. There was no need to be arrogant; he told us that it was going to be hard for everyone.[25]

Sometimes in other classes, students would curry favor with a professor by asking for private lessons for pay, but Brigitte Buxtorf recalls,

> We wondered if we should ask for private lessons with Mr. Crunelle. We had saved up and asked him and he said "Never! You don't need that, you have the lessons here." He was very honest, he could have taken advantage of it and said yes, but he told us he would never do that.[26]

His manner was formal. Waln relates that "Each student greets the teacher by a handshake as he enters and leaves the room, and assumes an attitude of grim silence during the observation of his colleague's lesson."[27] Students did not dare address him as Monsieur Crunelle but rather *maître*, the custom prior to May 1968. He had no trace of a northern accent but spoke like a true Parisian. He always dressed in a coat and tie, a practice which originated early in his career:

> [Louis] Ganne took him to a tailor and had him fitted with the regulation tail suit. He was a stickler for his musicians being well-turned out

(among the rich and famous). Crunelle himself was always very well-turned out, in class and in performance—I would consider his appearance, immaculate.[28]

Crunelle always wore his Chevalier de la Légion d'honneur medal, which he had received on August 31, 1955. This honor, established by Napoleon in 1802, is accorded to those with a minimum of twenty years of distinguished public service or twenty-five years of professional activity.

Despite Crunelle's formality, "He also had a joking side; he used to tell little stories, comic anecdotes in class to lighten the atmosphere."[29] He laughed a lot. For instance, he related that

> An admirer approached Florent Schmitt after the performance of *Salomé* and asked him: "Dear *maestro*, I thought there were only two pedals on the harp?" Schmitt, facetious as usual, replied: "Madame, you must be confusing it with a bicycle!"[30]

The *maître* was extremely demanding of students, never allowed a mistake, and required perfect rhythm. Crunelle specified whether to count subdivisions or whole beats in different sections of a piece. He often tapped the beat with a pencil and taught how to keep time by tapping one's foot, even in complex meters:

> He trained us to conduct very small meter patterns with the big toe, the foot resting on the heel, without beating time on the floor (a big no-no.). First, we made big patterns with the foot. Later, we made small patterns with the big toe inside the shoe. Finally, the patterns became so tiny, they were almost mental. We started out playing and foot-conducting scales and etudes.[31]

Crunelle had "a very systematic method; we went step-by-step."[32] He wrote an article around 1950, "On the Management of Time in the Study of the Flute," which outlined his approach to practicing tone and technique.[33] Classes started with *sons filés*, long tones, which he recommended practicing for half an hour daily. These consisted of ascending and descending octaves with various dynamics to perfect *legato* coordination of embouchure and air speed in register changes. According to Alexander Murray, "Crunelle was always after a soft, clear *timbré*. That's when you give an extra squeeze. You get the edge tone in it."[34] Referring to his smaller, tighter sound, typical of his era, Brigitte Buxtorf noted,

> We weren't yet talking about the diaphragm, nor about supporting the sound through it, and we were developing the facial musculature enormously, with the tension of the lips and this kind of technique that was already starting to go out of fashion.[35]

Crunelle never spoke about vibrato, as he considered it a natural part of the sound. He used Moyse's book, *De la sonorité*, at least in his earlier years.[36] He was concerned about the optimal position of the headjoint; Isabelle Chapuis recalled, "He marked the position of the headjoint on the body with red fingernail polish so we would not roll in."[37]

Technique, his primary consideration, was the next element of his practice scheme. He recommended devoting half an hour daily to scales and another hour to other technical studies. Students memorized exercises from Taffanel and Gaubert's *Seventeen Big Daily Finger Exercises for Flute* with many varied articulations, including doubling each note for double tonguing and tripling each note for triple tonguing. He also taught Marcel Moyse's *Daily Exercises* and the *7 Daily Exercises*, op. 5 by Matheus André Reichert (1830–1880).

Crunelle taught articulation in the French manner, with the tongue forward, protruding between the lips. He insisted on clear tonguing.

Études and solos encompassed the third part of Crunelle's practice scheme, with a recommended hour of daily practice. Isabelle Chapuis, who studied with him from 1961 to 1969, first as a private student and then in the flute class at the Conservatory, said, "I did so many etudes, so many! I would cover six etude books a year." Michael Scott related,

> There was an etude every week; whether it's perfect or not, you go on to the next one. The whole point was to teach us how to sight-read. We'd get up in front of everybody else, all playing the same study. There's no difference between the first year and the fifth year. Students were under a lot of pressure to try and keep up. At the time, I thought it was fearful, but in hindsight, it was very good, it motivated the students.[38]

In about 1950, the professors at the Conservatory drew up a list of pedagogical works used in their classes, and Crunelle listed the following études:

Joachim Andersen (1847–1909), *24 Etudes*, op. 15
Joachim Andersen, *School of Virtuosity for the Flute*, op. 60
Joachim Andersen, *24 Technical Etudes*, op. 63
Theobald Boehm, *24 Caprice-Etudes*, op. 26
Paul Jeanjean (1874–1928), *Études modernes*

In addition, students recalled that he occasionally taught the following:

Marcel Bitsch (1921–2011), *12 Etudes*
François-Julien Brun (1909–1990), *Études de virtuosité*
Pierre Camus, *12 Études*
Anton Bernhard Fürstenau (1792–1852), *Bouquet des tons*, op. 125
Ernesto Köhler (1849–1907), *Virtuoso Etudes*, op. 75
Heinrich Soussmann (1796–1848), ed. Moyse, *24 Études journaliers*, op. 53

Some students related that he did not cover sight-reading per se—that skill was developed through learning études, playing in orchestra and chamber music, and studying solfège. But others insisted that he gave specific, practical advice for sight-reading. Isabelle Chapuis remembers him saying many times: "Like an army general! Leave the dead and wounded behind. Keep going until the end."[39] Regarding the *déchiffrages*, Michael Scott added,

> You got sixty seconds to look at it, and as I was reading it through, Crunelle was suggesting the height of the music stand, and he said, "look at the music." I never should have taken my eyes off the music in those sixty seconds. We got quite a bit of instruction on how to sightread, how to beat time, with our foot.[40]

When Crunelle placed the *déchiffrage* on the stand at the *concours*, "He would put his finger on the tricky part" as a hint to the student.[41]

He taught how to practice and would zero in on the specific difficulty of a passage, emphasizing the optimal grouping of notes.[42] He stressed the importance of practicing slowly, suggested practicing études one phrase at a time, and often told students to practice a phrase backwards.[43] He gave students many alternate fingerings to facilitate difficult passages or to improve intonation. For instance, he advised using harmonic fingerings for the last line of Jolivet's *Chant de Linos*. He taught when to use each of the three fingerings for B-flat (thumb B-flat, "one-and-one" B-flat, and B-flat lever) and advocated leaving right-hand fingers down to simplify technique.[44] His detailed approach to technique included an innovative use of recording:

> When we went to work at his apartment, he used a tape recorder; it was quite rare at the time and there were none at the Conservatory. He asked us to play, record ourselves and then asked us what we thought of what we had just done before making us listen.[45]

Morceaux de concours dominated the solo repertoire covered in class, a frustration to some students. In his 1950 list, Crunelle included these solos:

Johann Sebastian Bach, Sonatas
Wolfgang Amadeus Mozart, Concertos
The following *morceaux de concours*:
Eugène Bozza (1905–1991), *Agrestide* (1942)
François-Julien Brun, *Un Andante et un Scherzo* (1948)
Henri Büsser, *Prélude et Scherzo*, op. 35 (1908), *Thème variée*, op. 68 (1919),
    Andalucia, op. 86 (1933)
Alfredo Casella (1883–1947), *Sicilienne et Burlesque* (1914)
Cécile Chaminade, Concertino, op. 107 (1902)[46]
Max d'Ollone (1875–1959), *Andante et Allegro en style ancien* (1926)
Henri Dutilleux, Sonatina (1943)
Alphonse Duvernoy, Concertino, op. 45 (1899)
Georges Enesco, *Cantabile et Presto* (1904)
Gabriel Fauré, *Fantaisie* (1898)
Louis Ganne, *Andante et Scherzo* (1901)
Philippe Gaubert, *Nocturne et Allegro Scherzando* (1906), *Fantaisie* (1920),
    Ballade (1928)
Gabriel Grovlez (1879–1944), *Romance et Scherzo* (1927)
Georges Hüe, *Fantaisie* (1913)
Jacques Ibert, Concerto (1934)[47]
André Jolivet, *Chant de Linos* (1944)
Henri Martelli, *Fantasiestück*, op. 67 (1947)
Émile Passani (1905–1974), Concerto (1949)
Albert Périlhou, *Ballade* (1903)
Pierre Sancan (1916–2008), Sonatina (1946)
Paul Taffanel, *Andante Pastorale et Scherzettino* (1907)
Henri Tomasi, Concertino in E major (1945)

In addition, he listed several works as *morceaux de concours* which were not written for the Conservatory yet molded in the same French style:

Philippe Gaubert, Three Sonatas (1917, 1924, and 1934)
Benjamin Godard, *Suite de trois morceaux*, op. 116 (1889)
Jules Mouquet, *La Flûte de Pan*, op. 15 (1904)
Charles-Marie Widor, Suite, op. 34 (1877)

Later, Crunelle taught the Flute Concerto (1956) by Jean Rivier (1896–1987) and more recent *morceaux de concours*,[48] especially those by Messiaen, Boutry, Gallois-Montbrun, and Rivier, composers who occasionally visited the class. Bach and Mozart were reserved for the most advanced flutists; Crunelle told his students, "To play *Chant de Linos*, it takes hours and hours. To play Bach or Mozart, it takes years and years."[49] Artaud explained:

In general, the students stayed at the Conservatory for three years, and so those in the third year, considered to be those who would graduate, had the right to play a movement of a Mozart concerto or of a Bach sonata.[50]

This approach mirrors that of Taffanel, whose students were restricted to a regime of exercises, scales, and studies, then proceeded to nineteenth-century virtuoso repertoire—more valuable for technical development than musical merit. "Not until a student had successfully performed some of this repertoire in the twice-yearly examinations would he be allowed to proceed to Bach, Handel, Mozart, or Saint-Saëns."[51] In Crunelle's view, Bach and Mozart presented interpretive problems that could undermine a student's success in a competition; he said, "Bach's music is obviously great but it's like the Bible: each has his own interpretation."[52]

Although he welcomed *morceaux de concours* in progressive styles, Crunelle never taught sonatas by Hindemith, Martinů, Poulenc, Prokofiev, or Reinecke, now considered standards. There were several reasons for the limited literature. The era of the flute soloist only began with Rampal, so Crunelle did not see the need to develop an extensive solo repertoire. The *morceaux de concours* were also a more efficient way to develop excellent tone and technique.[53] Although his 1950 repertoire list includes orchestral excerpts from the Taffanel and Gaubert *Complete Method*, he rarely taught them, focusing on material and skills needed for the *concours*.

His interpretation was based on faithfulness to the composer: "We always sought clean playing, perfect accuracy, total respect for the text, these were above all his criteria."[54] He encouraged personality in performance: "When he found our interpretation a little weak, he encouraged us with a nudge of the elbow in the ribs."[55] One had to find a color appropriate to the music; he said, "Debussy is beyond the notes, it is your soul. You must reveal your soul."[56] For Mozart's Concerto in G Major, he advised, "The concerto is huge, the opening is joyful, it's grandiose. You can't play in an inhibited, shy way; you must play wide open."[57]

Pierre-Yves Artaud related that "We were obsessed with the problem of memorizing."[58] This focus on memory is exceptional in wind pedagogy, which historically has prepared students for an orchestral rather than a solo career, and memorization is less common than among pianists, singers, and string players.[59] Students played each solo studied in class by memory from the moment they started learning it. Crunelle taught students to use different modes of memory: analytical, visual, tactile, and aural. He divided up each piece into sections—conforming with the musical structure—which he outlined in contrasting bold-colored ink to enhance visual memory. In class he would ask students to play the various sections of the piece in random order. He would mark the reprise of a theme with a drawing of an eye.[60]

A pianist visited the class to accompany every student at least once a month. Roger Boutry (1932–2019) accompanied the class from 1949 to 1955;[61] his Concertino was the *morceau de concours* in 1955, and he became a renowned conductor, pianist, arranger, and composer. The regular pianist in the 1960s was Annette Monteille, and the Conservatory paid her for seventeen hours of accompanying per month.[62]

The last month of the school year was devoted to the new *morceau de concours*. Crunelle had gone over the piece with the composer beforehand, and at the first class after the piece was released, he talked the students through it; as Renaud François related,

He said: "Pay attention to the third page, start your work there because that is where it gets complicated." He told us that to put us at ease without revealing the piece, without cheating, but he warned us to guide us in our work.[63]

Betty Bang observed,

The constant repetition of many students playing the same piece taught one the music by ear and gave each student the combined insights of the other players. I remember the day when a talented Swiss girl [Brigitte Buxtorf] for the first time played the solo as if it were music. At the next session, many others were able to follow her lead.[64]

Crunelle prepared students for the experience of playing on stage in the *concours*: "He taught us not to get overwhelmed by the jury which was seated just beyond the stage by directing one's attention to the monumental chandelier of the Salle Berlioz."[65] At the *concours*, he turned pages for the pianist, a reassuring presence for the students. He told students to relax, to play naturally, and not to force. His comments put students at ease.[66]

Although his repertoire was narrow, Crunelle gave students tools that could be applied to other music: "He tried to give us the means to manage on our own by giving us skillful and astute advice, and that was very valuable because it led to very secure playing."[67] He helped Brigitte Buxtorf prepare for a competition after she had left the Conservatory, and she was astonished that he had such insight into a complex contemporary work.[68] Many of his former students, including Pierre-Yves Artaud and Renaud François, made careers in new music.

He provided students the grounding that could take them in various directions, or as Isabelle Chapuis said, "When you have the basics, you can fly better."[69] When students finished their studies, Crunelle told them, "You are musicians, I don't have to tell you what to do, you already know it, and if you don't know it you will never know it."[70] After students left the Conservatory, he helped them with their careers: "He was very attentive and followed his students. As soon as I got my prize, he gave me some gigs to get started."[71]

Crunelle "was a mixture of rigor and liberty."[72] He taught his interpretation of a piece and did not accept contrary ideas, especially regarding where to breathe. For instance, in Dutilleux's Sonatina, he absolutely forbade students to breathe at the beginning of the coda, on the barline at rehearsal 16. Dutilleux himself endorsed this idea when he visited the class.[73] Several of Crunelle's students showed me their music with his markings in blue and red ink. He also marked discretionary breathing spots in parentheses. As Leone Buyse relates,

One huge difference between the French and the American educational systems is that the student is never expected to question. The teacher presents his knowledge in a very dogmatic manner . . . M. Crunelle, whenever showing me a new piece for the first time, goes through the piece completely marking all the breaths, tempi, etc., as if I never had any ideas of my own. I may never disagree with him, either.[74]

The authenticity of Crunelle's interpretation derives from personal experience; he had of course met Philippe Gaubert, Louis Ganne, and most of the composers whose music he taught. He had played Enesco's *Cantabile et Presto* with the composer at the piano. He recalled seeing Debussy.[75] He knew Louis Fleury, the dedicatee of Debussy's *Syrinx*, and insisted on Fleury's interpretation of the piece.[76] "It was like an aura surrounding him, that he'd been immersed with these people."[77]

The French educational system has become less rigid since May 1968, but there is still less emphasis on personal choice than in America and a sense that there is a proper or correct way to do something.[78]

On the other hand, Crunelle sometimes let students do things their own way. If a flutist had a peculiar hand position or way of tonguing, he would not correct it if the outcome was successful.[79]

Crunelle employed his rigorous training in solfège in class; he and Ulysse Delécluse, professor of clarinet, "made constant use of singing their interpretation in solfeggio, a device of syllables which each performer must thoroughly master."[80] He demonstrated on the flute frequently in earlier years but later less often, and his playing was impressive. Renaud François remarked,

> He always played with finesse and a very high precision of attack, and I considered that the sound of my dreams. When he played, I thought it was angelic, an extraordinary purity of sound. I remember when he played the solo of the scene of the Elysian Fields by Gluck in 1964. We were alone in the classroom, and it was like crystal, beautiful![81]

Ida Ribera remarked, "He had a superb sound that we all wanted to imitate. When he played, the flute was always beautiful, a warm and very colorful sound."[82] Brigitte Buxtorf said, "Each time Mr. Crunelle picked up the flute, he always had a better sound than any of his students . . . He never struggled to demonstrate or to show us his abilities."[83] Bernard Pierreuse recalls, "He had excellent technique and would often astonish us by playing such and such a difficult passage, sometimes with a Gitane held between two fingers of the right hand!"[84]

Women in the Flute Class

Crunelle's era at the Conservatory coincided with an increase in the number of women accepted into the flute class and leading professional careers, a trend which has continued. While feminism has a long tradition in France, it has not always achieved its goals, and women's gains have come later than in some other nations. The Vichy regime was a setback to women who sought careers outside of the home. Women have been more prominent in some musical activities than others, so before World War II there were numerous women composers, singers, pianists, and string players, but few wind players. Today, throughout the world the number of girls who take up the flute vastly outnumbers the number of boys, and more and more women perform and teach professionally. But in the nineteenth century, women flutists were extremely rare.[85]

Georgette Réné (b. 1892) earned a second prize in flute at the Paris Conservatory in 1913, studying with Hennebains. Lucy Dragon was the first woman to win a first prize in 1917. A gifted flutist, she had difficulty finding a position in an orchestra; a music director complained that "her presence would distract her colleagues tempted to look at her legs."[86] Nonetheless, she carved out a singular career, being one of the first flutists to play on the radio.[87] Crunelle's sister Suzanne followed Dragon in 1921. The following is a complete list of first prizes in flute that women earned through 1971:

1917 Lucy Dragon
1921 Suzanne Crunelle
1944 Gisèle Chauvin
1946 Régine Fischer
1951 Odette Ernest (married name Dias)
1957 Marguerite Chartois (known as Ida, married name Ribera)
1958 Colette Peaucelle, Josiane Harbonnier
1959 Brigitte Buxtorf
1960 Hirohiko Kato
1968 Elisabeth Richard, Arlette Leroy (married name Biget)
1969 Gladys Ohier
1970 Isabelle Chapuis, Annu Utagawa
1971 Geneviève Amar

By the end of Crunelle's years, there was an average of three or four women in the class, and a handful of them never won a first prize.

Crunelle encouraged Odette Ernest and Isabelle Chapuis, who both studied with him privately before entering the Conservatory, to pursue the flute. Brigitte Buxtorf believed she was given the same support as men in her class: "I think I was very lucky. At no time did I feel that the girls were less fortunate than the boys. There was real equality, both at the Conservatory and in the orchestra."[88] On the other hand, Chapuis recalls male students making sexist jokes directed at women in the orchestra and at student conductors.[89]

May 1968

France is still divided over the events of May 1968 in Paris and elsewhere. At the time, there was widespread dissatisfaction with higher education, which was considered elitist and authoritarian. Overreaction to what began as small protests quickly ballooned into a nationwide crisis. In March, students at the University of Paris in Nanterre to the west of the city occupied buildings on campus. They were protesting the Vietnam War and demanding the right to spend the night in each other's dorm rooms. The university was subsequently closed, and in solidarity, students at the Sorbonne began protests on May 3. Hundreds were arrested and the Sorbonne was also closed. Soon the protests became nationwide, and students erected street barriers and threw paving stones at the police. A general strike supported the students.

At the Conservatory on May 19, students voted 352 for and 127 against the following resolution:

> Given the general protest movement in France and given the position taken by the vast majority of French musicians in favor of a reform of the structures of music in France, we propose a boycott of classes for a period of fifteen days, renewable by decision of a general assembly meeting at the end of this period, the creation of study commissions at all levels for the purpose of developing the necessary reforms and studying the problems of postponing the *concours*.[90]

Many faculty members were sympathetic with the students:

> Gathered in a special meeting on May 20, the professors "affirm their solidarity with the students in the struggle undertaken by all the students for the improvement of all that concerns their studies and their future," declare

themselves "intent on increasing their own action to make the various necessary reforms as soon as possible in support of their students" and "ready to collaborate in any effective and constructive work in this direction."[91]

Crunelle was not among them:

He was mad with rage following the stories that had happened at the Conservatory in May 1968. He had been, unlike other people like André Jolivet whom I knew, angry at the students who had damaged things.[92]

Students continued their boycott and occupation of the Conservatory while various meetings were held, most importantly with Marcel Landowsky (1915–1999), Director of Music, Lyrical Arts, and Dance at the Ministry of Cultural Affairs. After he said he favored some of their proposed reforms, the boycott was called off in late June. The flute *concours* for that year was delayed until September 24, and the general situation in France calmed down over the summer vacation.

Some reforms were enacted at the Conservatory. Its *Conseil supérieur* (governing council) was restructured to include student representation. Composition classes now included a greater diversity of musical styles. In 1973, the Conservatory created the *Diplôme d'études supérieures musicales* or DESM, requiring either (1) a *baccalauréat*[93] and three Conservatory prizes, or (2) a university diploma and two Conservatory prizes. This new degree placed less emphasis on virtuosity and more on musical ability enhanced by general cultural knowledge. The culture of the Conservatory did not change as quickly as students had hoped. One of their demands was not met until more than forty years later; *élèves* only recently became *étudiants*. Both terms translate as "students," but *élèves* attend elementary schools, and *étudiants* attend universities. Noémi Lefebvre also remarked, "If the term *maître* has been used less after 1968, the instrumental classes remain marked by the autocratic authority of the teacher."[94]

8

Crunelle and the *morceaux de concours*

The first "Golden Age" of *morceaux de concours* for flute was during the tenure of Paul Taffanel with well-known works by Chaminade, Fauré, Enesco, Ganne, Gaubert, and Taffanel. The commissioning program, however, waned during the 1920s and 1930s, resulting in pieces that have fallen out of the repertoire. This can be attributed to two factors: the Conservatory Director Henri Rabaud's conservatism and Marcel Moyse's lack of interest in modern music aside from Ibert's Concerto. Ibert wrote his Concerto for Moyse, who subsequently recorded it, and the third movement of the Concerto was the *morceau de concours* for 1934, but not commissioned by the Conservatory.

The flute commissions took on new life during the tenure of Gaston Crunelle, due to Director Claude Delvincourt's interest in the *morceaux de concours* and Crunelle's openness to newer music. Pierre-Yves Artaud contrasts the attitudes of Moyse and Crunelle; he observed a masterclass with Moyse in which *le maître* refused to teach the Prokofiev Sonata, saying, "It's not music" ("*Ce n'est pas de la musique*"):

> Modern composers were not interesting for him [Moyse]. Crunelle was the opposite, he was extremely open. Not much music escaped his notice, because he didn't impose his personal opinions, he did not despise it.[1]

Thus, unlike Moyse, Crunelle's reason for not teaching repertoire such as sonatas by Hindemith, Martinů, and Prokofiev was not a repugnance for their style but rather a decision to focus on the *morceaux de concours*, many of which were stylistically advanced during his era.

Crunelle regularly advised composers who were commissioned by the Conservatory director to write the annual *morceaux de concours*, and according to Renaud François, he could have influenced the director's decision about which composers to invite: "He had a lot of powers, he could choose the juries, the works, in any case suggest them. He was very smart and manipulated things."[2] Delvincourt secured major composers with a more progressive vision than in past years—especially Dutilleux, Jolivet, and

Gaston Crunelle and Flute Playing in Twentieth-Century France. Leonard Garrison, Oxford University Press.
© Oxford University Press 2024. DOI: 10.1093/9780197778579.003.0008

Messiaen (Appendix 5 provides a complete list of the commissioned pieces from Crunelle's years).[3]

Aside from the works by Gaubert, Dutilleux, Sancan, Jolivet, and Messiaen, these pieces are not widely performed; in fact, out of twenty-eight works commissioned, fourteen have not been recorded.[4] Kathleen Cook's doctoral dissertation provides detailed descriptions of the works through 1955, and Melissa Colgin covers those written from 1955 to 1990.[5] As in previous eras, all the composers were French, except for the Polish Antoni Szałowski (1907–1973), the Belgian Marcel Poot (1901–1988), and the Italian Luigi Cortese (1899–1976). The only women composers were Jeanine Rueff (1922–1999) and Ginette Keller (1925–2017). Most were on the faculty of the Conservatory, and many were Prix de Rome winners, including Bozza, Dutilleux, Sancan, Dupont, Boutry, Gallois-Montbrun, Gallon, Chaynes, Petit, and Aubin.

All the *morceaux de concours* fulfill their function as contest pieces, combining lyrical passages with technically challenging ones. Cook notes that those written between 1941 and 1955 are more difficult than those written previously, but Colgin finds various levels of difficulty after 1955. Stylistically, Colgin groups the pieces into the following categories:[6]

Conservative: Boutry, Gallois-Montbrun, Brun, Gallon, Casadesus, Aubin, Hubeau
Progressive: Poot, Cortese, Hugon, Bondon
Atonal or serial: Chaynes, Petit, Keller

She finds that several works from the years 1955–69 "stand out as superior contributions to the repertoire. They are Gallois-Montbrun's *Divertissement* (1956), Chaynes's *Variations sur un tanka* (1962), Rivier's *Ballade* (1966), and Keller's *Chant de Parthénope* (1968)."[7]

Before each piece was published, Crunelle met with the composer and suggested changes; as Pierre-Yves Artaud relates, "Gaston often influenced the composers."[8] For instance, in the Sonatina by Dutilleux, he asked in the composer to add thirteen measures of piano solo at the beginning of the *Animé* section at rehearsal number 8 to give the flutist a chance to rest. After rehearsal 10, Crunelle suggested the flutter-tongue *ad libitum* as an alternative to the original triple tonguing. He also requested revisions to the cadenza before rehearsal 16 to avoid awkward fingerings involving low C-sharp and suggested that Dutilleux rewrite the coda from rehearsal 16.[9] According to

André Jolivet's diary, Crunelle met with him on February 21 and 24, 1944, and the composer spoke with Crunelle on May 18 regarding *Chant de Linos*; the *concours* was held on May 23.[10] Crunelle asked Luigi Cortese to add a cadenza to his *Introduzione e Allegro* to conform to a higher level of difficulty.[11] Indeed, a cadenza had become *de rigueur*; of twenty-eight *morceaux de concours* from Crunelle's years, only nine lack cadenzas.[12] After meeting with Crunelle, the composers sometimes visited the flute class to offer their input on preparing the performances.

The selection of the *morceau de concours* for 1941 was probably left to Crunelle, as the disarray of the previous year precluded the commissioning of a new work. Gaubert's *Fantaisie* was a natural choice, as it had been the piece with which Crunelle won his *prix d'excellence* in 1920, and Gaubert could have attended the *concours* in June 1941.

The first *morceau de concours* of the new era was *Agrestide* (1942) by Eugène Bozza, who had recently won the Prix de Rome and became a prolific composer of music for winds. The title derives from the adjective *agreste*, or "rustic." It is a challenging work in three sections: (1) a pastorale, connected by a cadenza to (2) a lyrical section in 6/8, requiring great finesse in the high register, and (3) an *Animé* in mixed meter.

The most popular work from Crunelle's era is Dutilleux's Sonatina (1943), one of four pieces Dutilleux wrote for the Conservatory's *concours*, along with his *Sarabande et cortège* (1942) for bassoon and piano, the Oboe Sonata (1947), and the *Choral, cadence et fugato* (1950) for trombone and piano. Dutilleux considered them early works, not representative of his mature style; the Sonatina, he remarks, "has been recorded many times abroad, although I have never wanted it to be recorded in France because it doesn't sound really like my music."[13] Considering their common ties to Douai, Crunelle and Dutilleux probably had a sympathetic relationship. Dutilleux's piece is the only *morceau de concours* from the modern era that Crunelle performed in public (aside from Jolivet's *Chant de Linos* in its version for quintet). The Sonatina is in three sections: (1) Allegretto in 7/8, with a cadenza leading to (2) an expressive Andante, and (3) a sprightly *Animé*, ending with a more elaborate cadenza and a coda.

The following year, Delvincourt commissioned another major composer, André Jolivet, whose *Chant de Linos*, discussed in Chapter 6 in its version for quintet, is one of the most difficult works written for the flute *concours*. As Jean-Pierre Rampal relates, most of the candidates for prizes found it too demanding to memorize:

In 1944, I obtained my First Prize in flute at the Paris Conservatory with the *Chant de Linos*. At the time, flautists were horrified by the modernity and difficulty of the work; so much so that I was one of the only ones, with Pol Mule, to play it by heart.[14]

Three other flutists, Gisèle Chauvin, Édouard Deuez, and Jacques Castagner received first prizes that year, and altogether, seven flutists out of sixteen—Deuez, Mule, Rampal, Jacques Royer, Paul Éthuin, Georges Savoy, and Serge Quillet—performed by memory.[15] The piece affirms Jolivet's searching for music's "ancient spiritual meaning" and his "continuing preoccupation with ritual; [it] exploits the flute's technical capabilities and reveals the influence of Le Flem's teaching in the contrapuntal independence of the lines."[16]

The 1945 required solo was the Concertino in E Major by Henri Tomasi, whose *Petite Suite de printemps* for quintet is discussed in Chapter 6. Without precedent for a *morceau de concours*, the Concertino is in three separate movements with a total duration of thirteen minutes, starting with a cadenza ushering in an *Allegretto giocoso*. The second movement is a lyrical *Largo* leading without pause into the finale, a *saltarello*.

Pierre Sancan wrote his Sonatina, one of the most enduring *morceaux de concours*, in 1946. A Prix de Rome winner, he was primarily a concert pianist, teaching piano at the Paris Conservatory from 1956 to 1985. In three sections played without a break, the Sonatina begins with a lyrical 6/8 with frequent hemiolas. A piano cadenza introduces an *Andante espressivo* in which the flute sustains long phrases. A flute cadenza connects directly to an *Animé*; just before the end, Sancan brings back the melody of the first section, a tradition going back to Fauré's *Fantaisie*.

Delvincourt tapped Henri Martelli to compose the *morceau de concours* in 1947, his *Fantaisiestück*. Despite the piece's German title, Martelli was French and studied with Widor at the Paris Conservatory. This work consists mostly of rapid tongued sixteenths and is too repetitious to elicit much artistic interest.

Studying with Philippe Gaubert at the Paris Conservatory, François-Julien Brun won a first prize in flute in 1926 and became the director of the Garde républicaine band. He composed *Un Andante et un Scherzo*, dedicated to Moyse, in 1948. He also wrote a set of *Études de virtuosité* that Crunelle often taught.

For the 1949 *concours*, French composer and pianist Émile Passani wrote his Flute Concerto in three movements. The first contains frequent changes of meter. An optional cadenza connects the slow movement to the finale, marked by challenging quick leaps.

André Pépin (1907–1985), who composed the 1950 *morceaux de concours*, earned a first prize in flute from the Paris Conservatory in 1928. His *Impromptu* is written in a conservative style, a *siciliano* with a cadenza in the middle.

The composer of the 1951 piece, Antoni Szałowski, was born in Poland and studied at the Warsaw Conservatory before emigrating to Paris in 1931 to study with Nadia Boulanger (1887–1979). Written in a Neoclassical style, his Concertino is a challenge to both the flutist and the pianist. The opening *Allegretto* contains both lyrical and technical elements. An extended cadenza connects to a brilliant *Allegro*.

Roger Nichols characterizes Delvincourt's commission of Olivier Messiaen to compose the 1952 *morceau de concours* "a fairly bold move," as "the shock waves from the performance of the *Turangalîla Symphony* at the Aix Festival in summer 1950 were still reverberating through France."[17] *Le Merle noir* is the first of Messiaen's many pieces based on specific birdsong, and the bird of the title is a thrush (*Turdus merula*) common to European woodlands and unrelated to the American blackbird. Messiaen captures its song accurately in two flute cadenzas. Each of these leads to a melodic section with shifting meters, presented in canon on its second appearance. The piece ends with a wild coda based on serialized pitch and rhythm, with disjunct leaps and rhythmic intricacies.[18]

Aulos by Jacque-Dupont (1906–1985) was the 1953 *morceau de concours*. In the traditional form for such works, it is in two sections, an *Andante ben moderato* and an *Allegro con spirito*, with a cadenza near the end of the first section. Jacque-Dupont won first prizes from the Conservatory in piano, harmony, and composition and was a Prix de Rome winner. He became director of the conservatory in Toulon. Most of his compositions are for piano.

The rarely performed *Diptyque* by Jeanine Rueff, written for the 1954 *concours*, is even more technically demanding than Jolivet's *Chant de Linos*. At the Conservatory, Rueff was an accompanist for the saxophone class of Marcel Mule and clarinet class of Ulysse Delécluse, and as a composer, she is best known for her works for those instruments. The title refers to a religious painting with two panels, and the piece has two sections. Cook relates the following:

Performing this work for the 1954 concours, Michel Debost received a first prize and recalls some comments by his teacher Gaston Crunelle pertaining to the articulation in *Diptyque*. Debost remembers that Crunelle told the students to feel the sextuplets in groups of four rather than each sextuplet in two groups of three. This would require double rather than triple tonguing and for some players may be easier.[19]

Roger Boutry's Concertino from 1955 is the fifth *morceau de concours* with the same title, following those of Duvernoy (1899), Chaminade (1902), Tomasi (1945), and Szałowski. As has been mentioned, Boutry served as accompanist for Crunelle's class from 1949 through 1955. He won a Prix de Rome in 1954. He became a conductor and taught harmony at the Conservatory from 1962 through 1997. The Concertino begins with a short premonition of its fast movement (*Allegro vivo*) and settles into a lyrical *Andante*. A brief flute cadenza precedes a scherzo-like *Allegretto*. The *Allegro vivo* receives full treatment, and a more extensive cadenza leads to the coda, *Vivace*. In a conservative style, the Concertino is less difficult than many of the works written in the same period.

Deserving of wider attention, the *Divertissement* (1956) by Raymond Gallois-Montbrun is an effective recital piece in the standard two-part format. Colgin characterizes the piece as "an example of effervescent French romanticism in the manner of Gabriel Fauré, Vincent d'Indy and Georges Auric."[20] The composer was born in colonial Vietnam and won the Prix de Rome in 1944. A violinist, he served as director of the Paris Conservatory from 1962 through 1983.

Nearly a decade after composing his first *morceau de concours* in 1948, *Un Andante et un scherzo*, François-Julien Brun wrote *Pastorale d'Arcadie* for the 1957 *concours*. The latter piece is in a light style and is cast in four sections played without a break: (1) *Allegro capriccioso*; (2) *Scherzando*; (3) *Lento espressivo*; and (4) reprise of the *Allegro*.

In 1958, Conservatory Director Raymond Loucheur turned to Noël Gallon, a Prix de Rome winner in 1910 who had taught at the Conservatory since 1920—first solfège, then counterpoint and fugue. According to Alain Louvier, "His compositions are marked by elegance and clarity, and by a discreet impressionism that veils his contrapuntal skill."[21] *Improvisation et Rondo* is lighter work in a conventional style.

The Belgian composer Marcel Poot wrote *Légende* for the 1959 *concours*. Having studied at the Brussels Conservatory, he became its professor of harmony and then director from 1949 to 1966. Colgin notes that the work's style is markedly different from that of *morceaux de concours* written by French composers.[22] *Légende* is marked by dissonance and asymmetric meters but holds limited artistic interest.

Robert Casadesus, whose quintet was discussed in Chapter 4, wrote the *morceau de concours* for 1960, his *Fantaisie*, op. 59. In a two-part form, the piece is conservative harmonically, with a key center of E minor/major, and poses fewer difficulties than other works of this period.

Introduzione e Allegro, op. 40 by Luigi Cortese was the commissioned work for the 1961 *concours*. Cortese studied in Paris with André Gedalge—who also taught Ravel, Enescu, Honegger, Ibert, Koechlin, Milhaud, and Schmitt—and in Rome with Alfredo Casella, whose style was a major influence. Cortese was director of the Liceo musicale in Genoa. In a more progressive style than the *morceaux* since 1954, his work presents technical challenges for both flutist and pianist. It is cast in a two-part form with a cadenza in the opening section.

In 1962, the flute *concours* featured Charles Chaynes's *Variations sur un tanka*, one of the most successful modern works. Chaynes (1925–2016) first studied at the Toulouse Conservatory and then at the Paris Conservatory as a student of Darius Milhaud. He won a Prix de Rome in 1951. From 1965 to 1975, he was director of the radio station France Musique, and then from 1975 to 1990 head of musical production at Radio France. His modernist language has elements in common with Messiaen, Dutilleux, and Jolivet. A tanka is a Japanese poetic form consisting of five lines with the syllabic pattern 5-7-5-7-7. Chaynes's piece consists of five variations dominated by meters and groupings of fives and sevens.

Pierre Petit (1922–2000) composed *Petite Suite*, the 1963 *morceau de concours*. A Prix de Rome winner in 1946, he taught the history of civilization at the Paris Conservatory and the École polytechnique and was an administrator for Radiodiffusion télévision française. In 1963, he succeeded Alfred Cortot as director of the École normale de musique. Colgin writes, "*Petite Suite*, a three-movement work, seems to poke fun at various compositional conventions with tongue-in-cheek humor."[23]

The *Concertino dell'amicizia* by Tony Aubin (1907–1981) was the *morceau de concours* for 1964. He won the Prix de Rome in 1930 and starting in 1945 taught composition at the Conservatory. Paul Griffiths remarks that "His compositions pursue the more harmonically rich and colourful aspects of the music of Ravel and Dukas."[24] This Neoclassical Concertino—*dell-amicizia* means "of friendship"—is in four sections: (1) *Allegretto*, (2) *Adagietto, calme*, (3) *Allegro*, and (4) reprise of the *Allegretto*.

The most substantial piece written for the *concours* is the four-movement Sonata (1965) by Georges Hugon (1904–1980), who taught solfège and harmony at the Paris Conservatory. His mostly atonal and rhythmically complex Sonata shows influences of the Second Viennese School of Schoenberg, Berg, and Webern. Movements III (*Larghetto*) and IV (*Final*) were required for the *concours*.

Jean Rivier was professor of composition at the Paris Conservatory from 1948 to 1966, and Crunelle performed and taught his Flute Concerto. Colgin finds that his *Ballade*, the *morceau de concours* for 1966, "is a worthy contribution to the repertoire."[25] With dissonant but not atonal harmony, the work is in ternary form, with slower outer sections framing a virtuosic *Allegro*.

Written in a conservative style, the *morceau de concours* for 1967 is the *Idylle* by Jean Hubeau (1917–1992). The composer was a pianist who entered the Paris Conservatory at age nine. He succeeded Claude Delvincourt as director of the Versailles Conservatory in 1942 after Delvincourt became director at the Paris Conservatory. From 1957 to 1982, Hubeau taught chamber music at the Paris Conservatory. *Idylle* is a tonal work in three sections: *Lento–Allegro–Lento*.

As mentioned in Chapter 7, the 1968 flute *concours* was delayed until September because of the student protests in May. The *morceau de concours* for that year was Ginette Keller's *Chant de Parthenope*, one of the best pieces from Crunelle's tenure. A student of Nadia Boulanger, Tony Aubin, and Olivier Messiaen—the last was her primary influence—Keller taught solfège and analysis at the Paris Conservatory and analysis at the École normale de musique. In Greek mythology, Parthenope was a siren who, failing to attract Ulysses, threw herself into the sea and drowned. Keller's atonal work begins with somber slow music, leading to a rhythmically complex and frantic dance, and concluding with more slow music fading into the depths.

The last *morceau de concours* from Crunelle's era was the *Mouvement chorégraphique* (1969) by Jacques Bondon (1927–2008). Originally a violinist, Bondon studied with Milhaud, Rivier, and Koechlin. He was a founder of the Orchestre de chambre de musique contemporaine, which became the Ensemble moderne de Paris. Driving chromatic sixteenths dominate *Mouvement chorégraphique*, but despite occasional moments of lyricism, it lacks interest for flutists or audiences.

Conservatory faculty usually composed the sight-reading pieces, and starting in 1961, the composer of the *morceau de concours imposé* also wrote the *déchiffrage*. The scores for the *déchiffrages* are held in the Archives nationales de France (ANF)[26] and will not be publicly available for many years due to copyright laws. One exception is Charles Koechlin's *Morceau de lecture pour la flûte*, op. 218 (1948), published by Billaudot. Some of the pieces are missing in the ANF, and some of them have no composer identified. The *concours* for entrance to the Conservatory often used previous sight-reading pieces, but sometimes a piece was newly composed. It is not known whether Crunelle worked with composers who wrote *déchiffrages*, but he did take copies of them home and later gave them to former students.[27]

Outside of the *morceaux de concours*, at least two other works were dedicated to Crunelle. Marcel Bitsch (1921–2011) studied composition at the Conservatory with Henri Büsser, won the *Prix de Rome* in 1945, and taught counterpoint and fugue at the Conservatory from 1961 until 1988. Crunelle often taught his set of études.[28] Gabriel Grovlez (1897–1944), who had composed the 1927 *morceau de concours* for flute, *Romance et Scherzo*, dedicated his Concertino to Crunelle.[29]

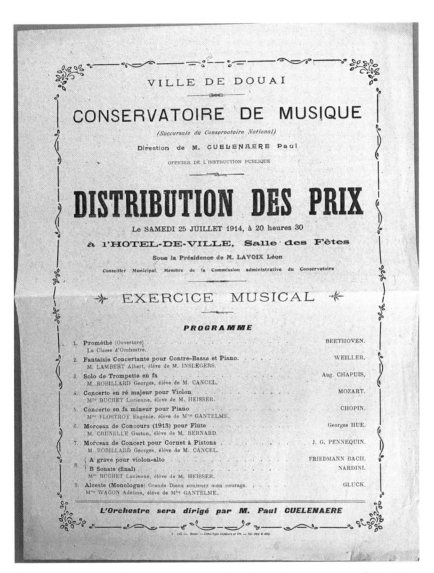

Figure 1 Program of first-prize winners of the Douai Conservatory, July 25, 1914.
Courtesy Archives municipales de Douai.

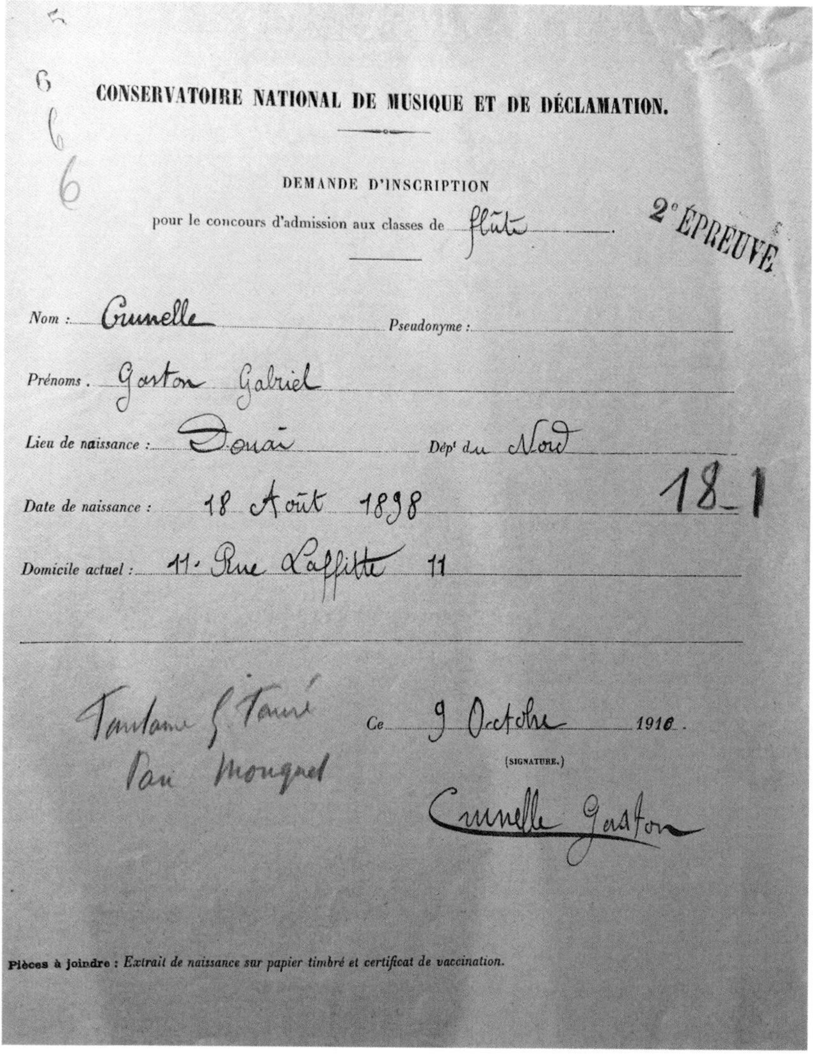

CONSERVATOIRE NATIONAL DE MUSIQUE ET DE DÉCLAMATION.

DEMANDE D'INSCRIPTION

pour le concours d'admission aux classes de flûte

2e ÉPREUVE

Nom : Crunelle *Pseudonyme :*

Prénoms. Gaston Gabriel

Lieu de naissance : Douai *Dép^t* du Nord

Date de naissance : 18 Août 1898 18_1

Domicile actuel : 11. Rue Laffitte 11

Toulouse ... Fauré
Pau Mouquet

Ce 9 Octobre 1916.

(SIGNATURE.)

Crunelle Gaston

Pièces à joindre : *Extrait de naissance sur papier timbré et certificat de vaccination.*

Figure 2 Gaston Crunelle's audition for the Paris Conservatory in 1916.
Courtesy Archives nationales de France.

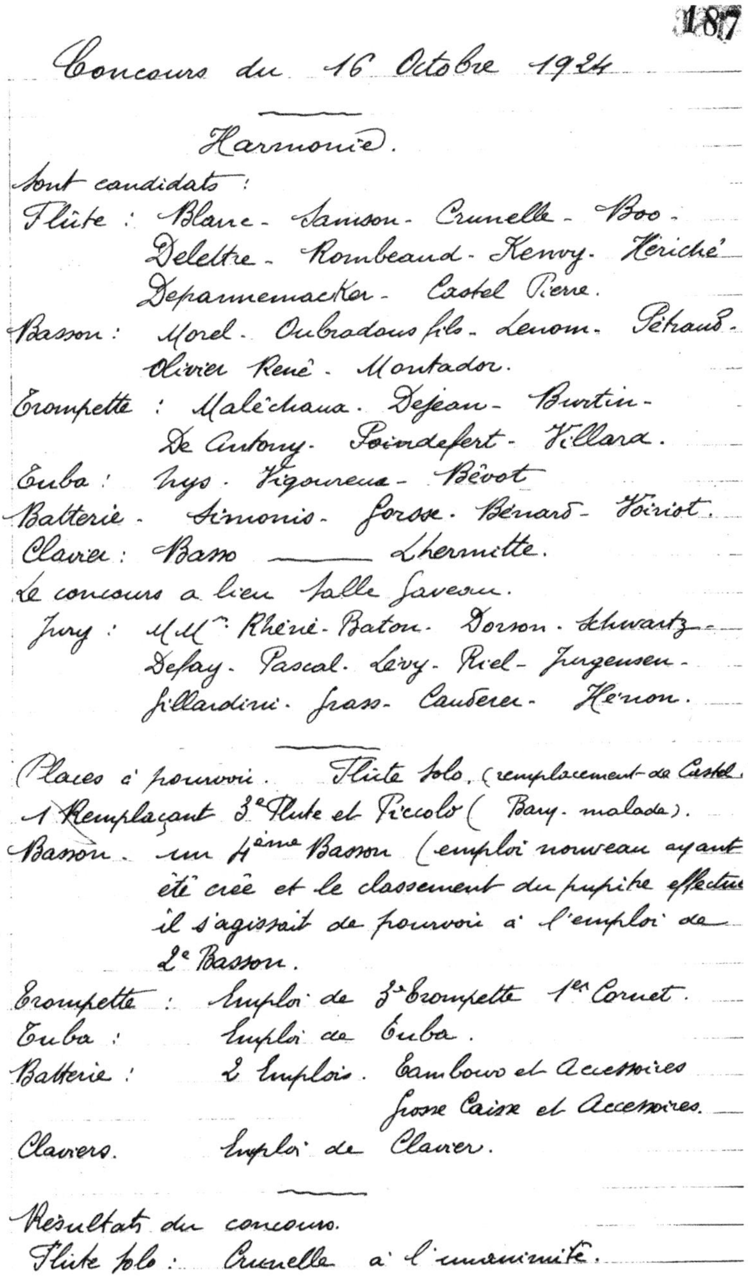

Concours du 16 Octobre 1924

Harmonie.

Sont candidats :

Flûte : Blanc - Samson - Crunelle - Boo -
Deletre - Rombeaud - Kenvy. Hériché
Deparnemacker - Castel Pierre.

Basson : Morel. Oubradous fils - Lenom - Pétraud -
Olivier René . Montador.

Trompette : Maléchaud. Déjean - Burtin -
De Antony. Poindefert - Villard.

Tuba : Inys. Vigoureux - Bévot

Batterie - Simonis - Forsse. Bénard - Hériot

Clavier : Basso _____ Lhermitte.

Le concours a lieu Salle Gaveau.

Jury : MM. Rhéné-Baton. Dorson. Schwartz _
Defay. Pascal. Lévy - Ricel - Jungensen -
Gillardini. Grass - Cauberei - Hernon.

(Places à pourvoir _____ Flûte solo. (remplacement de Castel
1 Remplaçant 3ᵉ Flûte et Piccolo (Bary. malade).

Basson _ un 4ᵉⁱᵉ Basson (emploi nouveau ayant
été créé et le classement du pupitre effectué
il s'agissait de pourvoir à l'emploi de
2ᵉ Basson.

Trompette : Emploi de 3ᵉ Trompette 1ᵉʳ Cornet.

Tuba : Emploi de Tuba.

Batterie : 2 Emplois. Tambour et Accessoires
grosse Caisse et Accessoires. _

Claviers. Emploi de Clavier.

Résultats du concours.
Flûte solo : Crunelle à l'unanimité.

Figure 3 Audition for principal flute of the Concerts Pasdeloup, 1924. *Courtesy Concerts Pasdeloup.*

Figure 4 Gaston Crunelle; photo taken during his mid-career period. Signed "To Isabelle Chapuis, very affectionately, G. Crunelle." *Courtesy Isabelle Chapuis.*

Figure 5 Members of the Quintette Pierre Jamet during the 1940s: René Bas, violin; Étienne Ginot, viola; Pierre Jamet, harp; Michel Frècheville, cello; and Gaston Crunelle, flute. *Courtesy Anne Ricquebourg.*

GASTON CRUNELLE

(*Croquis Jan Mara.*)

Figure 6 Caricature of Gaston Crunelle in *Les ondes*, October 17, 1943. *Courtesy Bibliothèque nationale de France.*

Figure 7 Gaston Crunelle's flute class at the Paris Conservatory in 1953. Michel Debost, who would win a first prize the next year, is in the center of the back row wearing a bow tie. Courtesy *Conservatoire national supérieur de musique et de danse de Paris*.

Théâtre Musical de Paris - Châtelet

Vendredi 16 septembre 1983 - 20 h 30

Jean-Pierre Rampal et ses amis

FLUTES

Jean-Pierre RAMPAL

— Pierre-Yves ARTAUD — Peter Lukas GRAF

— Julius BAKER — Shigenori KUDO

— Edouard BECKETT — Christian LARDE

— Poul BIRKELUND — Alain MARION

— Gaston CRUNELLE — Milan MUNCLINGER

CLAVECIN

Richard SIEGEL

— G.-F. TELEMANN
Sonate à quatre en ré majeur
— G.-F. HAENDEL
Duo en mi mineur
— A. REICHA
Andante et scherzo (quatuor)
— J.-L. TULOU
Allegro en fa majeur (trio)
— J. FELD
Cassation (9 flûtes)

— G.-F. TELEMANN
Sonate à 3 flûtes et continuo en ré mineur
— KULHAU
Trio en sol mineur
— BOIMORTIER
Quintette

Figure 8 Rampal International Competition program, 1983. Crunelle's last public performance. *Courtesy Denis Verroust.*

9

Crunelle's Retirement and Legacy

Crunelle was set to retire from the Paris Conservatory in June 1968. Rampal, however, could not start teaching that fall due to his many concert engagements, so Crunelle taught during the 1968–69 year. Leone Buyse reported that "He's very dynamic for a seventy-year-old: white hair, blue eyes, and really sweet."[1] After his retirement, he was flute professor at municipal conservatories in Paris's sixteenth arrondissement and in Villejuif, a southern suburb, and continued to welcome former students in his apartment. After his wife Raymonde died on June 13, 1977, he moved into a less expensive apartment down the street at 24 rue Raynouard.

On April 11, 1982, he was promoted at the age of 83 to *officier* of the *Légion d'honneur*, and many former students including Christian Lardé and Michel Debost attended the ceremony. In 1980 and 1983, he was on the jury for the International Jean-Pierre Rampal Competition. The 1983 concert featuring all the judges was the last time he played in public (see Figure 8).

Gaston Crunelle died at age ninety-one on January 12, 1990, and on March 15, a funeral mass was held in his honor at the Baroque Église Saint-Roch de Paris, an appropriate place to honor a great musician. Jean-Baptiste Lully regularly attended mass there, François-Joseph Gossec's *Messe des morts* and Hector Berlioz's *Messe solennelle* were first performed there, and the funerals of Ferdinando Paër (1771–1839) and Luigi Cherubini were held there. After Crunelle's death, Jean-Claude Diot established the Association Gaston Crunelle, which placed a marker on Crunelle's grave in Clamart, a Parisian suburb; today the grave seems forlorn and neglected. On February 9, 1994, the Association Gaston Crunelle presented a concert in his memory at the Auditorium Debussy-Ravel in Neuilly-sur-Seine, a wealthy western suburb. Performers included his former students Geneviève Amar, Brigitte Buxtorf, Jean-Claude Diot, Gérard Grognet, Eric Groussard, Elisabeth Guestault-Richard, Marc Honorat, Jean-Claude Marin, and Jean-Pierre Rampal.

Gaston Crunelle and Flute Playing in Twentieth-Century France. Leonard Garrison, Oxford University Press.
© Oxford University Press 2024. DOI: 10.1093/9780197778579.003.0009

Crunelle's World and Modern Musical Life

Crunelle worked in a small, elite community of musicians, most of whom held first prizes from the Paris Conservatory. Most musical activity took place within a circumscribed area on the Right Bank—the second, eighth, ninth, and seventeenth arrondissements. The neighborhood around the Conservatory in rue de Madrid was filled with music stores, publishers, and instrument makers. Crunelle knew most French composers from Fauré through Messiaen and Dutilleux. In his career, the same names come up repeatedly in different contexts. For example, Roger Désormière, his classmate at the Conservatory, became his conductor in the legendary recording of *Pelléas et Mélisande*. Fernand Oubradous, another classmate, revived Taffanel's Société des instruments à vent as the Association des Concerts de chambre de Paris and invited Crunelle to perform many times. René Bas, Étienne Ginot, Georges Blanpain, and Robert Krabansky, his colleagues in the Quintette instrumental de Paris, also played with him in the Opéra-Comique.

Musical life in France has changed a great deal since Crunelle's era. Paris, despite its musical riches, is no longer the undisputed capital of classical music and is rivaled by Amsterdam, Berlin, London, New York, Tokyo, and Vienna. Music is more decentralized in France. Many music businesses still grace the neighborhood of the old Conservatory on rue de Madrid, but the catalogs of some traditional publishers previously located there have been taken over by international conglomerates, and since 1990, the Conservatory has occupied a modern building at 209 avenue Jean Jaurès as part of the Cité de la musique complex in the Parc de la Villette, in the remote nineteenth arrondissement, the northeastern corner of Paris.

Most major concerts also take place in the Villette, and most operas have been performed in the Opéra Bastille since it opened in 1989. Orchestras and opera companies in cities such as Lyon, Marseille, Toulouse, Bordeaux, Strasbourg, and Lille have received a larger share of government funding and have become more prominent.

Today's musical landscape is more variegated. Groups such as the Ensemble intercontemporain founded by Pierre Boulez in 1976 specialize in new music. The avant-garde has progressed beyond the serialism of the 1950s and 1960s to spectral music and other advanced styles, and the simplifying tendencies predominant in American minimalist composers are less apparent in French music. Early music is flourishing, with such ensembles as Les Arts florissants, Les Musiciens du Louvre, and Le Concert spirituel.

Flute playing today is much different than in Crunelle's era. Flutes now have more reliable intonation and more secure mechanisms, and French flutists favor instruments from America and Japan. The tone is fuller and more flexible than in the first half of the twentieth century, with a slower vibrato. Pedagogy now emphasizes the use of various breathing muscles and the relation of the body to the flute, a subject absent from Crunelle's teaching. Modern flutists play with less rhythmic freedom. Repertoire casts a wider net, from Baroque music through recent works employing extended techniques. Most flutists, even when playing modern instruments, are sensitive to Baroque style, using less vibrato and less of a sustained sound.

The Paris Conservatory has also evolved and offers a wider range of degrees in many disciplines. Some of the traditions unique to the institution have been replaced by practices conforming to the Bologna Process, an agreement first forged in 1999 between various European countries standardizing educational systems and outcomes. A flutist may now study for three years toward a diploma in the first cycle—equivalent to an American Bachelor's degree—for two years in the second cycle—the equivalent of a master's degree—or the third cycle with various specialties leading to a doctorate.[2] Students have individual lessons rather than three group meetings per week but are welcome to attend their colleagues' lessons. There are still *concours d'entrée*, but they now occur in the spring. At the end of the year, the Conservatory holds *examens publics* or *épreuves publics* (public exams) or *récitals fin d'année* rather than *concours*. There is still a jury, but the first and second prizes are no longer given, and the Conservatory no longer commissions *morceaux de concours*.

The Paris Conservatory is still an elite institution,[3] but other schools have benefitted from decentralization. Besides independent music schools such as the École normale de musique, founded in 1919, and the Schola Cantorum of Paris, founded in 1894, there are now four categories of state-sponsored conservatories in France in ascending order of prominence:

Conservatoires à rayonnement communal (CRC)
Conservatoires à rayonnement départemental (CRD)
Conservatoires à rayonnement régional (CRR)
Conservatoires nationaux supérieurs de musique (CNSM) in Paris et Lyon

The European Union has also had an effect, and musicians trained in other parts of Europe play in French orchestras, now populated with alumni of many different institutions.

In 2018, the Association française des orchestres (OFF) adopted a Charter for Gender Equality in Orchestras and Opera Houses, and representation of women is making slow but steady progress. In the 2016–17 season, thirty-eight percent of musicians in orchestras were women, a 5 percent increase over the previous decade. Flute sections were slightly ahead of the curve, with women holding 40 percent of positions.[4] The OFF does not address other measures of diversity such as race, religion, or sexual orientation, and the French census has never included questions about such matters except in the Vichy era, when the government sought to identify Jewish people.

Crunelle's Legacy

Crunelle's obscurity in the anglophone world is due to his complete absence from Claude Dorgeuille's *The French Flute School* and the unflattering portrait in Sir James Galway's *The Man with the Golden Flute*. Dorgeuille was devoted to Le Roy, who showed disdain for and jealousy of Crunelle. Although Le Roy was a noted chamber musician and soloist, he never held the important orchestral and teaching positions in France that Crunelle had, and as we have seen, Le Roy wanted Crunelle's job at the Paris Conservatory. Renaud François, Crunelle's student who took chamber music classes with Le Roy relates:

> René Le Roy was very *bourgeois*, from the better half, elegant, refined. He lived in luxurious Parisian apartment houses. He always wore a very nice suit and was a bit full of himself, sure of himself, he thought he was a great master. He did not like Gaston Crunelle, they were not from the same world. Gaston Crunelle came from a more populist background and was more accessible . . . Le Roy lived in a worldly realm, high society, cultured people, surrounded by industrialists, and he liked that. Crunelle was simpler and liked everyone. Le Roy related to people who came from a good background.[5]

Gaston Crunelle was undisputedly one of the great flutists and pedagogues of the twentieth century. Unlike René Le Roy and his commissions, Marcel

Moyse and his many publications, or Paul Taffanel and Philippe Gaubert with their many compositions, Crunelle's legacy rests solely upon his playing and teaching, which have unfortunately faded from view over time. He was not an innovator, but his career demonstrates the hallmarks of the great tradition of flute playing in France—tasteful phrasing, flexible tone color, and impeccable technique.

Crunelle's high standards influenced an entire generation, and his former students have led active careers throughout the world. Jean-Pierre Rampal, Sir James Galway, and Maxence Larrieu became international soloists and recording artists, although each of them studied with him briefly. Michel Debost and Christian Lardé are widely recorded flutists whom Crunelle influenced greatly. Others became flutists in orchestras, professors of flute, conductors, composers, and specialists in early music or new music (see Appendix 4).

Thanks to his close collaboration with composers, the *morceaux de concours* written during his tenure suit the flute beautifully. Some of the lesser-known ones are worth adding to the standard repertoire.

Crunelle's performing repertoire was much more extensive than the limited literature he taught at the Conservatory. He was a leading orchestral flutist, and his exquisite solo and chamber music recordings are hard to find but some of the best of the era. His records of Bach and French Baroque music are important milestones in the revival of older music, and his performances of Mozart's Concerto for Flute and Harp with Pierre Jamet are justly famous. His elegant style and refined tone are perfectly suited to French chamber music of the early and mid-twentieth century by Debussy, Françaix, Koechlin, Pierné, Ravel, and Roussel.

Gaston Crunelle Discography

Compiled by Susan Nelson

Using the Discography

Entries for 78-rpm and long-playing recordings are arranged as shown below. In the case of multiple takes recorded on the same date, issued takes have been underlined. Single-sided numbers in brackets are given for Gramophone Company recordings made before 1936.

Composer, work(s)
> Performers
>> recording location, recording issue or copyright date
>> matrix and take numbers (for 78-rpm discs), catalog number [single-sided number]
>>> Long-playing and compact disc reissues

Record Labels, Catalog Number Prefixes, and Numerical Series for 78-rpm Recordings

L'Anthologie sonore   (France, 12-inch)
> Original French pressings had white and purple or black and gold labels. American pressings were issued exclusively by the Gramophone Shop, Inc., New York City, and the record labels displayed the Gramophone Shop banner motif above the spindle hole. The issues first bore bright gold and black labels; subsequent labels were bright yellow and black, similar to the first design. The last American issues had smaller labels with a dull gold and black design.

Decca
> G (US, 10-inch, from Parlophone masters)
> 20000 (US, 10-inch, from Odéon masters)

Disques de l'Oiselet (Oiseau-Lyre)
> DO (France, 10-inch)

The Gramophone Company
> Crunelle's recordings for the French branch of the Gramophone Company, all double-sided, appeared on both the "Disque Gramophone" and "La Voix de son Maître" labels.
> DA (International, 10-inch, red label)
> DB (International, 12-inch, red label)
> K (France, 10-inch, green label; later plum or green)

> SL (France, 12-inch, blue label)
> W (France, 12-inch, black label)

Lumen
> 32000 (France, 12-inch, red label)
> 30000 (France, 12-inch)

Odéon
> 250000 (France, 10-inch)

Parlophone
> 22000 (France, 10-inch)

Pathé Frères
> X96000 (France, 10-inch, black label)
> PDT (France, 12-inch, red label)

Victor
> 14000 (US, 12-inch, Red Seal)
> JD (Japan, 12-inch, Red Seal)

Libraries, Institutions, and Resources Referred to in the Discography, With Abbreviations Used

Bibliothèque nationale de France (BNF): the national library of France
Gallica: the digitized collection of the BNF
Gramophone Co. Discography (GCD): A database incorporating the research of Dr. Alan Kelly with more recent additions, created by Stephen Clarke and Roger Tessier
Institut national de l'audiovisuel (INA): the national radio and television archives of France
WERM: *The World's Encyclopedia of Recorded Music*. A monumental listing of the 78 rpm and long-playing classical recordings commercially available between 1950 and 1955.
Worldcat: the international library database managed by OCLC

Acknowledgments

Special acknowledgment is made to Peter Adamson for his assistance with details of Gramophone Company recordings; Christopher Steward, for many excellent transfers of Crunelle's recordings and for his very generous sharing of information; and William Shaman for his advice on discographic format and assistance with transferring recordings.

78-rpm Recordings: Solo and Chamber Ensemble

1. Gluck, Christoph Willibald, *Armide*, Act IV: Sicilienne
    Gaston Crunelle, flute; pianist unidentified
    recorded Paris, December 8, 1924
    BL 189-1, 2   Gramophone Company: K2972 [239154]
2. Chopin, Frédéric, *Waltz in D-flat Major*, op. 64/1 ["Minute Waltz"]
    Gaston Crunelle, flute; pianist unidentified
    recorded Paris, February–March 1929
    95215-3   Parlophone: 22.215
                US Decca: G-20536

3. Camus, Pierre, *Badinerie*
 Gaston Crunelle, flute; pianist unidentified
  recorded Paris, February–March 1929
  95216-1   Parlophone: 22.215
         US Decca: G-20536

4. Chrétien, Hedwige, *Vision*
 Gaston Crunelle, flute; Lucien Petitjean, piano
  recorded Paris, March 24, 1933
  0PG 674-1,2   unpublished
  recorded Paris, June 28, 1933
  0PG 674-3   Gramophone Company: K6999 [50-3132]

5. Camus, Pierre, *Badinerie*
 Gaston Crunelle, flute; Lucien Petitjean, piano
  recorded Paris, March 24, 1933
  0PG 675-1,2   Gramophone Company: K6918 [50-3017]

6. Godard, Benjamin, *Suite*, op. 116: Idylle
 Gaston Crunelle, flute; Lucien Petitjean, piano
  recorded Paris, March 24, 1933
  0PG 676-1,2   Gramophone Company: K6918 [50-3018]

7. Chopin, Frédéric (arr. Taffanel), a) *Prelude*, op. 28/7; b) *Waltz in D-flat Major*, op.64/1 ["Minute Waltz"]
 Gaston Crunelle, flute; Lucien Petitjean, piano
  recorded Paris, March 24, 1933
  0PG 677-1,2   Gramophone Company: K6999 [50-3131]

8. Bach, Johann Sebastian, *Cantata No. 212, Mer hahn en neue Oberkeet*, BWV 212
 Jeanne Guyla, soprano; Martial Singher, baritone; Gaston Crunelle, flute; chamber orchestra conducted by Gustave Bret
  recorded Paris, March 28, 1934
  Pt. 1: 2PG 1455-1,2 Gramophone Company: DB4939 [52-1300]
      -1 Victor: 14416, JD 848
  Pt. 2: 2PG 1456-1,2 Gramophone Company: DB4939 [52-1301]
      -1 Victor: 14416, JD 848
  Pt. 3: 2PG 1457-1,2 Gramophone Company: DB4940 [52-1302]
      -1 Victor: 14417, JD 849
  Pt. 4: 2PG 1458-1,2 Gramophone Company: DB4940 [52-1303]
      -1 Victor: 14417, JD 849

9. Anonymous, *Danses du 13e siècle*: a) English dance; b) French dance; c) English dance "Stantipes"
 Gaston Crunelle, piccolo; Albert Debondue, musette; Clayette, tambour
  recorded Paris, issued 1935
  AS 37   Anthologie sonore: 16
    Reissues:
    LP: Haydn Society AS2 [set HS.AS-A] (1954)

10. Anonymous, *Danses du 14e siècle*: a) French "Estampie" b) Italian Ballo "Il lamento de Tristano"
 Gaston Crunelle, piccolo; Albert Debondue, musette; Clayette, tambour
  recorded Paris, issued 1935
  AS 38   Anthologie sonore: 16
    Reissues:
    LP: Haydn Society AS2 [set HS.AS-A] (1954)

11. Bach, Johann Christian, *Quintet in D Major*, B.75
    Gaston Crunelle, flute; Louis Gromer, oboe; Jean Fournier, violin; Pierre Villain,
    viola; Pierre Fournier, cello
        recorded Paris, 1937
        Allegro
        AS 115   Anthologie sonore: 50
        a) Andantino, b) Allegro assai
        AS 116   Anthologie sonore: 50
            Reissues:
                CD: *Oboe Archive, France, Vol. 2: 1927–1938*, Oboe Classics CC 2305 (2016)
12. Bach, Johann Sebastian, *Magnificat*, BWV 243: Esurientes, implevit bonis
    Lina Falk, contralto; Gaston Crunelle, Albert Manouvrier, flute; Ruggero Gerlin,
    harpsichord
        recorded Paris, issued ca. 1938
        YL 113   Lumen: 32051, 3.20.004
13. Clérambault, Louis-Nicolas, *Léandre et Héro*
    Martha Angelici, soprano; Gaston Crunelle, flute; Jean Fournier, violin; Victor
    Clerget, viola da gamba; Pauline Aubert, harpsichord
        recorded Paris, 1941
        Pt. 1: AS 226-1   Anthologie sonore: 105
        Pt. 2: AS 227-1   Anthologie sonore: 105
        Pt. 3: AS 228-1   Anthologie sonore: 106
        Pt. 4: AS 229-1   Anthologie sonore: 106
14. Ravel, Maurice, *Shéhérazade*: La Flûte enchantée (poem by Tristan Klingsor)
    Leïla Ben Sedira, soprano; Gaston Crunelle, flute; Rose Dobos?, piano
        recorded Paris, January 12, 1942
        0LA 3697-1   Gramophone Company: DA4938
15. Boieldieu, François-Adrien (arr. Büsser), *La Fête du village voisin*, Act I: Profitez de la
    vie
    Leïla Ben Sedira, soprano; Gaston Crunelle, flute; Pierre Jamet, harp
        recorded Paris, January 12, 1942
        0LA 3698-1   Gramophone Company: DA4938
16. Rameau, Jean-Philippe, *Hippolyte et Aricie*: Rossignols amoureux
    Leïla Ben Sedira, soprano; Gaston Crunelle, flute; Pierre Jamet, harp
        recorded Studio Albert, Paris, January 12, 1942
        2LA 3699-1   Gramophone Company: W1507
            Reissues:
                LP: *The Record of Singing*, Volume Three 1926–1939, EMI (13 discs, 1984)
                CD: *The Record of Singing*, Volume Three 1926–1939, Testament (10 discs, 1999)
                CD: *300 ans d'Opéra à Bruxelles/Théâtre royal de la monnaie/Konninklijk
                    muntschouwburg*, Malibran Music CDRG 169D (4 discs)
17. Taffanel, Paul, *Quintet*
    (Société des instruments à vent: Gaston Crunelle, flute; Myrtil Morel, oboe; Pierre
    Lefebvre, clarinet; Jean Devémy, horn; Fernand Oubradous, bassoon)
        recorded Studio Pelouze, Paris, January 26, 1943
        Allegro con moto
        2LA 3951-1   Gramophone Company: W1567

Andante
2LA 3952-1   Gramophone Company: W1567
a) Andante; b) Vivace
2LA 3953-1   Gramophone Company: W1568
18. Pierné, Gabriel, *Pastorale*, op. 14, no. 1
     (Société des instruments à vent: Gaston Crunelle, flute; Myrtil Morel, oboe; Pierre
     Lefebvre, clarinet; Jean Devémy, horn; Fernand Oubradous, bassoon)
     recorded Studio Pelouze, Paris, January 26, 1943
     2LA 3954-1,2   Gramophone Company: W1568

*Gramophone Company matrices 2LA 3955–3956: not traced. Matrices 2LA 3957–3958 were
the Quintette Pierre Jamet performance of Ravel's Introduction and Allegro. See Appendix 3.*

19. Couperin, François, *Les Goûts-réunis*, No. 9 in E Major ["*Ritratto dell'amore*"]: *Le Charme,
     La Noble fierté* (Sarabande), *L'Enjouement*
     Gaston Crunelle, flute; Victor Clerget, viola da gamba; Pauline Aubert, harpsichord
     recorded Paris, copyright 1943
     AS 241-1   Anthologie Sonore: 116
20. Mozart, Wolfgang Amadeus, *Concerto in C Major for Flute and Harp*, K. 299
     Gaston Crunelle, flute; Pierre Jamet, harp; orchestra conducted by Gustav Cloëz
     recorded Paris, issued ca. 1946
     Allegro (first part)
     AS 265-1   Anthologie sonore: 122
     Allegro (second part)
     AS 266-1   Anthologie sonore: 122
     Allegro (conclusion) (cadenza by Reynaldo Hahn)
     AS 267-1   Anthologie sonore: 123
     Andantino (first part)
     AS 268-1   Anthologie sonore: 123
     Andantino (conclusion) (cadenza by Reynaldo Hahn)
     AS 269-1   Anthologie sonore: 124
     Rondo (first part)
     AS 270-1   Anthologie sonore: 124
     Rondo (second part)
     AS 271-1   Anthologie sonore: 125
     Rondo (conclusion) (cadenza by Reynaldo Hahn)
     AS 272-1   Anthologie sonore: 125
       Reissues:
       LP: Disques Adès M30 AS528 (1962)
       CD: *Pour célébrer Mozart*, Adès ADE 694 (5 discs, 1990)
       CD: *Pierre Jamet & son quintette*, Timpani 2C2122 (2 discs, 2007)
21. Migot, Georges, *Petits Préludes*
     Gaston Crunelle, flute; Jean Pasquier, violin
     recorded Paris, issued ca. 1946–47?, copyright 1950
     a) *Calandres* b) *Farlouses*
     XL 199-1   Lumen: 30100, 2.06.014
     a) *Rousselines* b) *Cochevis*
     XL 200-1   Lumen: 30100, 2.06.014

22. Debussy, Claude, *Sonata No. 2 for flute, viola, and harp*
>   Gaston Crunelle, flute; Georges Blanpain, viola; Pierre Jamet, harp
>> recorded Studio Albert, Paris, July 1, 1948
>> Pastorale (first part)
>> 2LA 5318-2   Gramophone Company: SL148
>> Pastorale (conclusion)
>> 2LA 5319-1   Gramophone Company: SL148
>> Interlude (first part)
>> 2LA 5320-1   Gramophone Company: SL149
>> Interlude (conclusion)
>> 2LA 5321-1   Gramophone Company: SL149
>> Final
>> 2LA 5322-1   Gramophone Company: SL150
>>> Reissues:
>>> CD: *Pierre Jamet & son quintette*, Timpani 2C2122 (2 discs, 2007)

23. Mozart, Wolfgang Amadeus, *Adagio and Rondo in C*, K.617
>> Yvette Grimaud, celeste; Gaston Crunelle, flute; Pierre Pierlot, oboe; Pierre Ladhuie, viola; Etienne Pasquier, cello; Fernand Oubradous, conductor
>> recorded Paris, issued 1949–50
>> Adagio (first part)
>> PART 4675-1   Disques de l'Oiselet: DO.1
>> Adagio (conclusion)
>> PART 4676-1   Disques de l'Oiselet: DO.2
>> Adagio with English commentary
>> PART 4840-1   Disques de l'Oiselet: DO.1
>> Rondo with French commentary
>> PART 4843-1   Disques de l'Oiselet: DO.2
>> Rondo (first part)
>> PART 4677- 1   Disques de l'Oiselet: DO.3
>> Rondo (second part)
>> PART 4678- 1   Disques de l'Oiselet: DO.3

24. Bach, Johann Sebastian, *Partita in A Minor*, BWV1013
>> Gaston Crunelle, flute
>> recorded Paris, issued 1949–50
>> Allemande, with commentary
>> PART 4949-1   Disques de l'Oiselet: DO.4
>> PART 4950-1 [E]
>> Courante, with commentary
>> PART 4951-1   Disques de l'Oiselet: DO.4
>> PART 4952-1 [E]
>> Sarabande
>> PART 4953-1   Disques de l'Oiselet: DO.5
>> Bourrée anglaise, with commentary
>> PART 4954-1   Disques de l'Oiselet: DO.5
>> PART 4955-1 [E]

25. a) Blavet, Michel, *Sonata*, op. 2/3 [La D'Hérouville]: Adagio; b) Naudot, Jacques-Christophe, *Sonata*, op. 1/4: Rondeau
>> Gaston Crunelle, flute; Pauline Aubert, harpsichord
>> recorded Paris, May 31, 1950
>> CPTX 935-1   Pathé: PDT 237

26. a) Boismortier, Joseph Bodin de, *Sonata*, op. 44/ 3: Adagio; b) *Sonata*, op. 19/ 6: Largo;
    c) Philidor, François Danican, *Le Polichinel*
       Gaston Crunelle, flute; Pauline Aubert, harpsichord
          recorded Paris, May 31, 1950
          CPTX 936-1   Pathé: PDT 237

78-rpm Recordings: Confirmed Orchestral Solos

For unconfirmed recordings, see the section on the recordings of the Pasdeloup and
Opéra-Comique Orchestras following the *Notes* to this discography.

27. Bizet, Georges, *Carmen*, Act III: Entr'acte
       Gaston Crunelle, flute; orchestra conducted by Désiré Inghelbrecht
          recorded Paris, issued 1933
          E 350122-MC   Pathé: X96265, PG50
28. Gluck, Christoph Willibald, *Orphée et Eurydice*, Act II: Scène des Champs-Élysées
       Gaston Crunelle, flute; orchestra conducted by Gustav Cloëz
          recorded Paris, 1933–34
          Pt. 1: Ki 5998-2   Odéon: 250.448; Decca: 20065
          Pt. 2: Ki 5999-1   Odéon: 250.448; Decca: 20065
29. Debussy, Claude, *Pelléas et Mélisande*
       Soloists, orchestra, and Yvonne Gouverné Chorus conducted by Roger Désormière
          recorded Paris, Salle du Conservatoire, April, May, October, and November, 1941
          2LA 3504–2LA 3545   Gramophone Company: DB5161–DB5180
             Reissues:
             LP: La Voix de son Maître FJLP5030–5032 (France, mono, 1954)
             LP: RCA Victor LCT 6106 (US, mono)
             45 rpm: RCA Victor WCT 61 (US, mono)
             LP: EMI *Plaisir musical* series, set C153.12513/15 (France)
             CD: EMI CHS 761038 2 (1988)
             CD: EMI Classics 3 457702, *Great Recordings of the Century* series (2006)

Long-Playing Recordings: Solo and Chamber Music

Note: ten-inch LPs are identified. All other issues are twelve-inch.

30. Bach, Johann Sebastian, *Concerto in F*, BWV1057 [based on *Brandenburg Concerto No. 4*, BWV1049]
       Gaston Crunelle, Jean-Pierre Rampal, flute; Céliny Chailley-Richez, piano; Association
    des Concerts de chambre de Paris conducted by Georges Enesco
          recorded Paris, issued September, 1953
          LP: Decca FAT 133068 (10-inch, mono, France, issued 1953)
             Decca FAT 173068 (mono, France, issued 1953)
             Reissues:
             CD: Oryx BHP 907 (UK)

31. Mozart, Wolfgang Amadeus, *Concerto for Flute and Harp*, K.299
    Gaston Crunelle, flute; Pierre Jamet, harp; Orchestre de la Camerata Academica du Mozarteum de Salzbourg conducted by Bernhard Paumgartner
        recorded October 15, 1954
        LP: Club français du disque 100 (mono, France)
            Histoire sonore de la musique CFD 423 (mono, France, issued 1966)
            [second and third movements only]
            Counterpoint/Esoteric CPT 609 (mono, US, issued 1964)
            Counterpoint/Esoteric CPTS 5609 (stereo, US, issued 1964)
            World Record Club TE-378 (mono, Australia, issued ca. 1965)
            World Record Club STE-378 (stereo, Australia, issued ca. 1965)
                Reissues:
            CD: Forgotten Records FR 1404 (France, 2017)
32. *La Palette orchestrale*, Side 2: Les Vents et la percussion
    Émile Vuillermoz (role unverified); "Dialogues interprétés par Cécile Demay et Henri Doublier."
        recorded Paris, copyright 1957
        LP: Club National du Disque CND1 (mono, France)
            Select SC 13006 (mono, Canada)
33. Barlow, Fred, *Pavane pour flûte et guitare*
    Gaston Crunelle, flute; Pierre Cotte, guitar
        recorded Paris, issued ca. 1961
        LP: Les amis de Fred Barlow INT 20115
34. Barlow, Fred, *Pavane pour flûte et guitare*
    Gaston Crunelle, flute;Pierre Cotte, guitar
        recorded Paris, copyright 1962
        LP: Erato LDE 20173 (mono, France)

Radio Broadcasts

This section includes only *extant* broadcasts, documented using the cataloging of the INA. The ID numbers included are those from the INA catalog.

35. Roussel, Albert, *Deux Poèmes de Ronsard*, op. 26
    Jean Planel, tenor, Gaston Crunelle, flute
    Broadcast, *Hommage à Albert Roussel*, recorded October 1, 1947 (broadcast date unverified)
        Network: X, produced by Radiodiffusion Française
        INA ID: PHD89009035
36. Vellones, Pierre, *Trio for flute, harp, and oboe*
    Gaston Crunelle, flute; Albert Debondue, oboe; Pierre Jamet, harp
    Broadcast, *Oeuvres de Pierre Vellones*, recorded July 15, 1948 (broadcast July 22, 1948)
        Network: X, produced by Radiodiffusion Française
        INA ID: PHD89009013
37. Vellones, Pierre, *Trio for flute, harp, and oboe*: second and third movements only
    Gaston Crunelle, flute; Albert Debondue, oboe; Lily Laskine, harp
    Broadcast, *Festival Pierre Vellones: 10ème anniversaire de sa mort*, recorded December 16, 1949 (broadcast December 21, 1949)
        Network: Paris Inter, produced by Radiodiffusion Télévision Française
        INA ID: PHD86039562

38. Ravel, Maurice, *Introduction and Allegro*
>   Gaston Crunelle, flute; Ulysse Delécluse, clarinet; Georges Enesco, violin; Gaston
>   Marchesini, cello; Pierre Jamet, harp
>   Broadcast, *Concert de musique de chambre,* recorded March 1, 1951 (broadcast date
>   unverified)
>>   Network: X, produced by Radiodiffusion Télévision Française
>>   INA ID: PHD85017147

39. Barlow, Fred, *Sonata*
>   Gaston Crunelle, flute; Jeanne Chailley Bert, harpsichord
>   Broadcast, *Musique de chambre: oeuvres de Fred Barlow, Ernest Moret, A. Gaillard,*
>   recorded October 20, 1952 (broadcast date unverified)
>>   Network: Programme National, produced by Radiodiffusion Télévision Française
>>   INA ID: PHD86054977

40. Roussel, Albert, *Deux Poèmes de Ronsard,* op. 26
>   Maria Beronita, soprano; Gaston Crunelle, flute
>   Broadcast, *Musique de chambre,* recorded May 23, 1953 (broadcast May 24, 1953)
>>   Network: Programme National, produced by Radiodiffusion Télévision Française
>>   INA ID: PHD86056080

41. Ravel, Maurice, *Introduction and Allegro*
>   Gaston Crunelle, flute; Ulysse Delécluse?, clarinet; Quatuor Pascal?; Pierre Jamet,
>   harp; Fernand Oubradous, conductor
>   Broadcast, *Association Concerts de Chambre de Paris: Concerts Oubradous,* recorded
>   November 29, 1953 (broadcast December 6, 1953)
>>   Network: Paris Inter, produced by Radiodiffusion Télévision Française
>>   INA ID: PHD90008894

42. Bach, Johann Sebastian, *Brandenburg Concertos*
>   Identified performers: Gaston Crunelle, flute; Robert Gendre, Louis Perlemutter,
>   violin; Colette Lequien, viola; Marcelle Charbonnier, harpsichord; Fernand
>   Oubradous, conductor; Association des Concerts de Chambre de Paris
>   Broadcast, *Concerts Oubradous diffusé le 21 février 1954,* recorded January 1, 1954
>   (broadcast February 21, 1954)
>>   Network: Paris Inter, produced by Radiodiffusion Télévision Française
>>   INA ID: PHD90008890

43. Zellbell, Ferdinand, *Concerto for flute and strings*
>   Gaston Crunelle, flute; orchestra not identified
>   Broadcast, *3ème partie: musiciens suédois peu connus de la fin du XVIIe siècle,* recorded
>   June 6, 1955 (broadcast March 22, 1956)
>>   Network: Programme National, produced by Radiodiffusion Télévision Française
>>   INA ID: PHD88000836

44. Roussel, Albert, a) *Deux Poèmes de Ronsard,* op. 26; b) *Trio,* op. 40
>   a) Flore Wend, soprano; Gaston Crunelle, flute; b) Quintette Pierre Jamet members
>   Broadcast, *Hommage à Albert Roussel,* recorded May 11, 1957 (broadcast July 29, 1957)
>>   Network: Paris Inter, produced by Radiodiffusion Télévision Française
>>   INA ID: PHD90009902

45. Debussy, Claude, *Sonata No. 2 for flute, viola and harp*
>   Gaston Crunelle, flute; Pierre Ladhuie, viola; Pierre Jamet, harp
>   Broadcast, *Musique de chambre française contemporaine,* recorded July 1,1958
>   (broadcast July 11, 1958)
>>   Network: PT, produced by Radiodiffusion Télévision Française
>>   INA ID: PHD90011125

Notes

1. The label identifies Crunelle as "Flûte-solo des Concerts Pasdeloup." The solo was coupled with:

   Zino Francescatti, violin; Georges Becker, piano: Handel, *Sonata in D Major:* Larghetto
      BS 294-2   26 Apr 1922   Gramophone Company: 88062, K2972

2. Matrix 95215-3 was reported from a Parlophone copy. American Decca G-20536 shows the same matrix as 95215-C.

4-7. The labels identify Crunelle as "1re Flûte solo des Concerts Pasdeloup."

6. A transfer of this recording is available on the website, "Robert Bigio Flute Pages." (http//www.robertbigio.com)

7. While the label credits the arrangement of the "Minute Waltz" to Taffanel, no arranger is identified for the *Prelude*.

8. The cantata is sung in French and presented in an abridged version on four sides. Crunelle is heard in the second and third parts. Victor labels identify him as "soloist of the Pasdeloup Orchestra." Takes for both the Gramophone Company and Victor issues have been confirmed from copies of the recordings in a private collection and in the Special Collections of the University of California, Santa Barbara, Libraries.

   The GCD shows shows Gramophone Company issues as having used second takes, but copies bearing second takes have not yet been reported.

9-10. On these two recordings for *L'Anthologie sonore*, included in the second volume of the series, Crunelle plays piccolo rather than flute. Debondue's instrument has no drone and plays only a melodic line. Crunelle is heard in the first and third dances of the first side of AS 16, and in the "Estampie" on the second side.

   Catalog records in the BNF give a copyright and recording date of 1935.

   The recordings were reissued on Record 2, "The 13th and 14th centuries," in the Haydn Society's *Vol. 1: Gregorian chant to the 16th century.*

   These recordings are available complete on Gallica.

   The recording that immediately precedes this one, Anthologie Sonore 15 (matrices AS35–36) is *Chansons françaises du 16e siècle*. Singer Marcelle Gerar is accompanied by an ensemble of "viols, flutes, and guitar;" only one flute is actually heard, and piccolo is used for one selection. Because of the sequence of matrix numbers, it is *possible* that Crunelle might have been the flutist for this recording as well, but record labels do not identify him or the other instrumentalists.

11. Issued in Volume 5 of *L'Anthologie sonore*. Cataloging records of the BNF note that it was recorded in 1937. The recording was listed in the *Gramophone Shop Supplement* for March 1938.

   The quintet is one of a group of six. Numbered in Ernest Warburton's complete edition as B.75, it is also identified in various sources as op. 11, no. 6. Contents of the Oboe Classics compact disc reissue have been made available on Spotify.

12. Listed in the *Gramophone Shop Supplement* for June 1938, coupled with the "Agnus Dei" from Bach's *Mass in B Minor.* Lumen 3.20.004 was a later re-numbering.

13. Issued in Volume 11 of *L'Anthologie sonore*. The cataloging record in the BNF states "Enr. 1941" for one copy of the recording and notes a copyright registration date of 1942 for another copy. The recording did not appear in *The Musical Quarterly's* record list until April 1947, suggesting that its issue and/or export may have been

delayed by the war. A transfer of the complete recording has been made available in the digital collection of the Médiathèque Musical de Paris at https://bibliotheques-specialisees.paris.fr.

14. Originally scored for voice and orchestra with a prominent solo flute part. Labels list the pianist as "Rose Bos," but researchers for the GCD have suggested that the Swiss pianist Rose Dobos, known to have accompanied Ben Sedira in recitals, is the performer.

15. Some sources, including the GCD, list a selection from Boieldieu's *Les Voitures versées* sharing this side, but this is not correct.

16. Performed with voice, flute, and harp. Gramophone Company ledger information identifies Rose Dobos as pianist, but piano is not used in either the Rameau or de Falla selections. The reverse side of the disc is Manuel de Falla's *Psyché* (see Appendix 3).

    The complete recording of the Rameau is available on Gallica. The Malibran Music compact disc transfer has been made available on Youtube and Spotify.

19. Issued in Volume 12 of *L'Anthologie sonore*. A copyright registration date of 1943 is given in the catalog of the BNF. The recording was not listed in *The Musical Quarterly* until April 1947, suggesting that the issue and/or export of the recording may have been delayed by the war.

    The excerpts from *Les Goûts-réunis* No. 9 occupied the final side of Anthologie sonore 115–116, a recording of Couperin's *Le Parnasse, ou l'apothéose de Corelli*, performed by the Versailles Chamber Ensemble led by Gustav Cloëz.

20. In Volume 13 of *L'Anthologie sonore*, listed in *The Musical Quarterly* for April 1947. Only first takes have been reported for all eight sides. Some postwar American pressings of matrix AS 270 are dubbings.

    The Disques Adès reissue was one of fourteen LPs presenting material from the original *L'Anthologie sonore* series. No other Crunelle performances appeared in the set.

    The complete concerto was included on the compact disc reissue, *Pierre Jamet & son quintette*, which appeared on Youtube, Spotify, and Naxos Music Library. A transfer of the complete work is also available at the Médiathèque Musical de Paris at https://bibliotheques-specialisees.paris.fr. Excerpts have been made available on Gallica.

21. Lumen 30097–30098 (matrices XL 207 through 210), orchestral music by Migot, are listed in the *Gramophone Shop Supplement*'s "French Importations" list for January 1947, but BNF cataloging records show the copyright registration date of Lumen 30100 as 1950. As copyright registration dates may not necessarily reflect the date of publication, it is possible that the *Petits préludes* may have been issued as early as 1946.

    Four of the six preludes were recorded. Lumen 2.06.014 was a later re-numbering.

22. The sixth side of this set, Debussy's *Fille aux cheveux de lin*, is performed by Jamet.

    The Timpani compact disc reissue, *Pierre Jamet & son quintette*, has been made available on Youtube, Spotify, and Naxos, and a complete transfer of the performance is also available on Gallica.

23. Introduced by Oiseau-Lyre in 1949–1950, the 78 rpm "Oiselet" series, which included only this recording and the one following, was intended to offer young listeners a "Discothèque de la jeunesse." An unrelated Oiseau-Lyre 45-rpm extended-play series, issued in the 1950s and 1960s, also used the name "Oiselet."

The Mozart *Adagio and Rondo* was issued on three ten-inch discs. The copy inspected included a mixture of French and English commentary, the result of a production accident, or perhaps an attempt to assemble the set from stray discs: the final record, DO. 3, was missing. Matrix numbers for the third disc have come from the website of the AHRC Research Centre at https://charm.rhul.ac.uk/index.html, and it is not indicated whether those sides have commentary. In addition, DO.2 was mislabeled, both sides identified as the conclusion of the Adagio. The spoken commentary, read by French music critic Bernard Gavoty, was illustrated with brief examples played by members of the ensemble.

24.   Listed in *The Musical Quarterly* for January 1950 and released as part of Oiselet set DO 4–6, with a third disc of Isabelle Nef playing Bach's *Prelude in C Minor* and *Suite in F Minor*. Two versions with different narration were issued; [E] has been added to distinguish matrices of the English-language version. Only one side, the "Sarabande," contains no commentary. The French commentary was written and read by music critic Bernard Gavoty. "Joe Birch," who read the English commentary, was in fact Joseph Birch Hanson, the second husband of Oiseau-Lyre founder, Louise Dyer-Hanson.

25–26. Pathé PDT237 was issued with the title *Au Jardin de la flûte de France*. Realizations of the figured bass were credited to "Borel."

    Transfers of both sides of the disc are available at the Médiathèque Musical de Paris at https://bibliotheques-specialisees.paris.fr.

26.   The record label identifies the composer of *Le Polichinel* as "V. Francis Philidor." The score is found in the collection, *Pièces pour la flûte traversière qui peuvent aussi se jouer sur le violon: Par M. François Philidor, Ordinaire de la Musique du Roy*, printed by J.B.-Christophe Ballard in 1716. The composer was François Danican Philidor (1689–1717), flutist of the Royal Chapel and the composer of many works for flute. He was a son of the better-known André Danican Philidor (1652–1730), known as *l'aîné* and later as *le père*. Works in the 1716 collection are in four suites; *Le Polichinel* is found in the *Suite in G*.

27.   The 1938 French Pathé catalog, *Répertoire des Disques Pathé*, identified Crunelle as soloist. The reverse side was the "Adagietto" from Bizet's *L'Arlésienne Suite No. 1*. The issue date of 1933 was taken from the catalog of the BNF, which notes "Datation d'après les suppléments du Répertoire phonographique de L'Office Générale de la Musique de 1933" (dating according to the supplement of the phonographic repertory of the General Office of Music of 1933): PG50 is a ten-inch, green label issue that couples the Act III Entr'acte with that of Act IV.

28.   Recorded in two parts, the flute solo on side two. The orchestra is shown on the label as "Paris Philharmonic," and Crunelle identified as the soloist.

29.   This recording is extensively documented in "L'Enregistrement historique de *Pelléas et Mélisande* en 1941" by Philippe Morin and Yannick Simon, *Cahiers Debussy* 37–38 (2013-2014), pp. 77–111. Recording details were assembled from studio logs, "rapports de cire" (literally "wax reports" documenting matrices), stock cards, and other materials from the factory archives of Pathé-Marconi at Chatou. The recording was done in three groups of sessions. Between April 24 and May 26, the entire work was recorded. After an approval and rejection process, twenty-five sides were re-recorded October 6 and 18. Finally, on November 17,

    the "Tower Scene" was re-recorded. The set was issued in 1942. The complete individual recording dates were April 24, 26, 28; May 3, 5, 6, 8, 12, 13, 15, 17, 19, 20, 25, 26; October 6, 8, 9, 13, 16, 18; November 17.

Recording dates cited in the GCD agree with those in Morin and Simon's account. As the two sources are based on Gramophone Company documents, both should be considered accurate.

The 2006 EMI *Great Recordings of the Century* compact disc and another complete version on the "Classical Moments" label have been made available on Youtube. The EMI reissue has also been made available on Spotify and Naxos Music Library. Excerpts from the first long-playing issue, La Voix de son Maître FJLP5030–5032, have been made available in the Gallica catalog.

30. First issued in a Decca series, *Hommage à J.S. Bach*. Both the ten-inch and twelve-inch LPs also included the *Concerto in A*, BWV1055, for harpsichord. The compact disc issue, from Oryx's *Bach Heritage Performances* series, was in the fourth volume of a four-disc set (BHP 904–907) that included many of the clavier concertos.

Decca's recordings of Enesco conducting Bach were made at pianist Chailley-Richez's urging, although Enesco was in poor health at the time. Recording of the series began in February 1953 with the concertos for one, two, and three pianos, and ended early in 1954. The September 1953 issue date has been taken from Denis Verroust's *Jean-Pierre Rampal: un demi-siècle d'enregistrements*.

Transfers of the complete concerto have been made available on the Baroque Music Library at https://www.baroquemusic.org/bmlcatalogue.html and on Musopen (https://musopen.org).

31. The original Club français du disque LP included commentary written and read by the French music critic Roland Manuel. Side 1 contains the concerto itself, side 2, Manuel's commentary. Club français du disque, active from 1953 until 1968, was the music branch of Le Club français du livre.

The *Histoire sonore de la musique* was a thirty-six-disc series of music from the fifteenth century through the Romantic era, published by Club français du disque.

Issues on Counterpoint/Esoteric and Australian World Record Club identify the orchestra as the Salzburg Mozarteum Orchestra. Only labels of the Club français du disque LP identify it as the Orchestre de la Camerata Académica du Mozarteum de Salzbourg.

It is possible that the LP did not appear quickly after the recording was made. A Club français du disque recording sheet provided the recording location, date, and a *fin de montage* ("end of editing") date of May 12, 1955. The sheet identifies the *monteur* (editor or engineer) as "Deloro." This may be the sound engineer Jean Deloron, known to have worked for several labels, including Adès, Boîte à musique, and Erato.

The Counterpoint/Esoteric issues were listed in the American Schwann catalog for June, 1964. The Australian World Record Club issues also included concertos for oboe (K.314) and horn (K.417).

Searches in the published history and chronology of the Salzburg Festival, *Festspiele in Salzburg*, by Josef Kaut (Salzburg: Residenz Verlag, 1965) and in the Salzburg Festival archives (https://archive.salzburgerfestspiele.at/en/archive) revealed no credited performances featuring Crunelle or Jamet. This, and the absence of any discernible audience noise in the recording itself, may indicate that this was not a live festival performance.

The performance *may* have been originally recorded for inclusion in Roland Manuel's radio broadcast series, *Plaisir de la musique*, which aired from 1944 until

1966. In 1956, a considerable part of the series was devoted to Mozart, to honor the bicentennial of the composer's birth. Although the INA holds recordings of many of Manuel's broadcasts, none including the *Concerto for Flute and Harp* featuring Crunelle and Jamet have been cataloged.

Manuel's commentary mentions the cadenzas and attributes them to "Claude Prieur," but he may have meant the flutist and conductor *André* Prieur.

Excerpts have been made available on the Gallica site.

32. Crunelle and eighteen other musicians are listed on the record jacket as providers of the "exemples instrumentaux." The demonstration of the flute consists of short passages (*not* orchestral excerpts) illustrating the instrument's range, trills, arpeggios, and various articulations, including flutter-tonguing. The piccolo is represented by a fragment of the chromatic scale, and alto flute is heard in a short solo from Ravel's *Daphnis et Chloé*.

Unidentified recorded excerpts from *Daphnis et Chloé* furnish two additional examples of flute and piccolo. While Crunelle played the brief live excerpts, it is not clear whether the included commercial recordings feature him as well. This seems unlikely, as no commercial Opéra-Comique recordings of *Daphnis et Chloé* have been documented.

Crunelle left the Pasdeloup Orchestra before the advent of long-playing recordings, and all the orchestral excerpts appear to be from post-war recordings. It is possible that he played the short alto flute solo from the ballet, as it is unaccompanied and does not sound as though it was taken from a recording.

Vuillermoz was a music critic and may have been responsible for the written commentary, which is read by Cécile Demay and Henri Doublier

Canadian Select labels note, "Avec licence Club National du Disque, France" and sides bear the numbers MSC 651, MSC 652.

33. Probably a private recording, produced by "Les Amis de Fred Barlow." This recording appears to have furnished the material for the Erato LP (item 34), as both feature the same repertory played by the same performers (with the exception of the *Enfantines* for harpsichord, added to the Erato issue) and both are identified as having been recorded by the Intersonor studios in Paris.

The remaining contents of the private LP, titled *Concert Fred Barlow*, are as follows:

Sinfonietta des saisons: l'Orchestre de Chambre de la RTF, conducted by Pierre Capdevielle

Droite dans la candeur; *When-Chun*; *La Fleur merveilleuse*: Ginette Guillamat, voice; Geneviève Joy, piano

Ave Maria: Maurice Duruflé, organ; unnamed child vocalist from Maîtrise de la RTF

Sonatine pour flûte, violon et piano: Jean-Pierre Rampal, flute; Roland Charmy, violin; Geneviève Joy, piano

Pater Noster: Chorale des Jeunesses Musicales de France conducted by Louis Martini.

Barlow (born Ferdinand Frédéric Barlow, 1881–1951) was largely self-trained, although he also had the advantage of studying with his cousin, Charles Koechlin, and with the organist and composer Jean Huré. The *Pavane* was originally part of a ballet, *Gladys*, first performed in Barlow's native Mulhouse in 1956. The flute and guitar version is an arrangement.

34. The liner notes by Roland Manuel and Roger Cotte are dated 1961. Denis Verroust's *Jean-Pierre Rampal: un demi-siècle d'enregistrements* shows January 19, 1962, as the date of copyright registration.

    An excerpt has been made available on Gallica.

35. A live concert at the Salle Érard, Paris, presumably broadcast on the same date. Other works on the program were Roussel's *Sérénade*, op. 30 (Quintette Pierre Jamet: Gaston Crunelle, flute; René Bas, violin; Georges Blanpain, viola; Robert Krabansky, cello; Pierre Jamet, harp); *String Quartet*, op. 45 (Pascal Quartet); *Sonatine* for piano (Hélène Pignari); and *Mélodies*, selected from different song sets (Ginette Guillamat, soprano; André Collard, piano). The surviving broadcast transcription is incomplete and does not include the Roussel *Sérénade*, so has not been included in Appendix 3.

36. Other works on the program were Vellones's *Rhapsodie* for saxophone, harp, and celeste, and the *Ballade* for two pianos.

37. A live concert from the École normale in Paris. An announcement in the broadcast noted that Lily Laskine was a last-minute replacement for Pierre Jamet.

    Other works featured in the broadcast were *Chine* (this may refer to the song "La Tchen," from Vellones' *Chansons d'amour de la vieille Chine*, or to the entire group of four songs), *Valse chromatique*, for piano, and *Épitaphes* (probably the *Cinq Épitaphes* for voice and piano).

38. A program of chamber music performed by professors of the Paris Conservatory. Other featured works were Beethoven's *Septet*, op. 20, and Schubert's *Octet*. Additional performers for the *Introduction and Allegro* have not been identified. Fernand Oubradous was listed as "director" for the broadcast, one in the series *Association des concerts de chambre de Paris*.

39. Further identification of Barlow's *Sonata* has not been encountered. Other works on the program were Ernest Moret's *6 Préludes* for piano, and André Gaillard's *Airs de la vieille Chine*.

40. Roussel's *Jazz dans la nuit*, probably performed by Beronita and pianist Odette Pigault, and Florent Schmitt's *Sonate libre* for violin and piano were also included in the program.

41. Described as a "Concert broadcast from the Salle Gaveau with the participation of Fernand Oubradous and given for the benefit of the social works of the National Conservatory of Music." The program included works by Ravel, Debussy, and Mozart. Delécluse and the Quatuor Pascal were not listed as performers for the *Introduction and Allegro*, but their presence on the program, and the absence of another clarinetist or string quartet, suggest that they *may* have played.

42. The broadcast is described as "Full hearing [*audition intégrale*] of the *Brandenburg Concertos* of Johann Sebastian Bach." Five concerti are then identified only by key: F major, G major, G major, D major, and B-flat major, leaving some doubt as to whether both the first and second concertos, in F major, were included.

43. The third in a series, *Aspects de la musique du passé en Suède*. This episode, and possibly the complete series, was produced by Roger Cotte. Other works on the broadcast were the *Variations sur une chanson suédoise* and *Variations sur sur la marche des séraphins de Suède* by "Wogler" (possibly the German composer George Joseph Vogler, 1749–1816, Kapellmeister to Gustave III of Sweden) and the Allegro from F.J. Berwald's *Quartet*, op. 3.

44. Although performers for the *Trio* (flute, viola, cello) are identified only as members of the Quintette Pierre Jamet, Crunelle is almost certainly the flutist. Other works on the program were Roussel's *Sérénade*, op. 30 (see Appendix 3), the *Sonata in D minor* for violin and piano (Suzanne Plazonich, Annik Février), *Cinq Mélodies chinoises* (Flore Wend, soprano), and *Impromptu*, op. 21 (Pierre Jamet, harp)

The program was broadcast in the series *Association des amis de la musique de chambre*.

45. Other works on the program were Roussel's *Sérénade*, op. 30, and Pierné's *Voyage au pays du Tendre*, both performed by the Quintette Pierre Jamet (see Appendix 3).

The broadcast also included songs by Fauré and Debussy, Milhaud's *Catalogue des fleurs*, and Poulenc's *Le Bestiaire*, all featuring soprano Irène Joachim. It was not indicated whether *Le Bestiaire* was the version with piano or instrumental ensemble.

Orchestral Recordings: The Pasdeloup and Opéra-Comique Orchestras

Crunelle is not identified as a participant in any of the following recordings—on labels, in company catalogs, or, in the case of the Gramophone Company recordings, in recording ledgers. As principal flutist of these orchestras, however, it is *likely* that he was present for most, if not all, of the recording sessions.

At the end this summary there is a short discography of selected recordings with significant passages for flute.

The Pasdeloup Orchestra

I. Gramophone Company, Ltd. recordings

Between 1923 and 1935 the Pasdeloup Orchestra made at least thirty 78-rpm recordings for the French branch of the Gramophone Company, labeled variously "Disque Gramophone" and "La Voix de son Maître." All were conducted by Piero Coppola. Crunelle's audition date for the orchestra, October 16, 1924, suggests that he did not play in the orchestra's recording of Berlioz's *Symphonie fantastique*, made at sessions on October 14, 17, and 18.

Two noteworthy performances from the following year, however, may be among the first Pasdeloup Orchestra recordings to include Crunelle: the ballet music from Gounod's *Faust*: seven selections, recorded on February 13, 1925, issued on two twelve-inch discs; and Honegger's *Pacific 231*, recorded five days later.

Later Gramophone Company issues included a complete or near-complete performance of Berlioz's *La Damnation de Faust*, recorded February 12–18, 1931, and issued on ten twelve-inch discs; Lalo's *Symphonie espagnole*, with violinist Henry Merckel (February 15, 1932); Debussy's *La Damoiselle élue* (November 27, 1934); and a series of excerpts from Wagner's operas and Strauss's *Salomé*, featuring soprano Marjorie Lawrence.

II. Pathé Frères recordings

Between 1928 and 1932 the Pasdeloup Orchestra, conducted by Désiré Inghelbrecht, made over a dozen 78-rpm recordings for Pathé. Except for Inghelbrecht's own *Sinfonia breve No. 1*, all appeared on twelve-inch discs. Works included Debussy's *Petite Suite* (Pathé X5480–5481), Ravel's *Ma Mère l'Oye* (Pathé X5485–5487), Borodin's "Polovetsian Dances" from *Prince Igor* (Pathé X5491–5492), and Berlioz' *Roman Carnival Overture* (Pathé X5538).

The 1933 Pathé catalog, *Disques à aiguille Pathé*, lists two other orchestral recordings conducted by Inghelbrecht: Pathé X96226-96227, incidental music from Bizet's *L'Arlésienne*; and Pathé X96229-96230, four selections from the ballet music in Delibes's *Lakmé*. The ensemble is identified only as "Orchestre" and the recordings are listed separately from those played by the Pasdeloup Orchestra, as well as being issued in Pathé's lower-priced green-label and black-label series. While it is possible that Pasdeloup Orchestra members *might* have participated in these additional recordings, it is more likely that the discs feature a studio orchestra.

No later 78-rpm Pathé recordings of the Pasdeloup have surfaced, except for Danièle Amfitheatrof's *Panorama américain*, conducted by the composer and issued on two twelve-inch discs (Pathé PDT40–41). The 1938 catalog, *Répertoire des disques Pathé*, noted that the recording was awarded a *Grand prix du disque* in the category of "jazz symphonique." *Panorama américain* was composed in 1935, so was likely recorded in 1936 or 1937. The work is scored for full orchestra (including three flutes, one doubling on piccolo), with the addition of three saxophones, steel guitar, and an augmented percussion section.

III. Decca Record Company, Ltd. recordings

The Pasdeloup Orchestra made at least two 78-rpm recordings for Decca conducted by Rhené Emmanuel Baton (Rhené-Baton): Franck's *Symphony in D Minor*, recorded between September and November, 1930 (French Decca T10008–T10012), and Honegger's *Le Chant de Nigamon*, issued in May, 1931 (British Decca K553). The orchestra also recorded Mozart's *Concerto in D Major*, K.357, with piano soloist Magda Tagliaferro and conductor Reynaldo Hahn (French Decca TF141–144, recorded ca. September, 1930–April, 1931).

The Opéra-Comique Orchestra

IV. 78-rpm recordings

Opéra-Comique Orchestra performances recorded by the French Gramophone Company between 1934 and 1952 consisted almost entirely of arias and other vocal or choral operatic excerpts. Conductors included Roger Désormière, André Cluytens, Eugène Bigot, Elie Cohen, and Albert Wolff. One of the few orchestral recordings was the overture to Gounod's *Mireille*, conducted by André Cluytens (Gramophone Company SL138, recorded in Paris on February 14, 1949).

Recordings on 78 rpm for other companies included an impressive legacy of complete or near-complete operas. Most were staples of the Opéra-Comique's repertory, including Emmanuel Chabrier's *L'Étoile*, conducted by Roger Désormière (Pathé PD 21–25, recorded 1943) and Offenbach's *Les Contes d'Hoffmann*, conducted by André Cluytens (French Columbia LFX794–809, recorded March 11 and 26, 1948). The other orchestral recordings consisted primarily of opera overtures, among them Boieldieu's *La Dame blanche* (Pathé PDT171, issued 1948) and Ferdinand Hérold's *Le Pré aux clercs* (French Columbia GFX131, copyright 1949), both conducted by André Cluytens.

V. Long-playing recordings

Long-playing discs brought a rapid increase in the recording of complete operas and large-scale instrumental works. Between 1951 and 1964, many Opéra-Comique performances were released by Decca, Columbia, Pathé-Marconi, Philips, and EMI. Conductors included Albert Wolff, André Cluytens, Elie Cohen, Pierre Monteux, Georges Tzipine, and Pierre Dervaux.

Among these long-playing issues were two important first recordings. The premier of Poulenc's *La Voix humaine* in 1959 was followed within months by a recording with the same performers: soprano Denise Duval and the Opéra-Comique Orchestra, conducted by Georges Prêtre. Initially issued as Ricordi 30 CA 001, the LP then appeared as Vox OPL160 in 1962, and Club National du Disque CND814 in 1963. Poulenc's *Les Mamelles de Tirésias*, premiered by the Opéra-Comique in 1947, was recorded under Cluyten's direction and issued in 1954 on French Columbia FCX230.

A Note on Orchestral Broadcasts

The first broadcasts of the Pasdeloup Orchestra took place in Paris in November, 1927. The broadcasts had originally been arranged by Achille Mestre, a professor of the Faculté de Droit de Paris and an amateur musician. Programs were to be aired over "Radio Tour Eiffel," which used transmitting facilities installed on the famous Paris landmark. However, the orchestra was apparently lured away by the PTT (Postes, Télégraphes et Téléphones) to broadcast via their station.

While it is possible that some of the Pasdeloup's pre-1945 broadcasts were transcribed, none are currently listed as extant in the catalog of the Institut national de l'audiovisuel.

The cataloged holdings of the INA include several Opéra-Comique broadcasts from the 1950s. Among these are complete performances of: Reynaldo Hahn's *Ciboulette* (March 25, 1953), Gounod's *Mireille* (March 12, 1954), Ravel's *L'Heure espagnole* (three performances in 1954–55, the first on June 30, 1954), Messager's *Monsieur Beaucaire* (December 10, 1955), and Charpentier's *Louise* (March 9, 1956).

Orchestra Recordings with Significant Passages for Flute

78-rpm Recordings

1. Rimsky-Korsakov, Nikolai, *The Tale of Tsar Saltan*: The Flight of the Bumblebee
   Pasdeloup Orchestra, conducted by Desiré Inghelbrecht
      recorded Paris, 1928   Pathé: X5485
2. Inghelbrecht, Désiré, *Sinfonia breve No. 1 di camera*
   Pasdeloup Orchestra, conducted by Désiré Inghelbrecht
      recorded Paris, issued 1931
         Tranquillo (first part)   Pathé: X8810
         Tranquillo (second part)   Pathé: X8810
         Pastorale (first part)   Pathé: X8811
         Pastorale (second part)   Pathé: X8811
         Finale (first part)   Pathé: X8812
         Finale (second part)   Pathé: X8812
      Reissues:
         CD: *Les Autographes vocaux*, Timpani 1C1201 (2012)
3. Strauss, Richard, *Salomé*: Danse des sept voiles
   Pasdeloup Orchestra, conducted by Piero Coppola
      recorded Paris, March 20, 1934
         Part 1: 2PG 1424-1   Gramophone Company: DB4932 [52-1286]
                       -2   unpublished
         Part 2: 2PG 1425-1   Gramophone Company: DB4932 [52-1287]
                       -2   unpublished
4. Boieldieu, François-Adrien, *La Dame blanche*: Overture
   Opéra-Comique Orchestra, conducted by André Cluytens
      recorded Paris, issued 1948   Pathé: PDT171
      Reissues:
         CD: *André Cluytens-Complete Mono Orchestral Recordings, 1943–1958*, Erato
         (2017)

Long-Playing Recordings

5. Bizet, Georges, *Carmen* (complete)
   Opéra-Comique Orchestra conducted by André Cluytens
      recorded Théâtre des Champs-Élysées, Paris, September 6–9, 1950
         issued 1950–1951   Pathé-Marconi: FCX101–103 (France, mono)
         issued 1951   Columbia Masterworks: SL109 (US, mono)
                                                  MOP33 (US, 78 rpm)
                                                  MOP4-33 (US, 45 rpm)
         issued ca. 1951–1952   Columbia: 33CX1016–1018 (UK, mono)
         issued ca. 1951–1952   Columbia: 33OCX1016–1018 (Australia and
                                   New Zealand, mono)
         issued ca. 1951–1952   Columbia: 33WCX1016–1018 (Germany,
                                   mono)

Complete reissues:

LP: Pathé-Marconi FCX35020–35022 (France, mono) issued ca.1966

LP: Pathé-Marconi Trianon TRI 33308–33310 (France, stereo compatible) issued ca.1978

LP: Pathé-Marconi Trianon 2 C127 73047–73049 (France, mono) issued ca. 1981

CD: EMI Classics CMS 5 65318 2 (2 discs, 1994)

CD: Naxos Historical 8.110238–39 (2 discs, 2003)

6. Bizet, Georges, *Carmen*

Opéra-Comique Orchestra conducted by Albert Wolff

recorded Paris, June–July, 1951

Decca: LXT2615–2617 (France, mono)

London: A4304 (UK, mono)

London: LLPA6 (US, mono)

Reissues:

CD: Preiser "Paperback Opera" 20016 (2002)

7. *French Overtures*

Opéra-Comique Orchestra, conducted by Albert Wolff

recorded La Maison de la Mutualité, Paris, June, 1951

Decca: LXT2625 (France, mono)

London: ARL749 (UK, mono)

Contents (overtures): Massenet, *Phèdre*; Lalo, *Le Roi d'Ys*; Saint-Saëns, *La Princesse jaune*; Berlioz, *Benvenuto Cellini*; Massenet, *Werther*: La Nuit de Noël, and Prelude

Reissues:

CD: Decca Eloquence 4802385 (2011): Saint-Saëns and Berlioz only

CD: *French Overtures*, Profound Classic Archive PCA-062 (2016)

8. Massenet, Jules, *Scènes alsaciennes*; *Scènes pittoresques*; *Phèdre*, Overture

Opéra-Comique Orchestra, conducted by André Cluytens

recorded Paris, September 26, 1952 (*Scènes alsaciennes*); October 12, 1953 (*Scènes pittoresques*; *Phèdre*, Overture)

Pathé: 33DTX159 (France, mono)

Reissues:

CD: *André Cluytens–Complete Mono Orchestral Recordings, 1943–1958*, Erato (2017)

9. Fauré, Gabriel, *Masques et Bergamasques*; *Dolly Suite*; *Pelléas et Mélisande Suite*

Opéra-Comique Orchestra, conducted by Georges Tzipine

recorded Paris, copyright 1956

Columbia: 33FCX463 (France, mono)

Columbia: 33CX1577 (UK, mono)

Angel Records: 35311 (US, mono, issued ca. 1957)

10. Massé, Victor, *Les Noces de Jeannette*

Opéra-Comique Orchestra conducted by Pierre Cruchon (orchestra) and Jack Collin (chorus)

recorded Paris

issued ca. 1961	Pathé: CPTPM130190 (France, stereo compatible)
issued ca. 1961	Pathé: ASTX130190 (France, stereo)
issued ca. 1965	Pathé: DTX 30190 (US Capitol import, mono)
issued ca. 1965	Pathé: ASTX 121 (US Capitol import, stereo)

Notes

1. "The Flight of the Bumblebee," along with the "Pavane de la belle au bois dormant" from Ravel's *Ma Mère l'Oye*, filled the final side of Dukas' *L'Apprenti sorcier*, issued as Pathé X5484–5485. The recording appeared on vertical- and lateral-cut discs with identical catalog numbers. Pathé X5486–5487 presented the remaining movements of *Ma Mère l'Oye*. The recording date was documented in Victor Girard and Harold Barnes' *Vertical-Cut Cylinders and Discs*, British Institute of Recorded Sound, 1964/1971.

    Pathé catalogs for 1929 and 1933 do not identify Crunelle as the soloist. Labels have not been inspected.
2. Issued on three ten-inch discs with blue and silver labels. The issue date was reported by the BNF, based on the recording's inclusion in the supplement *Pathé. La Vie phonographique* (February, 1931). The *Sinfonia breve* is scored for strings, harp, and single woodwinds, with a small brass section and percussion in the second and third movements. There are short solo passages for flute, particularly in the first movement and at the end of the Finale.

    The compact disc reissue, *Les Autographes vocaux*, has been made available on Spotify and YouTube.
4. The Erato compact disc reissue, *André Cluytens-Complete Mono Orchestral Recordings, 1943–1958*, has been made available on Spotify.
5. The principal singers were Solange Michel (*Carmen*); Raoul Jobin (*Don José*); Michel Dens (*Escamillo*); and Martha Angelici (*Micaela*). The performance used the Opéra-Comique version of the opera, with spoken dialogue. The recording date was cited in notes for the EMI Classics compact disc reissue.

    The list of LP issues provided here is selective as the complete opera has been reissued many times Excerpts have also appeared in a wide variety of long-playing and digital formats and combinations.

    The Naxos compact disc reissue has been made available on Youtube and Naxos Music Library.
6. The principal singers were Suzanne Juyol (*Carmen*); Libero De Luca (*Don José*); Janine Micheau (*Micaela*); and Julien Giovannetti (*Escamillo*).
7. The London LP was titled *Famous Overtures No. 5*.

    The Decca Eloquence compact disc reissue has been made available on Spotify.

    The complete Profound Classic Archive reissue has been made available on the Youtube channel of the Orchestra of the Théâtre-National de l'Opéra-Comique.
8. The Erato compact disc reissue has been made available on Spotify and YouTube.
9. Excerpts from the *Pelléas et Mélisande Suite*, including the beginning of the "Sicilienne," are available on Gallica.
10. The cast included Liliane Berton (*Jeannette*), Michel Dens (*Jean*), and Robert Manuel (narrator).

    The American Capitol LP import was reviewed in *American Record Guide* for February,1965. The disc had a green French Pathé Marconi *Plaisir Musical* (series) label. Described in a review as "almost complete," the performance included the well-known "Air du Rossignol," with its significant flute obbligato. Excerpts from this recording, including one from the first cadenza of the "Air du rossignol," are on Gallica.

    Berton's "Air du Rossignol" has been made available on Youtube on the channel of "78-45-33 Tours/CD."

Works Written for the Quintette instrumental de Paris

Absil, Jean (1893–1974), *Concert à 5*, op. 38 (1939) [I. *Introduction et Allegro*; II. *Andante con moto*; III. *Finale: très vite*]. Published by CeBeDeM in 1957. Duration: 12:00. The Quintette Pierre Jamet (QPJ) gave the premiere in Paris on May 3, 1953.

Amellér, André (1912–1990), *Suite française dans le goût romantique*, op. 33 (1947) [I. *Prélude à la douleur de vivre*; II. *Équivoque*; III. *Scintillante lune*; IV. *Rondes printanières*]. Unpublished manuscript available at www.ameller.org/fr/eformation. php. The QPJ gave the premiere for the Concerts de musique de chambre de Paris on November 20, 1948. Amellér revised the work in 1960.

Andriessen, Hendrik (1892–1981), *Variations sur un thème de Couperin*. Published by Donemus/Darmstadt in 1949. There is no record of the premiere.

Béclard d'Harcourt, Marguerite (1884–1964), *En regardant Watteau* (1928) [I. *Le Parc*; II. *Les Amants*; III. *L'Indifférent*; IV. *Les danseurs rustiques*]. Published by Fortin (Salabert) in 1942. Premiered by Gaston Crunelle, flute, Pierre Jamet, harp, Jean Pasquier, violin, Pierre Pasquier, viola, and Nelly Gauthier, cello, on a program of music by women composers for Le Triptyque on March 9, 1941, at the Hôtel de Sagonne.

Bernard, Robert (1900–1971), *Quintette en mi* [I. *Allegro tranquillo*; II. *Très lent*; III. *Vivace*]. Unpublished. The QPJ gave the premiere at the École normale de musique on May 21, 1947.

Bloch, André (1873–1960), *Petite Suite dominicale* [I. *À l'Église*; II. *Intermède sur le nom JAMET*; III. *Angelus*; IV. *Finale*]. Unpublished. The QPJ premiered his work in the Salle du Conservatoire on March 17, 1946.

de Bréville, Pierre (1861–1949), *Trois Pièces*. Unpublished. This work cannot be found but is mentioned in Jacques Tilley's profile of the QPJ.[1]

Brown, Charles (1898–1988), *Concert en l'honneur de la nativité* [I. *Allegro*; II. *Andante*; III. *Final: Allegro avec joie*]. Unpublished. Duration: 14:45. The QPJ gave the premiere at the Schola de Saint-Étienne in Bourges on December 15, 1953.

Casadesus, Robert (1899–1972), *Quintet*, op. 10 (1927) [I. *Sinfonia: Allegro moderato*; II. *Barcarola*; III. *Saltarello*]. Published by International Music Company. Duration: 10:00. The QIP performed the premiere for the SMI at the École normale de musique on February 28, 1931.

Cras, Jean (1879–1932), *Quintette* (1928) [I. *Assez animé*; II. *Animé*; III. *Assez lent*; IV. *Très animé*]. Published by Maurice Sénart (Salabert) in 1930. Dedicated to the QIP. Duration 21:00. The QIP gave the premiere at the SN on May 17, 1930.

Damase, Jean-Michel (1928–2013), *Quintette*, op. 2 (1947) [I. *Allegro moderato*; II. *Andante*; III. *Allegro vivace*]. Published by Henry Lemoine. Duration: 19:45. There is no record of the premiere of this piece, but the QIP's recording was released in 1962.

Demarquez, Suzanne (1891–1965), *Variations, Interlude et Tarantelle sur un thème populaire corse*. Unpublished. Duration: 10:30. The QPJ gave the premiere for Le Triptyque on December 22, 1942, at the École normale de musique.

Dequin, Georges, *Quatre Chansons de Bilitis*. Unpublished. The work was first performed by the QIP for the SN on May 16, 1925, in the Salle Gaveau.

Desportes, Yvonne (1907–1993), *Aubade*, op. 62 (1946). Unpublished. Duration: 10:00. The QPJ gave the first performance of *Aubade* at the École normale de musique on May 21, 1947.

Desportes, Yvonne (1907–1993), *Suite de danses* [I. *Tango*; II. *One Step*; III. *Rumba*; IV. *Valse*]. Unpublished. Duration: 11:00. The QIP gave the premiere on April 28, 1934, for the SN at the École normale de musique.

d'Indy, Vincent (1851–1931), *Suite en parties*, op. 91 (1927) [I. *Entrée en sonate*; II. *Air désuet, pour flute (Modéré, sans lenteur)*; III. *Sarabande avec deux doubles (Assez lent)*; IV. *Farandole variée en Rondeau (Avec entrain)*]. Published by Heugel in 1930. Dedicated to René Le Roy and the QIP. Duration: 16:30. The QIP gave the premiere at the École normale de musique for the SN on May 17, 1930.

Françaix, Jean. (1912–1997), *Quintette* (1933) [I. *Prélude*; II. *Scherzo*; III. *Andante*; IV. *Rondo*]. Published by Schott. Duration: 9:15. The QIP gave the premiere for Le Triton at the École normale de musique on May 24, 1935.

Gaillard, Marius-François (1900–1973), *Cinq Moudras su un rubayat à sept notes* (1934) [I. *La terre s'éveille (the earth is awakening)*; II. *Le lotus s'ouvre (the lotus opens)*; III. *L'abeille tournoie autour des fleurs (the bee swirls around the flowers)*; IV. *Les cimes des arbres se balancent (the tops of the trees are swaying)*; V. *Le paon salue le soleil (the peacock greets the sun)*]. Unpublished. The QIP first performed this piece on May 6, 1937 in the Salle Chopin. Radio-Paris broadcast their performance on July 21, 1943, and they recorded it in 1942 or 1943 (see Appendix 3).

Gretchaninov, Alexander[2] (1864–1956), *Scherzo*, op. 140 (1930). Unpublished. Gretchaninov was a prolific Russian-born composer who lived in France from 1925 to 1939 and then moved to New York. He wrote symphonies, operas, liturgical music, songs, and chamber music.

Jolivet, André (1905–1974), *Chant de Linos* (1944). Published by Costallat in 1944 (Leduc, 1954). Duration: 11:00. The quintet version was performed by the QIP in the Salle du Conservatoire on June 1, 1945.[3]

Jongen, Joseph (1873–1953), *Concert à cinq*, op. 71 (1923) [I. *Décidé*; II. *Calme*; III. *Très décidé*]. Published by CeBeDeM. Duration: 23:00. The QIP gave the premiere at their first concert on May 27, 1924, in the Salle des agriculteurs.

Koechlin, Charles (1867–1950), *Primavera Quintet*, op. 156 (1936) [I. *Allegro quasi allegretto*; II. *Adagio*; III. *Intermezzo*; IV. *Final*]. Published by Max Eschig. Duration: 14:00. The QPJ gave the public premiere for Le Groupement des compositeurs de Paris at École normale de musique on March 14, 1944 (The QPJ had given a private performance on June 10, 1943, at the home of Mme. Amos).

Koechlin, Charles (1867–1950), *Quintet No. 2*, op. 223 (1949). [I. *Allegro (non troppo)*; II. *Intermezzo*; III. *Andante con moto (Soleil au matin)*; IV. *Final: Allegro con moto*]. Published by Max Eschig. Duration: 16:15. The QPJ gave the premiere on October 21, 1952, in the Salle Berlioz at the Conservatory, and French radio broadcast the performance (see Appendix 3).

Labey, Marcel (1875–1968), *Suite*, op. 37 (1938) [I. *Canzone*; II. *Scherzo*; III. *Rondo*]. Unpublished. Duration: 17:00. Dedicated to the QIP, the piece was premiered by André Prieur, flute, Th. Raabe, violin; Gisèle Weber-Labey, viola; Edwige Bergeron, cello, and Bernard Galais, harp, in the Salle Gaveau for the École César Franck, where

Labey was director, and subsequently performed by the QPJ on Radio-Paris on
December 12, 1943.

Lajtha, Laszlo. (1892–1963), *Les Marionettes*, op. 26 (1937) [I. *Marche des trois pantins*;
II. *La Nuit dans la forêt*; III. *Menuet royale*; IV. *Chamailleries*]. Published by Editio
Musica Budapest. Duration: 25:45. Flutist Gaston Crunelle, violinist Janine Andrade,
violist Alice Merckel, cellist Charles Bartsch, and harpist Micheline Kahn performed
the premiere for Le Triton on March 20, 1939, at the École normale de musique.

Lajtha, Laszlo (1892–1963), *Sérénade*. Unpublished. The QIP performed the premiere for
Le Triton on May 9, 1938, at the École normale de musique.

Lang, Max (1917–1987), *Prélude, danse, air et finale* (1942). Unpublished. The QPJ gave
the premiere on May 20, 1950.

Lesur, Daniel (1908–2002), *Suite médiévale* (1945) [I. *Monodie*; II. *L'Ange de Sourire*; III.
Symphonie; IV. *Complainte*; V. *Danse*]. Published by Durand. Duration: 12:45. The
QPJ gave the premiere at the École normale de musique on May 21, 1947.

Loucheur, Raymond (1899–1979), *Quatre Pièces en quintette* (1953) [I. *Allegretto
scherzando*; II. *Lento*; III. *Moderato*; IV. *Vivo*]. Published by Billaudot in 1973.
Duration: 14:30. The QPJ gave the premiere for the SN on February 21, 1958. The
Quintette Marie-Claire Jamet recorded this work on LP in 1964 (Erato STE50152),
and their recording has been rereleased on CD.

Malipiero, Gian Francesco (1882–1973), *Sonata a cinque* (1934). Published by Ricordi.
Duration: 14:45. The QIP gave the premiere on May 24, 1935, for Le Triton at the
École normale de musique.

Manen, Christian (1934–2020), *Quintette*, op. 33 (1958). Published by Lemoine in 1970.
The date of the premiere is not known.

Manziarly, Marcelle de (1899–1988), *Quintette*. Unpublished. The QIP gave the premiere
for SN at the Salle Chopin on February 22, 1936.

Maugüé, Jules (1869–1953), *Suite mythologique* (1930) [I. *Napées* ; II. *Ægipans* ; III.
Bacchantes]. Unpublished.[4] The QIP gave the première for the SN on April 28, 1934,
at the École normale de musique.

Margoni, Alain (b. 1934), *Quintette*. Unpublished. Duration: 19:20. The QIP gave the
premiere at the Festival des nuits de Sceaux on June 4, 1961, at a concert of new works,
and French radio broadcast this program on June 8.

Martelli, Henri (1895–1980), *Quintette*, op. 73 (1951). Unpublished. The QPJ gave the
premiere on November 28, 1951, for Les Amis de la musique de chambre at 24 place
Malesherbes in Paris and subsequently performed it on French radio on January
26, 1952.

Orban, Marcel (1884–1958), *Trois danses* (1948) [I. *Fantasque*; II. *Gracieuse*; III.
Rustique]. Published in Paris in 1948.[5] Duration: 9:00. The QPJ gave the premiere for
the SN at the École normale de musique on June 16, 1950.

Pierné, Gabriel (1863–1937), *Voyage au pays du Tendre* (1935). Published by Leduc in
1938 and 1951. Duration: 11:45. The QIP gave the premiere on 8 May, 1936, over
French national radio.

Pierné, Gabriel (1863–1937), *Variations libres et final*, op. 51 (1933). Published by
Salabert in 1932. Duration 11:00. Dedicated to the QIP. The QIP gave the premiere at
the SN on April 1, 1933, at the École normale de musique.

Pierné, Paul (1874–1952), *Variations au clair de lune* (1935). Published by Lemoine in
1935. The QIP gave the premiere for the SN at the Salle Chopin on February 22, 1936.

Pillois, Jacques (1877–1935), *Cinq haïkaï: Épigrammes lyriques du Japon* (1926) [I. *Prière d'orphelin: Modérément lent* (Orphan's Prayer: Moderately Slow); II. *Jour de l'an japonais: Vif et joyeux* (Day of the Japanese Year: Fast and Joyous); III. *Chagrin d'amour* (Love's Sorrow); IV. *Solitude (Aubade à la lune)* (Solitude: Dawn Serenade to the Moon); V. *Rêves de guerriers morts* (Dream of Dead Warriors)]. Published by Durand in 1926. Duration 10:30. The QIP gave the premiere on January 9, 1926 for the SN in the Salle Érard.

Ropartz, Guy (1864–1955), *Prélude, Marine et Chansons* (1928) [I. *Prélude*; II. *Marine*; III. *Chansons*]. Published by Durand in 1928. Duration: 12:30. Dedicated to the QIP. The QIP gave the premiere on November 24, 1928, in the Salle Érard.

Roussel, Albert (1869–1937), *Sérénade*, op. 30 (1925) [I. *Allegro*; II. *Andante*; III. *Presto*]. Published by Durand. Duration: 15:30. Dedicated to René Le Roy. The QIP gave the premiere in the Salle Gaveau on October 15, 1925, for the SMI.

Schmitt, Florent (1870–1958), *Suite en rocaille*, op. 84 (1934) [I. *Sans hâte*; II. *Animé*; III. *Sans lenteur*; IV. *Vif*]. Published by Durand. Duration: 13:45. The QIP gave the premiere on May 24, 1935, for Le Triton at the École normale de musique.

Scott, Cyril (1879–1979), *Rapsodie arabesque* (1926). Unpublished. Dedicated to René Le Roy. The QIP gave the premiere on November 24, 1928, in the Salle Érard.

Smit, Léo (1900–1943), *Quintette* (1928) [I. *Allegro*; II. *Lento*; III. *Allegro vivace*]. Published by Donemus. Duration: 21:00. The QIP gave the premiere for the SMI on April 20, 1929, in the Salle de la société des concerts du conservatoire.

Sohy, Charlotte (1887–1955), *Triptyque champêtre*, op. 21 (1925) [I. *Enchantement matinal*; II. *Au fil de l'eau*; III. *Danse au crepuscule*]. Unpublished.[6] Duration: 13:30. The QIP gave the premiere for the SN in the Salle Érard on January 9, 1926.

Spelman, Timothy Mather (1891–1970), *Poème: Le Pavillon sur l'eau* (1925). Published by Chester. The QIP gave the premiere of the *Poème* in 1933.

Tomasi, Henri (1901–1971), *Petite suite de printemps*. Unpublished. The QIP performed the premiere at the École normale de musique for Le Triton on May 9, 1938.

Tournier, Marcel (1879–1951), *Suite*, op. 34 (1928) [I. *Soir*; II. *Danse*; III. *Lied*; IV. *Fête*]. Published by Lemoine in 1929. Duration: 13:45. The QIP gave the premiere on May 28, 1928, in the Salle Érard.

Woollett, Henri (1864–1936), *Nocturne, Sérénade*. Unpublished. The QIP gave the premiere at the SN at the Salle Gaveau on May 5, 1928.

Quintette instrumental de Paris Discography

Compiled by Susan Nelson

Record Labels, Catalog Number Prefixes, and Numerical Series for 78-rpm Recordings

Action artistique (Association française d'action artistique)
> AA (France, 10- and 12-inch)

Columbia
> LFX (France, 12-inch)
> 68000 (US, 12-inch)

Elite Special
> ER; 8900 (Switzerland, 10-inch)

The Gramophone Company
> DA (International Celebrity, 10-inch, red label)
> DB (International Celebrity, 12-inch, red label)
> E (UK, 10-inch, black label)
> K (France, 10-inch, green label)
> W (France, 12-inch, black label)

Victor
> 4200 (US, 10-inch, Red Seal)
> 11100 (US, 12-inch, Red Seal)
> JD (Japan, 12-inch, Red Seal)

78-rpm Recordings

1. Scarlatti, Alessandro (realization by Germaine Tailleferre), *Sonata for flute and strings* [D Major]
    (Quintette instrumental de Paris: René Le Roy, flute; René Bas, violin; Pierre Grout, viola; Roger Boulmé, cello; Pierre Jamet, harp)
    recorded Paris, November, 1929
    a) Allegro moderato b) Adagio
    BS 4367–2   Gramophone Company: K5920 [50–822], E608
                               Victor: 4250
    Fugue
    BS 4368–2   Gramophone Company: K5920 [50–823], E608
                               Victor: 4250

Largo
BS 4369–2   Gramophone Company: K5921 [50–824], E609
                          Victor: 4251

Allegro
BS 4370–1   Gramophone Company: K5921 [50–825], E609
                          Victor: 4251

2. d'Indy, Vincent, *Suite en parties*, op. 91
   (Quintette instrumental de Paris: René Le Roy, flute; René Bas, violin; Pierre Grout, viola; Roger Boulmé, cello; Pierre Jamet, harp)
   recorded London, Studio 2, Abbey Road, May 25, 1933
   Entrée en sonate
   2B 6564–2   Gramophone Company: DB2009 [32–3755]
                         Victor: 11168, JD297
   a) Air désuet b) Sarabande (first part)
   2B 6565–1   Gramophone Company: DB2009 [32–3756]
                         Victor: 11168, JD297
   Sarabande (conclusion)
   2B 6566–2   Gramophone Company: DB2010 [32–3757]
                         Victor: 11169, JD298
   Farandole variée
   2B 6567–2   Gramophone Company: DB2010 [32–3793]
                         Victor: 11169, JD298
      Reissues:
      LP: *The Great Flautists*, Volume II, Pearl GEMM 302 (1986)
      CD: *The Great Flautists*, Volume II, Pearl GEMM CD 9302 (1990)
      CD: *Pierre Jamet & son quintette*, Timpani 2C2122 (2 discs, 2007)

3. Pierné, Gabriel, *Variations libres et final*, op. 51
   (Quintette instrumental de Paris: René Le Roy, flute; René Bas, violin; Pierre Grout, viola; Roger Boulmé, cello; Pierre Jamet, harp)
   recorded Paris, December 1933
   Pt. 1: CLX 1740–1   Columbia: LFX331, 68689-D
   Pt. 2: CLX 1741–1   Columbia: LFX331, 68689-D
   Reissues:
      CD: *Pierre Jamet & son quintette*, Timpani 2C2122 (2 discs, 2007)

4. Schmitt, Florent, *Suite en rocaille*, op. 84
   (Quintette instrumental de Paris: René Le Roy, flute; René Bas, violin; Pierre Grout, viola; Roger Boulmé, cello; Pierre Jamet, harp)
   recorded Paris, Studio Albert, February 8, 1936
   Sans hâte
   0LA 870–1   Gramophone Company: DA4882
   Animé
   0LA 871–1   Gramophone Company: DA4882
   Sans lenteur
   0LA 872–1   Gramophone Company: DA4883
   Vif
   0LA 873–1   Gramophone Company: DA4883
      Reissues:
      CD: *Pierre Jamet & son quintette*, Timpani 2C2122 (2 discs, 2007)

5. Falla, Manuel de, *Psyché* (poem by Georges Jean-Aubry)
   Leïla Ben Sedira, soprano (Quintette Pierre Jamet: Gaston Crunelle, flute; René Bas,
   violin; Etienne Ginot, viola; Marcel Frécheville, cello; Pierre Jamet, harp)
      recorded Paris, January 12, 1942
      2LA 3700-1   Gramophone Company: W1507
      Reissues:
      LP: *Manuel de Falla, ses amis et ses interprètes,* EMI 2C 153 16.241–16.242
         (2 discs, 1979)
      CD: *Manuel de Falla/Grabaciones historicas/78 rpm and live concerts,*
         Almaviva DS 0121 (1996)

6. Pierné, Gabriel, *Voyage au pays du Tendre*
   (Quintette Pierre Jamet: Gaston Crunelle, flute; René Bas, violin; Etienne Ginot,
   viola; Marcel Frécheville, cello; Pierre Jamet, harp)
      recorded Paris, Studio Pelouze, November 16, 1942
      Pt. 1: 0LA 3770-2   Gramophone Company: DA4944
      Pt. 2: 0LA 3771-3   Gramophone Company: DA4944
      Pt. 3: 0LA 3772-3   Gramophone Company: DA4945
      Pt. 4: 0LA 3773-3   Gramophone Company: DA4945
      Reissues:
      CD: *Pierre Jamet & son quintette,* Timpani 2C2122 (2 discs, 2007)

7. Ravel, Maurice, *Introduction and Allegro*
   (Quintette Pierre Jamet: Gaston Crunelle, flute; René Bas, violin; Etienne Ginot,
   viola; Marcel Frécheville, cello; Pierre Jamet, harp); André Vacellier, clarinet;
   Octave Marchesini, violin
      recorded Paris, Studio Pelouze, February 3, 1943
      Pt. 1: 2LA 3957-1,2 Gramophone Company: W1562
      Pt. 2: 2LA 3958-1,2 Gramophone Company: W1562

8. Pierné, Paul, *Variations au clair de lune*
   (Quintette Pierre Jamet: Gaston Crunelle, flute; René Bas, violin; Etienne Ginot,
   viola; Marcel Frécheville, cello: Pierre Jamet, harp)
      recorded France, 1942 or 1943
      Pt. 1: PARTX 1854-1 Action Artistique: AA-7
      Pt. 2: PARTX 1855-1 Action Artistique: AA-7

9. Gaillard, Marius-François, *Cinq Moudras sur un rubayat à sept notes*
   (Quintette Pierre Jamet: Gaston Crunelle, flute; René Bas, violin; Etienne Ginot,
   viola; Marcel Frécheville, cello: Pierre Jamet, harp)
      recorded France, 1942 or 1943
      Pt. 1: PARTX-1885   Action Artistique: AA-17
      Pt. 2: PARTX-1886   Action Artistique: AA-17

10. Roussel, Albert, *Sérénade,* op. 30
    (Quintette Pierre Jamet: Gaston Crunelle, flute; René Bas, violin; Georges Blanpain,
    viola; Robert Krabansky, cello; Pierre Jamet, harp)
       recorded Studio Pelouze, Paris, May 24, 1946
       Allegro
       2LA 4604-1   Gramophone Company: DB11124
       Andante (first part)
       2LA 4605-1   Gramophone Company: DB11124

Andante (conclusion)
2LA 4606-1   Gramophone Company: DB11125
Presto
2LA 4607-1   Gramophone Company: DB11125
   Reissues:
   CD: *Pierre Jamet & son quintette*, Timpani 2C2122 (2 discs, 2007)

11. Françaix, Jean, *Quintette*
   (Quintette Pierre Jamet: Gaston Crunelle, flute; René Bas, violin; Georges Blanpain, viola; Robert Krabansky, cello; Pierre Jamet, harp)
   recorded France, copyright registered 1950
   Prelude: Andante tranquillo
   4284   Elite Special: ER3009, 8943
   Scherzo
   4285   Elite Special: ER3010, 8944
   Andante
   4286   Elite Special: ER3009, 8943
   Rondo
   4287   Elite Special: ER3010, 8944
   Reissues:
   CD: *Pierre Jamet & son quintette*, Timpani 2C2122 (2 discs, 2007)

Long-Playing Recordings

12. Ropartz, Guy, *Prélude, Marine et Chansons*
   (Quintette Pierre Jamet: Gaston Crunelle, flute; Pierre Jamet, harp; René Bas, violin; Georges Blanpain, viola; Robert Krabansky, cello)
   recorded 1956
   LP: Ducretet Thomson 300 C 023 (10-inch, mono, France, issued ca. 1958)
   Reissues:
   CD: Forgotten Records FR 460 (France, 2010)

13. Falla, Manuel de, *Psyché* (poem by Georges Jean-Aubry)
   Pierrette Alarie, soprano; Quintette Pierre Jamet
   recorded Paris, Théâtre Apollo, October 16, 1956
   LP: Ducretet Thomson 260-C-088 (10-inch, mono, France, copyright 1958)
   Reissues:
   CD: *Les introuvables de Manuel de Falla*, EMI Classics 5692352 (4 discs, 1996)

14. Françaix, Jean, *Quintette*; Lesur, Daniel, *Suite médiévale*; Damase, Jean-Michel, *Quintette* op. 2
   (Quintette instrumental de Paris: Gaston Crunelle, flute; René Bas, violin; Pierre Ladhuie, viola; Pierre Coddée, cello; Bernard Galais, harp)
   copyright 1962
   LP: Discophiles français DF 730.062 (mono, France)
     Discophiles français DF 740.014 (stereo, France)

Radio Broadcasts

This section includes only *extant* broadcasts, documented primarily through the cataloging of the INA. The ID numbers included are those from the INA catalog.

15. d'Indy, Vincent, *Suite en parties*, op. 91
   (Quintette Pierre Jamet: Gaston Crunelle, flute; René Bas, violin; Georges Blanpain, viola; Robert Krabansky, cello; Pierre Jamet, harp)
   Broadcast, *621ème Concert de la Société Musical de Paris*, recorded April 30, 1948 (broadcast date unverified)
       Network: X, produced by Radiodiffusion Française
       INA ID: PHD85025285

16. [Selection of works by Gabriel Pierné, program not identified]
   (Quintette Pierre Jamet: Gaston Crunelle, flute; René Bas, violin; Georges Blanpain, viola; Robert Krabansky, cello; Pierre Jamet, harp)
   Broadcast, *Oeuvres de Gabriel Pierné, et le Quintette Instrumental Pierre Jamet*, recorded November 22, 1948 (broadcast December 5, 1948)
       Network: X, produced by Radiodiffusion Française
       INA ID: PHD860233396

17. Pierné, Gabriel, *Voyage au pays du Tendre*; Roussel, Albert, *Sérénade*, op. 30
   (Quintette Pierre Jamet: Gaston Crunelle, flute; René Bas, violin; Georges Blanpain, viola; Robert Krabansky, cello; Pierre Jamet, harp)
   Broadcast, *Quintette instrumental Pierre Jamet*, recorded July 19, 1949 (broadcast July 20, 1949)
       Network: Programme National, produced by Radiodiffusion Télévision Française
       INA ID: PHD86059783

18. Ropartz, Guy, *Prélude, Marine et Chansons*
   (Quintette Pierre Jamet: Crunelle is the only member individually identified)
   Broadcast, *Musique de chambre*, recorded June 28, 1952 (broadcast June 29, 1952)
       Network: Programme National, produced by Radiodiffusion Télévision Française
       INA ID: 86004185

19. Jongen, Joseph, *Concert à cinq*, op. 71: Finale (Trés décidé)
   (Quintette Pierre Jamet: Gaston Crunelle, flute; René Bas, violin; Georges Blanpain, viola; Robert Krabansky, cello; Pierre Jamet, harp)
   Broadcast, *Concert de la guilde*, recorded and broadcast November 9, 1952
       Network: Paris Inter, produced by Radiodiffusion Télévision Française
       INA ID: PHD90010913

20. Koechlin, Charles, *Quintet No. 2*, op. 223
   (Quintette Pierre Jamet: Gaston Crunelle, flute; René Bas, violin; Georges Blanpain, viola; Robert Krabansky, cello; Pierre Jamet, harp)
   Broadcast, *Concert de musique de chambre*, recorded and broadcast October 10, 1953 (live broadcast)
       Network: Programme National, produced by Radiodiffusion Télévision Française
       INA ID: PHD86056337

21. Brown, Charles, *Concert en l'honneur de la nativité*; Demarquez, Suzanne,
    Variations, Interlude et Tarantelle sur un thème populaire corse
    (Quintette Pierre Jamet: Gaston Crunelle, flute; René Bas, violin; Georges Blanpain,
    viola; Robert Krabansky, cello; Pierre Jamet, harp)
        Broadcast, *Concert de musique de chambre*, recorded and broadcast February 27, 1954
            Network: Programme National, produced by Radiodiffusion Télévision Française
            INA ID: PHD86056717
22. Malipiero, Gian Francesco, *Sonata a cinque*
    (Quintette Pierre Jamet: Gaston Crunelle, flute; Robert Quattrochi, violin; Marcel
    Quattrochi, viola; Robert Krabansky, cello; Pierre Jamet, harp)
    Broadcast, *Concert de musique de chambre*, recorded and broadcast June 19, 1954
        (live concert)
            Network: Programme National, produced by Radiodiffusion Télévision Française
            INA ID: PHD86033823
23. Schmitt, Florent, *Suite en rocaille*, op. 84
    (Quintette Pierre Jamet)
    Broadcast, *Couleurs instrumentales*, recorded June 21, 1956 (broadcast September
        26, 1956)
            Network: F4, produced by Radiodiffusion Télévision Française
            INA ID: PHD89017655
24. Koechlin, Charles, *Primavera Quintet*, op. 156
    (Quintette Pierre Jamet: Gaston Crunelle, flute; René Bas, violin; Georges Blanpain,
    viola; Robert Krabansky, cello; Pierre Jamet, harp)
    Broadcast, *Charles Koechlin*, recorded October 9, 1956 (broadcast October 21, 1956)
            Network: Programme National, produced by Radiodiffusion Télévision Française
            INA ID: PHZ13005919
25. Roussel, Albert, (a) *Deux Poèmes de Ronsard*, op. 26; (b) *Trio*, Op. 40; (c) *Sérénade*,
    Op. 30
    a: (Flore Wend, soprano; Gaston Crunelle, flute); b: Quintette Pierre Jamet
    Broadcast, *Hommage à Albert Roussel*, recorded May 11, 1957 (broadcast July 29, 1957)
            Network: Paris Inter, produced by Radiodiffusion Télévision Française
            INA ID: PHD90009902
26. Roussel, Albert, *Sérénade*, op. 30; Pierné, Gabriel, *Voyage au pays du Tendre*
    Quintette Pierre Jamet
    Broadcast, *Musique de chambre française contemporaine*, recorded July 1, 1958
        (broadcast July 11, 1958)
            Network: PT, produced by Radiodiffusion Télévision Française
            INA ID: PHD90011125
27. Pierné, Gabriel, *Voyage au pays du Tendre* (excerpt)
    Quintette Pierre Jamet
    Broadcast, *Actualités de midi*, recorded and broadcast July 3, 1958
            Network: France II Régionale, produced by Radiodiffusion Télévision Française
            INA ID: PHD94000722_00
28. Schmitt, Florent, *Suite en rocaille*, op. 84; Mozart, W.A., *Quartet in A major*, K.298;
    Telemann, G.P., *Sonata for flute, violin, viola, cello, harp*
    (Quintette instrumental de Paris: Gaston Crunelle, flute; René Bas, violin; Pierre
    Ladhuie, viola; Pierre Coddée, cello; Bernard Galais, harp)

Broadcast, *Quintette instrumental de Paris du 12 février 1961*, recorded November 20, 1960

(broadcast February 12, 1961)

Network: France III Nationale, produced by Radiodiffusion Télévision Française
INA ID: PHD99280744

29. Margoni, Alain, *Quintette*

(Quintette instrumental de Paris: Gaston Crunelle, flute; René Bas, violin; Pierre Ladhuie, viola; Pierre Coddée, cello; Bernard Galais, harp)

Broadcast, *Jeunes compositeurs*, recorded June 4, 1961 (broadcast June 8, 1961)

Network: France IV Haute-Fidélité, produced by Radiodiffusion Télévision Française
INA ID: PHD90011293

30. Koechlin, Charles, *Primavera Quintet*, op. 156

(Quintette instrumental de Paris: Gaston Crunelle, flute; René Bas, violin; Pierre Ladhuie, viola; Robert Krabansky, cello; Bernard Galais, harp)

Broadcast, *Musique de chambre*, recorded June 1, 1962 (broadcast June 15, 1962)

Network: France III Nationale, produced by Radiodiffusion Télévision Française
INA ID: PHD99280043

31. Malipiero, Gian Francesco, *Sonata a cinque*

(Quintette instrumental de Paris: Gaston Crunelle, flute; René Bas, violin; Pierre Ladhuie, viola; Robert Krabansky, cello; Bernard Galais, harp)

Broadcast, *Musique de chambre*, recorded October 6, 1962 (broadcast October 17, 1962)

Network: France III Nationale, produced by Radiodiffusion Télévision Française
INA ID: PHD89009182

32. Absil, Jean, *Concert à 5*, op. 38

(Quintette instrumental de Paris: Gaston Crunelle, flute; René Bas, violin; Pierre Ladhuie, viola; Robert Krabansky, cello; Bernard Galais, harp)

Broadcast, *Musique de chambre*, recorded November 5, 1962

(broadcast November 30, 1962)

Network: France III Nationale, produced by Radiodiffusion Télévision Française
INA ID: PHD89009158

33. Cras, Jean, *Quintette*

(Quintette instrumental de Paris)

Broadcast, *Musique de chambre*, recorded January 15, 1963 (broadcast January 23, 1963)

Network: France III National, produced by Radiodiffusion Télévision Française
INA ID: PHD89009127

34. Pierné, Gabriel, *Voyage au pays du Tendre*

(Quintette instrumental de Paris: Gaston Crunelle, flute; René Bas, violin; Pierre Ladhuie, viola; Robert Krabansky, cello, Bernard Galais, harp)

Broadcast, *Hommage à Gabriel Pierné*, recorded October 25, 1963, Salle du Conservatoire (broadcast October 29, 1963)

Network: X, produced by Radiodiffusion Télévision Française
INA ID: PHD99279593

35. Pierné, Gabriel, *Voyage au pays du Tendre*

(Quintette instrumental de Paris: Gaston Crunelle, flute; René Bas, violin; Pierre Ladhuie, viola; Michel Tournus, cello; Bernard Galais, harp)

Broadcast, *Musique de chambre*, recorded, February 1, 1965 (broadcast February 14, 1965)

> Network: France Culture, produced by Office Nationale de Radiodiffusion Télévision Française
> INA ID: PHD99279595

Additional Quintette Broadcasts

Some broadcasts featuring the Quintette were issued in the *Masterworks from France* series of transcription discs, produced as part of the "French Broadcasting System in North America" program. Collector Gordon Skene has made three of these performances available on his Past Daily website (https://pastdaily.com). Dates given there are approximations from material that accompanied the discs and from Skene's research. One of the performances is Suzanne Demarquez's *Variations*, confirmed through listening to be that from the February 27, 1954 broadcast listed above (item 21). The following two, however, have not yet been conclusively linked to any extant broadcasts held by the INA:

Koechlin, Charles, *Primavera Quintet*, op. 156 (Quintette Pierre Jamet)
Posted at: https://pastdaily.com/2017/05/14/charles-koechlin-1952-past-daily/
> Although Skene identifies this as part of a memorial concert and broadcast on October 21, 1952, reviews and other sources confirm that the second *Primavera Quintet*, Op. 223, was featured on that program. The recording posted on Skene's website is Op. 156. It is possible that this is a performance from a broadcast that has not survived in another form, a broadcast performance from 1956 that has not been conclusively identified (see note for item 24), or a broadcast performance from 1962 (see item 30). The October 21, 1952 concert is either not in the INA collection or has not been cataloged.

Pierné, Gabriel, *Variations libres et final*, op. 51 (Quintette Pierre Jamet)
Posted at: https://pastdaily.com/2017/01/29/pierne-1955-past-daily/
> Identified by Skene as a 1955 broadcast. The posted recording has not yet been linked to a specific broadcast.

Notes

1. Record labels identify the work as *Sonata for Flute and Strings* and note, "basse chiffrée réalisée par Germaine Tailleferre." The piece is often identified as Scarlatti's *Flute Concerto in D Major*. It is one of the *Sette sonate per flauto e archi*, first published in 1725. Reviewed in the American periodical, *Disques*, 1/10 (December 1930): p. 418.
2. The *Suite en parties* was written for the Quintette and premiered by them on May 17, 1930.
3. The *Variations* were written for the Quintette and premiered by them on April 1, 1933.
2–4. The Timpani compact disc reissue, *Pierre Jamet & son quintette,* has been made available on Naxos Music Library, Youtube, and Spotify.

4. The arrangement of the movements over four sides has not been confirmed from discs. The *Suite en rocaille* was written for the Quintette and premiered by them on May 24, 1935.
5. The reverse side of the disc is the "Rossignols amoureux," from Rameau's *Hyppolite et Aricie*, performed with voice, flute, and harp (see entry in Appendix 1). Gramophone Company ledger information apparently does not name Bas for the de Falla, but violin can clearly be heard in the recording. Ledger information also identifies Rose Dobos as pianist, but piano is not used in either the Rameau or de Falla selections.

    Aubry (1882–1950), born Jean-Frédéric-Emile Aubry, was a music critic, editor, and translator, most notably of the works of Joseph Conrad. A lengthy excerpt has been made available on Gallica. A complete version has been made available on Youtube.
6. The Timpani compact disc reissue, *Pierre Jamet & son quintette*, has been made available on Naxos Music Library, Youtube, and Spotify. The *Voyage* was written for the Quintette and premiered by them on May 8, 1936.
7. Issued first takes have been reported for both sides. Gramophone Company ledgers indicate that both first and second takes were made on February 3, and that the second takes were issued, although the GCD currently reports first takes only. Copies of the discs have not been inspected.
8. According to the name authority file of the BNF, the releases of the Association française d'action artistique (French Association for the Promotion of the Arts) were all recorded between November 1, 1942, and November 10, 1943. AA-7 was a 12-inch disc. The *Variations* were written for the Quintette and premiered by them on February 22, 1936.
9. See note for item above. AA-17 was a 10-inch disc
10. The Timpani compact disc reissue, *Pierre Jamet & son quintette,* has been made available on Naxos Music Library, Youtube, and Spotify. A transfer is also available in the Médiathèque Musicale de Paris, accessed at https://bibliotheques-specialis ees.paris.fr.

    The *Sérénade* was written for the Quintette and premiered by them on October 15, 1925.
11. Listed in the first supplement of *WERM*. The copyright date is from the catalog of the BNF. The Timpani compact disc reissue gives a recording date of "ca. May, 1950." The arrangement of movements on the four sides has not been confirmed from discs. The recording location has not been confirmed, but it was very likely to have been Paris.

    Established in 1940, Elite Special was a label of the Swiss record company Turicaphon AG, founded in 1930 by Hans Oestreicher.

    The Timpani compact disc reissue, *Pierre Jamet & son quintette,* has been made available on Naxos Music Library, Youtube, and Spotify.

    The *Quintette* was written for the Quintette and premiered by them on May 24, 1935.
12. Ropartz's *Sonata* for violin and piano, performed by Dévy Erlih and Maurice Bureau, occupied the remaining one and a half sides of the Ducretet Thomson LP. The Forgotten Records compact disc reissue gives June 18, 1956, as the recording date for the violin sonata, and 1956 for the quintet. The copyright registration date, taken from a catalog of the BNF, is 1958. The recording was also first listed in the French record catalog *Disques* in 1958. The *Prélude, Marine et Chansons* was written for the Quintette and premiered by them on November 24, 1928. Excerpts from the LP have been made available on Gallica.

13. The Ducretet LP included other works by de Falla: the *Concerto* for harpsichord, the *Hommage à Debussy*, and the *Soneta à Cordoba*, none of which involved the Quintette Pierre Jamet members. Ensemble members for *Psyché* are not named on the record labels or jacket.

14. The copyright date is from the catalog of the BNF. The works by Françaix and Lesur are on side 1, the Damase on side 2. All three works were written for the Quintette, which first performed the *Suite médiévale* on May 21, 1947, and the Françaix on May 24, 1935. Excerpts from all three works on the LP have been made available on Gallica.

15. Works by Henri Dutilleux, Jeanine Rueff, Raymond Loucheur, and Marcel Labey, not involving Crunelle or the Quintette, were in the broadcast. The *Suite en parties* was written for the Quintette and premiered by them on May 17, 1930.

16. Other performers in the broadcast were Bernard Demigny, baritone, and pianists Henriette Roget and Odette Pigault.

17. The *Voyage* was written for the Quintette and premiered by them on May 8, 1936. The *Sérénade* was also written for the Quintette and premiered on October 15, 1925.

18. The broadcast also included works by Georges Enesco and Marcel Bertrand that did not feature Crunelle or the Quintette. *Prélude, Marine et Chansons* was written for the Quintette and premiered by them on November 24, 1928.

19. The broadcast also presented an extensive program of Chopin's piano compositions, a Vivaldi concerto for four violins and orchestra featuring the Hewitt Chamber Orchestra, and a piece for four pianos by pianist Kouguell Arkadie, who was one of the performers.
    The *Concert à cinq* was written for the Quintette and premiered by them on May 27, 1924.

20. Other works on the broadcast were Ropartz's *1ère Sonate* for cello and piano, and four songs by Louis Aubert: *Hélène, Silence, Aigue-Marine*, and *Sérénade mélancolique*.
    The *Quintet No. 2* was written for the Quintette and premiered by them on October 21, 1952.

21. Other works in the broadcast were Jacques Canet's *Trio d'anches*; Arthur Honegger's *Trois Poèmes de Jean Cocteau*; Albert Roussel's *Jardin mouillé* and *Jazz dans la nuit*; and Jean Rivier's *Musique pour piano*.
    Suzanne Demarquez's *Variations, Interlude et Tarantelle* was among the French broadcasts distributed on long-playing discs by the French Broadcasting System in North America (see note above, "Additional Quintet Broadcasts"). A transfer of this recording has been made available at the website https://pastdaily.com, under the topic "Pierre Jamet Quintet."
    The works by Brown and Demarquez written for the Quintette and premiered by them, the Brown on December 15, 1953, and the Demarquez on December 22, 1942.

22. Other works in the broadcast included Manuel Rosenthal's *Les petits métiers* for piano, Henri Sauguet's *Neige*, and Margaret Béclard-d'Harcourt's *Rhapsodie péruvienne pour trio d'anches*. None of these featured Crunelle or the Quintette. The Malipiero *Sonate* was written for the Quintette and premiered by them on May 24, 1935.

23. The broadcast also included Tony Aubin's *Six Poèmes de Verlaine* for voice and piano.
    The *Suite en rocaille* was written for the Quintette and premiered by them on May 24, 1935.

24. Part of a broadcast series, "Musiciens français contemporains." Other works by Koechlin in the broadcast included the *Pièces enfantines* for piano, *Sept Chansons*,

and the *Sonata*, op. 70 for horn and piano. The INA catalog identifies the quintet only as "Primavera," with no opus number or other designation.

25. Performers for the *Trio* (flute, viola, cello) and *Sérénade* (flute, violin, viola, cello, harp) were identified only as members of the Quintette Pierre Jamet. Part of a broadcast series, *Association des amis de la musique de chambre*. Other works in the broadcast were Roussel's *Sonata in D minor* for violin and piano, *Cinq Mélodies chinoises*, and the *Impromptu*, op. 21, for harp, performed by Pierre Jamet.

    The *Sérénade* was written for the Quintette and premiered by them on October 15, 1925.

26. Individual members of the quintet were not identified. The broadcast also included Debussy's *Sonata No. 2* for flute, viola and harp, performed by Crunelle; violist Pierre Ladhuie, and Jamet, so their presence is known (see entry in Appendix 1). Other works in the broadcast included songs by Fauré and Debussy, Milhaud's *Catalogue des fleurs*, and Poulenc's *Le Bestiaire*, all featuring soprano Irène Joachim. It is not indicated if *Le Bestiaire* was the version using piano or that with chamber ensemble.

    Part of a broadcast series, *Festival de Vichy*.

    Both the *Sérénade* and the *Voyage* were written for the Quintette and premiered by them, the *Sérénade* on October 15, 1925, and *Voyage* on May 8, 1936.

27. A daily news broadcast that included a segment devoted to the Vichy Music Festival. An excerpt from the "Concert dans le Théâtre des Fleurs" featured the Quintette Pierre Jamet, performing part of *Voyage au pays du Tendre*. The *Voyage* was written for the Quintette and premiered by them on May 8, 1936.

28. From a concert at the Salle Gaveau by L'Association des concerts du chambre de Paris under the direction of Fernand Oubradous.

29. A broadcast from the Festival des Nuits de Sceaux. The other composers represented in the broadcast were Charles Chaynes, Henry Dillon, André Lavagne, and Francis Miroglio. Margoni's *Quintette* was written for the Quintette and premiered by them on June 4, 1961.

30. Works by Gabriel Fauré and Louis Aubert, not featuring Crunelle or the Quintette, were also on the broadcast. The *Primavera Quintet* was written for the Quintette and premiered by them on March 14, 1944.

31. Works by Béla Bartók, Manuel de Falla, and Maurice Ravel, not featuring Crunelle or the Quintette, were also on the broadcast. The Malipiero *Sonate* was written for the Quintette and premiered by them on May 24, 1935.

32. Works by Henri Tomasi and Arthur Honegger, not featuring Crunelle or the Quintette, were also on the broadcast. The Absil *Concert à 5* was written for the Quintette and premiered by them on May 3, 1953.

33. Individual performers were not identified in the surviving broadcast recording. Works by Maurice Emmanuel, Pierre de Bréville, and Gabriel Fauré, not featuring Crunelle or the Quintette, were also on the broadcast. The Cras *Quintette* was written for the Quintette and premiered by them on May 17, 1930.

34. Pierné's *Sonata da camera*, op. 48, was in the broadcast, but performers were Jean-Pierre Rampal, flute, Geneviève Marinet, cello, and Jean Doyen, piano. The *Voyage* was written for the Quintette and premiered by them on May 8, 1936.

35. Songs by Henri Duparc and Gabriel Fauré were also in the broadcast. The *Voyage* was written for the Quintette and premiered by them on May 8, 1936.

Crunelle's Students Who Won
First Prizes in Flute

Year	Name[a]	Career Accomplishments
1941	Rémy Cotton	Flutist, Opéra-Comique Principal flutist, Orchestre national des pays de la Loire
	René Goube	
	Maurice Werner	
1942	Eugène Boutleux	Professor, Amiens Conservatory
	Jacques Tiberge	Principal flutist, Orchestre national du capitole de Toulouse Professor, Toulouse Conservatory
	Maurice Vautrin	
	Lucien Martin	
	Henri Boulet	
1943	Jean Étienne	Professor, Rouen Conservatory Principal flutist, Théâtre des arts de Rouen
	Raoul Le Toumelin	
	Pierre Marillier	Professor, Lille Conservatory
1944	Pol Mule	Conductor, Orchestre de Nice
	Gisèle Chauvin	
	Édouard Deuez	Flutist, Musique de l'air
	Jacques Castagner	Flutist, Quintette à vent de Paris and in Boulez's Domaine musical
	Jean-Pierre Rampal	International recording artist Professor, Paris Conservatory
1945	Jacques Royer	Flutist, Paris Opéra
	Georges Savoy	
1946[b]	Michel Plockyn	Principal flutist, Paris Opéra
	Charles Barelle	
	Paul Éthuin	
	Gilbert Leuk	
	Jean Loisel	Director, Conservatory of the fourth arrondissement of Paris
1947	Jacques Mule	Professor, Nancy Conservatory
1948	Jack Darraud	Flutist, Musique de l'air
	Marius Beuf	Professor, Lyon Conservatory
	Christian Lardé	Recording artist Professor of chamber music, Paris Conservatory
	Edmund Œchslin	

Year	Name[a]	Career Accomplishments
1949	Serge Fournier Jean Chérigié	Conductor, Toledo Symphony Orchestra
1950	Jean Puech Frédéric Pellini Frédéric Morvillez	Flutist, Garde républicaine
	Pierre Cazaux	Professor, Clermont-Ferrand Conservatory and Principal flutist, Orchestre symphonique de Clermont-Ferrand
1951	Odette Ernest (Dias) Maxence Larrieu	Principal flutist, Orquestra Sinfônica Brasileira International recording artist Professor, Lyon Conservatory and Geneva Conservatory
1952	Daniel Morlier Alexander Murray	Professor, Mulhouse Conservatory Principal flutist, London Symphony Orchestra Professor, Michigan State University and the University of Illinois
	Régis Calle	Professor, Schola Cantorum of Paris Principal flutist, La Musique des gardiens de la paix
1953	Gerhard Schaub Jacques Rocheblave Louis Hebral	
1954	Michel Clergue Jacques Le Troquer Michel Debost	Principal flutist, Orchestre de la Société des Concerts du Conservatoire and Orchestre de Paris Professor, Paris Conservatory and Oberlin Conservatory of Music
	Michel Debels Georges Tessereau	Professor, Montpellier Conservatory
1955	Jean Saillard Maurice Chevry Georges Gueneux	Flutist, Orchestre philharmonique de Radio France
1956	Claude Delbarre Cyrille Fontevielle Gabriel Ballot	Professor, Saint-Étienne Conservatory Professor, Lyon Conservatory
	Pierre Bardon	Professor, Aix-en-Provence Conservatory
1957	Marguerite Chartois (Ida Ribera)	Professor, Orléans Conservatory and numerous regional conservatories; assistant to Jean-Pierre Rampal at the Paris Consevatory
	Claude Grognet Henri Beridot Ulrich Meyer	Principal flutist, Opera of Monte Carlo

Year	Name[a]	Career Accomplishments
1958	Jean-Claude Diot	Principal flutist, Orchestre national d'Île-de-France
	Félix Manz	Professor, Aubervilliers-La Corneuve Conservatory
		Flutist, Orchestre de la garde républicaine
	Francis Gabin	
	Colette Peaucelle	Conductor, Orchestre de la garde républicaine
	André Guilbert	Flutist, Opera of Monte Carlo
	Josiane Harbonnier	
1959	Brigitte Buxtorf	Principal Flute, Orchestre de la Suisse Romande
		Professor, Lausanne Conservatory
	Philippe Bender	Music director, l'Orchestre régional de Cannes-Provence-Alpes-Côte d'Azur
	Jacques Blaevoet	
	Henri Dufour	Professor, Grenoble Conservatory
1960	Hirohiko Kato	
	Claude Vacellier	
	Gabriel Fumet	Recording artist
	Carlos Leresche	Composer of popular songs and film music
1961	Jean-Claude Hermenjat	Principal flutist, Orchestre de la Suisse Romande
	Bernard Trémolières	Professor, Poitiers Conservatory
	Pierre Séchet	Baroque flutist
1962	Jean-Claude Gérard	Principal flutist, Staatsoper Hamburg
	Guy Cottin	Professor, Nantes Conservatory, and principal flutist, Orchestre philharmonique du pays de la Loire
	Francis Loriaux	
	Maurice Pruvot	Piccolo, Orchestre de Paris
		Professor, Créteil and Evreux Conservatories
1963	Jacques Delacôte	Conductor of many orchestras
	Gérald Jemain	Professor, Le Mans Conservatory
	Gilbert Boulot	
1964	Marc Honorat	Professor, Angers Conservatory
		Principal flutist, Orchestre national des pays de la Loire
		Composer and flutist
	Renaud François	Professor, Lyon Conservatory
		Director, Versailles Conservatory
		Flutist, Orchestre symphonique de Strasbourg
	André Descos	
	Jean-Claude Marin	
1965	Christian Cheret	Principal flutist, Paris Opéra
	Edward Beckett	Freelance flutist, London
		Professor, Guildhall School of Music and Drama
	Jean-Pierre Lebocq	Flutist, Orchestre philharmonique de Nice
	Paul Ferraris	Conductor, composer

Year	Name[a]	Career Accomplishments
1966	Bernard Pierreuse	Author of *Flûte littérature*
		Principal Flute, Orchestre philharmonique de Liège
	Pierre Biget	Professor, Orléans Conservatory
	Jean-Claude Dhainaut	Professor, Conservatoire de la Vallée de la Chevreuse
1967	André Guérin	Professor, Chambéry Conservatory
1968	Jean-François Blondeau	Flutist, Taffanel Wind Quintet
	Pierre Caron	Flutist, Garde républicaine
	Elisabeth Guestault-Richard	Professor, Argenteuil Conservatory
	Arlette Leroy (Biget)	Professor, Orléans Conservatory
		Flutist, Arcadie Flute Quartet
	Jean-Louis Potrel	
1969	Philippe Sabouret	
	Pierre-Yves Artaud	Professor, Paris Conservatory
	Bernard Demottaz	
	Gladys Ohier (Boucher)	Principal flutist, Orchestre national de Bretagne
		Professor, Rennes Conservatory
	Xavier Pillot	Professor, Marly-le-Roy Conservatory
1970[c]	Georges Lambert	Principal Flute, Orchestre national des Pays de la Loire; author of *Méthode pour la flûte traversière* and other flute studies
	Isabelle Chapuis	Principal Flute, Opera San Jose
		Senior Lecturer, San Jose State University
	Annu (Anne) Utagawa	
	André Salm	Recording artist, flutist in Les joueurs de flûte
		Principal flutist, Bamberger Symphoniker
1971	Geneviève Amar	Principal flutist, Orchestre philharmonique de Radio France

[a] The order of prize winners reflects the number of votes each received from the jury, who would also vote to approve the *premier nommé* ("the first named").

[b] From 1946 to 1953 there were two flute classes each year; thus, only students of Crunelle are listed above. Students of Moyse who won a first prize were Régine Fischer in 1946; Aurèle Nicolet and Raymond Guiot in 1947; Robert Jupin and Lucien Vialet in 1948; and Peter-Lukas Graf, Jean Doussard, and Jean Patéro in 1949. Since Moyse left before the end of the school year in 1949, Roger Cortet took over his studio, and his student, Charles Dagnino, won a first prize in 1950. Cortet continued as a temporary professor through 1953, and his students who won first prizes were Charles Dagnino in 1950; Pierre Destremau and Conrad Klemm in 1951; Jean Eustache and Jean Ornetti in 1952.

[c] Crunelle retired in 1969, and Rampal was the teacher for the 1970 and 1971 *concours*, but all first-prizes winners listed here for those years had started their studies with Crunelle.

Other former students:

Juho Alvas, Principal flutist, Helsinki Philharmonic Orchestra; Professor, Sibelius Academy

Jean-Louis Beaumadier, piccolo soloist, former professor, Marseilles Conservatory

Francette Beurnier (Vernet), Professor, Conservatoire à rayonnement départemental de Fresnes

Leone Buyse (*classe des étrangers*), Acting Principal flutist, Boston Symphony Orchestra, and Professor, Rice University Shepherd School of Music

Sir James Galway, International recording artist, Principal Flute, Berlin Philharmonic

Gérard Grognet (second prize, 1969), professor, Clichy Conservatory and Courbevoie Conservatory

Eric Groussard (studied privately with Crunelle), Professor, Conservatoire à rayonnement départemental de Fresnes

Dorothy Antoinette Handy-Miller (*classe des étrangers*), Flutist, Richmond Symphony, Professor, Virginia State University, Director, National Endowment of the Arts Music Program[1]

John Harrison Hicks, Professor, University of Texas at Austin

Betty Bang Mather (*classe des étrangers*), Professor, University of Iowa

Mary Louise Nigro Poor, Professor, Beloit College, author[2]

Günter Rumpel, Principal flutist, Tonhalle-Orchester Zürich

Michael Scott, Professor, University of Sydney Conservatorium of Music

Gretel Yvonne Andrus Shanley, Flutist, Rochester Philharmonic and National Symphony Orchestra

Tim Wilson (*classe des étrangers*), Principal flutist, Hong Kong Philharmonic

Bernard Wystraete, jazz flutist

Gérard Zinsstag, composer

Morceaux de concours imposés and déchiffrages, 1940–1969

Year	Morceau imposé, difficulty level,[a] and recordings	Dedication	Duration	Déchiffrage composer
1941	Philippe Gaubert (1879–1941), *Fantaisie* (Leduc),[b] 6 Numerous recordings	Léopold Lafleurance	6:30	?
1942	Eugène Bozza, (1905–1991), *Agrestide*, op. 44 (Leduc), 8–9 Numerous recordings	Gaston Crunelle	8:30	Jean-Roger Ducasse (1873–1954)
1943	Henri Dutilleux (1916–2013), Sonatina (Leduc), 7–8 Numerous recordings	Gaston Crunelle	9:00	Jacques Chailley (1910–1999)
1944	André Jolivet (1905–1974), *Chant de Linos* (Leduc), 8 Numerous recordings	Gaston Crunelle	11:00	Henri Martelli (1895–1980)
1945	Henri Tomasi (1901–1971), Concertino in E Major (Leduc), 7 Recording: *Carl Petkoff: Flute Recital Recordings 1950–1960* (produced by Joe Armstrong, 2001	Gaston Crunelle	13:00	?
1946	Pierre Sancan (1916–2008), Sonatina (Durand), 8 Numerous recordings	Gaston Crunelle	9:30	René Guillou (1903–1958)
1947	Henri Martelli (1895–1980), *Fantasiestück*, op. 67 (Billaudot), 8 No recording	Claude Delvincourt	8:45	Jean Rivier (1896–1987)
1948	François-Julien Brun (1909–1990), *Un Andante et un Scherzo* (Billaudot), 8 No recording	Marcel Moyse	8:15	Charles Koechlin (1867–1950)
1949	Émile Passani (1905–1974), Concerto (Billaudot), 8 No recording	Marcel Moyse and Gaston Crunelle	12:30	?

Year	*Morceau imposé*, difficulty level,[a] and recordings	Dedication	Duration	*Déchiffrage* composer
1950	André Pépin (1907–1985), *Impromptu* (Leduc), 7–8 No recording	Gottfried Maag	9:30	Roger Désormière (1898–1963)
1951	Antoni Szałowski (1907–1973), Concertino (Amphion), 8 No recording	none	12:00	?
1952	Olivier Messiaen (1908–1992), *Le merle noir* (Leduc), 8 Numerous recordings	none	6:00	?
1953	Jacque-Dupont (1906–1985), *Aulos*, op. 37 (Leduc), 7–8 No recording	Gaston Crunelle and Roger Cortet	8:00	?
1954	Jeanine Rueff (1922–1999), *Diptyque* (Leduc), 8 Recording: *Ladies First: Komponistinnen gestern & heute*, Ana Ioana Oltean, flute; Simon Bucher, piano (ARS, 2010)	Gaston Crunelle	8:45	Charles Jay (1911–1988)
1955	Roger Boutry (1932–2019), Concertino (Leduc), 8 No recording	Gaston Crunelle	9:00	André Bloch (1873–1960)
1956	Raymond Gallois-Montbrun (1918–1994), *Divertissement* (Leduc), 9 Recording: *La Flûte au Conservatoire de Paris*, Claude Régimbauld, flute; Claude Webster, piano (ATMA Classique, 1999)	Gaston Crunelle	8:00	?
1957	François-Julien Brun (1909–1990), *Pastorale d'Arcadie* (Leduc), 9 No recording	his father	9:00	Maurice Franck (1897–1983)
1958	Noël Gallon (1891–1966), *Improvisation et Rondo* (Max Eschig), 6–7 Recording: *The French Flute 1920–30*, Bent Larsen, flute; Sverre Larsen, piano (Classico CLASSCD 160, 1997)	Gaston Crunelle	7:15	Valérie Soudères (1914–1995)

Year	*Morceau imposé*, difficulty level,[a] and recordings	Dedication	Duration	*Déchiffrage* composer
1959	Marcel Poot (1901–1988), *Légende* (Max Eschig), 7 Recording: *Le Flûtiste et son siècle*, Denis-Pierre Gustin, flute; Carmen-Elena Rotaru, piano (Cypres CYP4615, 2002)	the professors of the Conservatoire Royal de Musique de Bruxelles	9:15	Tony Aubin (1907–1981)
1960	Robert Casadesus (1899–1972), *Fantaisie*, op. 59 (Durand), 6–7 No recording	Jean Gallon	6:00	Pierre Petit (1922–2000)
1961	Luigi Cortese (1899–1976), *Introduzione e Allegro*, op. 40 (Ricordi), 7–8 Recording: *Icarus: Works for Flute and Piano*, Roberto Cognazzo, flute; Mario Carbotta, piano (Nuova Era 7185, 1993)	none	7:00	Luigi Cortese
1962	Charles Chaynes (1925–2016), *Variations sur un tanka* (Leduc), 8 Recording: *La Flûte au Conservatoire de Paris*, Claude Régimbauld, flute; Claude Webster, piano (ATMA Classique, 1999)	none	9:00	Charles Chaynes
1963	Pierre Petit (1922–2000), *Petite Suite* (Leduc), 7 No recording	Gaston Crunelle	8:00	Pierre Petit
1964	Tony Aubin (1907–1981), *Concertino dell'amicizia* (Leduc), 8 No recording	none	9:00	Tony Aubin
1965	Georges Hugon (1904–1980), Sonata (four movements of which third and fourth form the *morceau de concours*) (Éditions musicales transatlantiques), 7–8 Recording: *Musique française du 20e siècle* Sophie Cherrier, flute; Jean-Marie Cotte, piano (Cybelia CY 701, 1983)	his father	16:00	Georges Hugon

Year	Morceau imposé, difficulty level,[a] and recordings	Dedication	Duration	Déchiffrage composer
1966	Jean Rivier (1896–1987), *Ballade* (Éditions musicales transatlantiques) Recording: *Rivier Revisited: Chamber Music for Flute*, Leone Buyse, flute; Logan Skelton, piano (Crystal Records CD319, 2002)	Gaston Crunelle	7:45	Jean Rivier
1967	Jean Hubeau (1917–1992), *Idylle* (Durand), 5–6 No recording	none	7:15	Jean Hubeau
1968	Ginette Keller (1925–2017), *Chant de Parthénope* (Max Eschig), 5–6 No recording	none	7:45	Jeannette Keller
1969	Jacques Bondon (1927–2008), *Mouvement chorégraphique* (Choudens), 5–6 No recording	none	9:00	Jacques Bondon

[a] Cook, "The Paris Conservatory and the 'Solos de Concours' for flute, 1900–1955," and Melissa Gail Colgin, "The Paris Conservatoire Concours Tradition and the Solos de concours for Flute, 1955–1990." Both authors use the European nine-point difficulty rating: 1–3 indicates easy, 4–6 moderately difficult, and 7–9 difficult.

[b] Originally written for the 1920 *concours*.

Notes

Chapter 1

1. See list in the "For Further Reading" section.
2. None of Crunelle's students, including Jean-Pierre Rampal, appear in bold type. Claude Dorgeuille, *The French Flute School, 1860–1950,* trans. Edward Blakeman (London: Tony Bingham, 1986).
3. Dorgeuille, *The French Flute School,* p. 66.
4. See Appendix 4 for first-prize winners who studied with Crunelle.
5. Galway, Larrieu, and Rampal all studied for less than a year with Crunelle, all three having had significant training before arriving at the Paris Conservatory. Galway left in 1961 to take a position at the Sadler's Wells Opera Company in London, and both Larrieu and Rampal earned a first prize in their first year of study after substantial training with Rampal's father, Joseph Rampal (1895–1983), professor of flute at the Marseilles Conservatory.
6. When Edward Blakeman interviewed Crunelle in his apartment on April 24, 1982, "He had a large collection of music and archive materials," Blakeman, email to author, March 13, 2019. Pierre-Yves Artaud said Crunelle gave some things to his students ("Il a donné beaucoup de choses à plusieurs élèves") but that his daughter "threw away most of the things that belonged to her father" ("j'ai l'impression qu'un peu elle a bazardé la plupart des choses qui appartenaient à son père"), Pierre-Yves Artaud, interview by author, Bourges, March 1, 2022. All translations in this book are by the author unless otherwise noted.
7. Gaston Crunelle, *Traits difficiles tirés d'œuvres symphoniques et dramatiques* (Paris: Alphonse Leduc, 1943). Part of a series of collections of orchestral excepts commissioned by Claude Delvincourt, director of the Paris Conservatory, this volume presents passages taken mostly from obscure pieces by Delvincourt, Jeanne Leleu, Jules Massenet, Maurice Ravel, and Marcel Samuel-Rousseau.
8. Jean-Claude Diot, "Gaston Crunelle: Le témoignage de Jean-Claude Diot," *Traversières* 72 (July–August–September 2022 Q3): p. 30.
9. Patricia George, "Lessons with the Masters: An Interview with Isabelle Chapuis," *Flute Talk* 31, no. 5 (January 2012): p. 14.
10. Jean-Pierre Rampal and Deborah Wise, *Music, My Love* (New York: Random House, 1989), p. 73.
11. "C'était quelqu'un qui voulait jouer 'autrement' de la flûte. Pour cela, il a été obligé de changer plus ou moins l'école en elle-même; c'est fatal." Denis Verroust, *Jean-Pierre Rampal: La flûte universelle* (Paris: Association française de la flûte "La Traversière" and Association Jean-Pierre Rampal, 2022), p. 214.

Chapter 2

1. Henri Dutilleux and Claude Glayman, *Henri Dutilleux: Music—Mystery and Memory. Conversations with Claude Glayman,* tr. Roger Nichols (London: Routledge, 2003), p. 10.

2. J. Andreas Löwe, "Richard Smyth and the Foundation of the University of Douai," *Nederlands Archief Voor Kerkgeschiedenis/Dutch Review of Church History* 79, no. 2 (1999): p. 152.

3. Guy Gosselin, *L'Âge d'or de la vie musicale à Douai 1800–1850* (Liège: Mardaga, 1994).

4. Dorgeuille, *The French Flute School,* p. 23.

5. Guy Gosselin, "Douai," in Joël-Marie Fauquet, *Dictionnaire de la musique en France au XIXe siècle* (Paris: Fayard, 2003).

6. The date of Léon Gaston Crunelle's death is not known.

7. Claudine and Jean-Paul Dewez, "Ascendance Crunelle," *Le lien généalogique du Douaisis* 39 (3ᵉ trimestre 2022): pp. 18–20.

8. Crunelle told students she was a *marchande de légumes,* a vegetable seller. Renaud François, interview by author, Paris, November 30, 2019.

9. Archives départementales du Nord. Their home no longer exists, and a more recent building stands on the same spot.

10. "A de la facilité et a fait des progrès sensibles," ANF, AJ/37/274 Classe de flûte de Tulou, www.siv.archives-nationales.culture.gouv.fr/mm/media/download/FRAN_0 181_04020_L-medium.jpg.

11. Robert Hériché, *À Propos de la flûte* (Paris: Gérard Billaudot, 1985), p. 123. Hériché reports that Bernard played third flute from 1861 to 1875, but Jean-Pierre Eustache lists him as second and fourth flute from 1860 to 1870 in a detailed "Tableau des flûtistes et des chefs d'orchestre de l'Opéra," shared widely among historians of flute playing in Paris. Constant Pierre reports that Bernard lived in Lille in 1900. Constant Pierre, *Le conservatoire national de musique et de déclamation: documents historiques et administratifs* (Paris: Imprimerie nationale, 1900), p. 697.

12. "M. Bernard, professeur de flûte au Conservatoire National de Douai, est mort il y a quelques jours. Premier Prix du Conservatoire de Paris, il a pendant 42 ans comme professeur, comme membre de l'Harmonie Municipale et de diverses Sociétés musicales de la Ville, fait preuve d'un très grand dévouement, ne ménageant jamais son concours que son talent rendait précieux," Archives de Douai Serie R, Section 1, 1R275.

13. Emmanuel Hondré, "Herman, Jules-Arthur Hermant dit Jules," *Dictionnaire de la musique en France au XIX siècle,* ed. Joël-Marie Fauquet (Paris: Fayard, 2003), p. 588.

14. Pierre Gervasoni, *Henri Dutilleux* (Paris: Actes Sud, 2016), p. 428.

15. One page of the program states that he won a *deuxième accessit* (a second certificate), but a later page identifies him as a first prize-winner in the *cours supérieur* (upper level). Archives municipals de Douai. The same program lists the name Suzanne Obez (b. 1898), sister of André Obez (1892–1975), who became a famous playwright—as a writer, he spelled his surname Obey. In 1928, he wrote an autobiographical novel, *Le Joueur de triangle* (The Triangle Player), about studying

music at the Douai Conservatory in 1910. In his Preface to the book, Henri Dutilleux praises Obey's musicianship—he was an accomplished pianist. The protagonist of the novel is a pianist but is required to perform on triangle in the Orchestre des concerts populaires, whose conductor is the conservatory's director, Guillaume Meulenaere—a character clearly modeled after the actual director, Paul Cuelenaere.

16. Harold Bauer, "The Paris Conservatoire: Some Reminiscences," *The Musical Quarterly* 33, no. 4 (October 1947): p. 539.

17. The official name is now the Conservatoire national supérieur de musique et de danse de Paris (CNSMDP).

18. "Une bibliothèque nationale de musique est formée dans le Conservatoire; elle est composée d'une collection complète des partitions et ouvrages traitant de cet art, des instruments antiques ou étrangers, et de ceux à nos usages qui peuvent par leur perfection servir de modèles." Constant Pierre, *B. Sarrette et les origines du Conservatoire national du musique et de déclamation* (Paris: Librairie Delalain Frères, 1895), p. 180.

19. Rémy Campos, *Le Conservatoire de Paris et son histoire: une institution en questions* (Paris: L'œil d'or, 2016), pp. 22–3.

20. Campos, *Le Conservatoire de Paris et son histoire*, p. 23.

21. Gail Hilson Woldu details these changes in "The Conservatoire before Fauré: The Years 1784–1905," from her dissertation, "Gabriel Fauré as Director of the Conservatoire national de musique et de déclamation, 1905–1920" (PhD dissertation, Yale University, 1983), pp. 41–57.

22. Campos, "La Classe," *Le Conservatoire de Paris et son histoire*, pp. 45–52.

23. Edward Blakeman, *Taffanel: Genius of the Flute* (Oxford: Oxford University Press, 2005), p. 11.

24. Henri Altès, *26 Selected Studies,* ed. Georges Barrère (New York: G. Schirmer, 1918).

25. Blakeman, *Taffanel: Genius of the Flute.*

26. Blakeman, *Taffanel: Genius of the Flute*, p. 187.

27. Blakeman, *Taffanel: Genius of the Flute*, p. 185.

28. Paul Taffanel and Philippe Gaubert, *Méthode complète de la flûte* (Paris: Alphonse Leduc, 1923). The popular extract is Taffanel and Gaubert, *Dix-sept grands exercices journaliers de mécanisme pour flûte* (Paris: Alphonse Leduc, 1958).

29. "Il était très dur, très exigeant. Il ne souriait jamais. Il avait son franc-parler et ce n'était pas toujours très agréable. Hennebains jouait beaucoup pendant les cours. Il jouait tellement bien que je n'avais qu'une envie : arriver à jouer comme lui. Avec Lafleurence, c'était tout autre chose. Il jouait aussi pendant les cours, mais beaucoup moins, et de toutes façons on n'avait pas très envie de l'imiter. Il jouait dur et n'avait pas la lumineuse sonorité d'Hennebains." Bernard Duplaix, "Lucy Dragon: 'Les aventures de Radiolette," *La Traversière* 47 (October 1994): p. 66.

30. Bernard Duplaix, "Léopold Lafleurance: un hérisson au cœur tendre," *La Traversière* 44 (Q1, 1994): p. 59.

31. Edward Blakeman, interview with Gaston Crunelle, April 24, 1982, documented in an email to the author, December 28, 2022.

32. René Dumesnil, "L'Enseignement," in Ladislas de Rohozinski, *Cinquante Ans de musique française de 1874 à 1925* (Paris: Les Éditions musicales de la librairie de France, 1926), pp. 191–92.

33. The city conservatory (Conservatoire à rayonnement régional de Paris) makes its present home in the rue de Madrid location. See Chapter 9 for an explanation of the hierarchy of conservatories in France. A CRR (Conservatoire à rayonnement régional) is one level below the "national superior" conservatories in Paris and Lyon.

34. Campos, *Le Conservatoire de Paris et son histoire*, p. 21.

35. Jacques Hillairet, *Dictionnaire historique des rues de Paris,* vol. 2, 7th ed. (Paris: Éditions de minuit, 1963), p. 86. A *collège* is roughly equivalent to an American middle school.

36. Gail Hilson Woldu, "Gabriel Fauré, directeur du Conservatoire: les réformes du 1905," *Revue de musicologie* 70, no. 2 (1984): pp. 199–228.

37. The end-of-year *concours* were traditionally open to the public, but because of public disruptions of the proceedings, Fauré banned the public except for critics in a 1915 decree. This policy remained in effect until the end of his term in 1920. See Chapter 6, "The Years 1906–1920," in Gail Hilson Woldu. "Gabriel Fauré as Director of the Conservatoire national de musique et de déclamation, 1905–1920," pp. 147–86.

38. Paul Rougnon, *Souvenirs de 60 années de vie musicale et de 50 années de professorat au Conservatoire de Paris* (Paris: Éditions Margueritat, 1925).

39. Sometimes spelled Glyzon.

40. "L'heure est à la virtuosité gratuite, les auteurs prenant un malin plaisir à accumuler des difficultés que l'on ne rencontre jamais sous cette forme dans la vie musicale normale: changements de clefs, pièges rythmiques, embûches pour l'intonation, chausse-trappes métriques et autres traquenards." Rémy Campos, *Le conservatoire de Paris et son histoire*, p. 57.

41. Maurice Emmanuel, *Histoire de la langue musicale* (Paris: Henri Laruens, 1911).

42. Gail Hilson Woldu. "Gabriel Fauré as Director of the Conservatoire national de musique et de déclamation, 1905–1920," pp. 88–90.

43. No copies of this piece have survived. Kathleen Roberta Cook, "The Paris Conservatory and the 'Solos de concours' 1900–1955" (DMA dissertation, University of Wisconsin, 1991), p. 78.

44. Sometimes spelled Bigerel.

45. Archives départementales du Nord.

46. Jean Guénel, "La Grippe « espagnole » en France en 1918–1919," *Histoire des sciences médicales* 38, no. 2 (2004): pp. 165–75.

47. Ann McCutchan, *Marcel Moyse: Voice of the Flute* (Portland, OR: Amadeus Press, 1994), p. 122.

48. Penelope Fischer, "Philippe Gaubert (1879–1941): His Life and Contributions as Flutist, Editor, Teacher, Conductor, and Composer" (DMA thesis, University of Maryland, 1982), p. 33.

49. Blakeman, *Taffanel: Genius of the Flute*, p. 143.

50. Blakeman, email to author, December 28, 2022.

51. *Le Courrier musical* (July 1920): p. 219.

52. "Un virtuose accompli que d'immédiats bravos désignent au prix d'excellence," *Le Ménestrel* (July 2, 1920): p. 271.

53. It is not known when Suzanne first started studying the flute. She is not listed in the 1914 program of the Douai Conservatory. Little trace remains of her subsequent career. On February 25, 1923, *Le Figaro* reported her playing in a private concert at the home of Baroness C. de Rochetaillée and Duchess de Broglie, and on December 2, 1927, *Le Ménestrel* reported on a concert of La Société "Entre soi" from Lille: "A charming flutist, Mme. Ginon-Crunelle, achieved great success in pieces by Bach, Mozart, and Enesco." ["Une charmante flûtiste, Mme. Ginon-Crunelle, a obtenu un vif succès dans des pièces de Bach, de Mozart, et d'Enesco."] *Le Ménestrel* (December 2, 1927): p. 500. Suzanne Crunelle married violist Étienne Ginot in 1925, but they divorced in 1932. Suzanne then married Jean Lixi in 1933. She died in 1944 (https://archives.paris.fr).

54. "Magnifique lot de treize flutes à la douzaine, présenté par M. Ph. Gaubert, auteur, par surcroît, du morceau de concours. Parmi ceux qui traduisirent le mieux la poésie et la bravoure ce cette *fantaisie*, M. Gaston Crunelle s'affirma le plus complet de tous et mérita l'excellence de son prix," Jean Poueigh, *Comœdia* (June 26, 1920): p. 1.

Chapter 3

1. The Salle Favart was restored in 2013.

2. *Carmen* has been performed more than 2,500 times at the Opéra-Comique, and the following operas have each been performed more than a thousand times: *Cavalleria Rusticana, Le Chalet, La Dame blanche, Le Domino noir, La Fille du regiment, Lakmé, Manon, Mignon, Le Noces de Jeannette, Le Pré aux clercs, Tosca, La Bohème,* and *Werther.* Stéphane Wolff, "The Opéra-Comique of Paris" *Opera* 12 No. 3 (March 1961): pp.160–65.

3. The orchestra folded in 1967 and was replaced by the Orchestre de Paris.

4. Eric Benoist, "Les grands concerts parisiens: Étude comparative des saisons 1930–1931 et 1937–1938," in Danièle Pistone, ed., *Musiques et musiciens à Paris dans les années trente* (Paris: Honoré Campion, 2000), pp. 259–70.

5. Roger Nichols, *The Harlequin Years: Music in Paris 1917–1929* (Berkeley: University of California Press, 2002), p. 178.

6. Henri Heugel, "Nouvelles diverses: Paris et départements," *Le Ménestrel* (March 12, 1905): p. 87.

7. The number of concerts in Paris declined from 1,810 in the 1924–25 season to 1,025 in 1938–39. Elizabeth Cook, Gordon A. Anderson, Thomas B. Payne, Daniel Heartz, Richard Freedman, James R. Anthony, John Eby, Beverly Wilcox, Paul F. Rice, David Charlton, John Trevitt, Guy Gosselin, and Jann Pasler. "Paris," *Grove Music Online.* 2001. https://doi.org/10.1093/gmo/9781561592630.article.40089.

8. Nichols, *The Harlequin Years: Music in Paris, 1917–1929,* p. 202.

9. Robert Hériché, "Erinnerung an Gaston Crunelle." *Tibia* 15, no. 3 (1990): p. 209.

10. "Les grands cinémas peuvent être qualifiés de 'refuges de premier prix de Conservatoire,'" Emmanuelle Toulet and Christian Belaygue, *Musique d'écran: l'accompagnement musical du cinéma muet en France 1918–1995* (Paris: Réunion de Musées Nationaux, 1994): p. 42.

11. "Il m'a toujours dit que l'époque du cinéma muet représentait une fortune, un âge d'or financier pour les musiciens, parce qu'ils jouaient trois fois par jour au cinéma," Michel Debost, interview by Pascal Gresset, *Tempo flûte: Revue de association d'histoire de la flute française* 6 (2012, no. 2): p. 4.

12. David Robinson, *Musique et cinéma muet* (Paris: Éditions de la Réunion des musées nationaux, 1995).

13. Hériché, "Erinnerung an Gaston Crunelle," p. 209. Hériché says the performance of *Les Saltimbanques* was at the Théâtre des Ternes, but the operetta was revived on July 10, 1920 at the Gaîté-Lyrique with the composer conducting (*Comœdia*, July 9, 1920, and *Le Ménestrel*, July 20, 1920) and was performed on November 13, 20, 27 and December 5, 12, 19, 1920 at the Trianon-Lyrique (*Le Guide du concert*).

14. Hériché, "Erinnerung an Gaston Crunelle." p. 210.

15. Denis Verroust, *Jean-Pierre Rampal (1922–2000) et les solistes de l'Orchestre du grand casino de Vichy* (Vichy: Musée de l'Opéra de Vichy, 2022), p. 11.

16. Vichy also provided a round-trip travel supplement to musicians. Archives of the Musée de l'opéra de Vichy.

17. Blakeman, *Taffanel: Genius of the Flute*, p. 195.

18. Archives of the Musée de l'opéra de Vichy.

19. *Le Figaro* (March 5, 1923): p. 5.

20. *Comœdia* (September 17, 1924): p. 5.

21. Conductor Walther Straram (1876–1933) led a series of concerts in Paris, mentioned above, that included many important premieres by Honegger, Messiaen, Ravel, and others.

22. *Comœdia* (August 25, 1926): p. 2.

23. *Comœdia* (September 10, 1930): p. 3.

24. ANF, F/21/4674.

25. Trevor Wye, *Marcel Moyse, An Extraordinary Man: A Musical Biography* (Cedar Falls, IA: Winzer Press, 1993), pp. 133–4.

26. Paris Archives, https://archives.paris.fr.

27. Archives départementales des Hauts de Seine, https://archives.hauts-de-seine.fr.

28. Nichols, *The Harlequin Years: Music in Paris 1917–1929*, p. 44.

29. Hériché, "Erinnerung an Gaston Crunelle," p. 210.

30. "La flûte solo se tailla un succès personnel," *Le Ménestrel* (January 2, 1925): p. 7.

31. January 21, 1928, October 13, 1928, October 13, 1929, March 1, 1930, May 2, 1931, October 9, 1932, December 10, 1932, January 16, 1937, April 15, 1938, May 13, 1938, March 17, 1940, December 22, 1940, January 4, 1942, April 12, 1942, and November 15, 1942.

32. "Louons M. Crunelle, dont la flûte agile et limpide chanta si agréablement," *Le Ménestrel* (May 8, 1931): p. 203.

33. "M. Crunelle joue la partie de flûte solo de façon remarquable. Elle m'a semblé d'ailleurs assez difficile, ce qui excuse certaines respirations mal placées," *Le Ménestrel* (January 16, 1925): p. 28.

34. "M. Crunelle qui avait quitté son pupitre de flûtiste pour nous offrir plus directement les dons exquis de la *Suite en si mineur* fut un dispensateur fervent de cette richesse éternelle." *Le Monde musical* (Nos. 1–2, January 1925).

35. "La *Suite en si mineur* de Bach, avec flûte-solo, rencontra en M. Crunelle un interprète fort habile et doué d'une jolie qualité de son, ce qui lui valut un succès personnel très vif." *Le Ménestrel* (February 4, 1927): p. 51.

36. *Le Guide du concert* (April 23, 1926): p. 818.

37. He was soloist in Brandenburg Concerto No. 2 on November 4 and 18, 1928, February 16, 1936, and October 30, 1938; No. 4 on February 26, 1927, and November 23, 1941; and No. 5 on November 20, 1926, December 31, 1932, and October 18, 1936.

38. "Le Concerto en fa majeur—proprement délicieux au sens classique—va aux nues. Albert Lévêque, au clavier, y rivalise de grâce et de pureté avec les flûtes de Crunelle et de Castel, en des arabesques et courbes divines." Roger Vanteuil, *Le Ménestrel* (November 4, 1938): p. 247. Albert Lévêque (1900–1970) was a French pianist and musicologist who specialized in Bach.

39. *Comœdia* (December 18, 1930): p. 2.

40. *L'Art musical* (November 6, 1936): p. 127, *L'Art musical* (December 17, 1937): p. 267, and *L'Art musical* (November 26, 1937): p. 214. The Église réformé de Paris Étoile is a Protestant church at 56 avenue de la Grande Armée in the seventeenth arrondissement near the Arc du triomphe.

41. *L'Art musical* (December 30, 1938): p. 342.

42. "L'adorable scherzo du Songe d'une Nuit d'Été fut enlevé avec toute la légèreté et toute la souplesse indispensables, et la flûte de M. Crunelle y inséra de la plus agréable façon ses notes d'une pureté cristalline." *Le Ménestrel* (October 16, 1925): p. 421.

43. *Le Ménestrel* (January 1, 1926): p. 4.

44. "L'aérien Scherzo du *Songe d'une nuit d'été*, de Mendelssohn, fut parfaitement exécuté en ce qui concerne les bois (et spécialement M. Crunelle)," *Le Ménestrel* (December 9, 1927): p. 511.

45. Performed on February 28, 1926, February 5, 1927, March 26, 1927, February 26, 1928, March 18, 1928, January 4, 1930, February 6, 1937, March 27, 1938, when he "received a loud applause" ("M. Crunelle se fit vivement applaudir dans *Le Vol du bourdon*"), *L'Art musical* (April 1, 1938): p. 674.

46. "L'*Ouverture su trois thèmes grecs* de Glazounow, la *Symphonie inachevée* de Borodine, le *Vol du Bourdon* de Rimsky-Korsakoff (bissé par le public et qui valut au flûtiste solo, M. Crunelle, un grande succès personnel), des fragment du *Coq d'Or* avaient précédé l'audition de ondes," *Le Ménestrel* (January 10, 1930): p. 11

47. Maurice Imbert, "Ce qu'on a entendu la semaine dernière dans les concerts symphoniques à Paris," *L'Art musical* (March 26, 1937): p. 598.

48. "Il convient de louer l'exécution de l'entr'acte de *Carmen*, avec son célèbre solo de flûte bien exécute ici par M. Crunelle." Émile Vuillermoz, "Chronique phonographique," *Le Temps* (June 18, 1933): p. 5.

49. Albert Debondue (1895–1984) was principal oboist of the Pasdeloup, oboist in the Opéra-Comique, and author of books of etudes for oboe.

50. André Vacellier (1909–1994) was principal clarinetist of the Orchestre Pasdeloup, a member of the Quintette à vent de Paris, and later principal clarinetist of the Opéra-Comique. He played the Paris premiere of Messiaen's *Quartet for the End of Time* and recorded the piece with the composer in 1956.

51. René Plessier, who won a first prize in bassoon at the Conservatory in 1932, was the principal bassoonist in the Pasdeloup and later in the Orchestre nationale de France, where he also played in the orchestra's wind quintet.

52. Marcel Richard was principal hornist in the Pasdeloup.

53. *Le Ménestrel* (March 10, 1939): p. 68.

54. *Le Figaro* (January 20, 1926): p. 5.

55. *La Parole libre* 71: p. 6.

56. Brega (1899–1990) was a frequent soloist in the 1920s and 1930s. She married composer Maurice Jaubert (1900–1940) in 1926, and Maurice Ravel served as a witness at the wedding. She became a member of the French resistance in World War II.

57. Gaston Marchesini (1904–1981) was principal cellist in the Pasdeloup and was active as a cellist from the 1920s through the 1960s. He recorded Ibert's Concerto for cello and wind instruments in 1947.

58. "Il faut louer le talent d'accompagnateur de M. Maurice Jaubert et aussi de M. Marcel Delannoy, et rendre hommage à la haute valeur de M.M. Crunelle et Gaston Marchesini, qui brillèrent dans l'accompagnement des *Chansons madécasses*," *Le Ménestrel* (January 21, 1927): p. 28.

59. Cahuzac (1880–1960) was principal clarinetist of the Opéra, professor of clarinet at the Paris Conservatory, and composer of many works for clarinet.

60. *Comœdia* (March 14, 1927): p. 5. The Krettly Quartet, with first violinist Robert Krettly (1891–1956), second violinist René Costard, violists Georges Taine and then François Boos, and cellists Pierre Fournier (1906–1986) and then André Navarra (1911–1988), was active in the 1920s and 1930s.

61. Louis Mercier was oboist in the wind quintet of the Garde républicaine, featured on the CD collection, *The Oboe: 1903–1953* (Oboe Classics CC2012).

62. Oboist Paul-Gustave Brun, who played English horn in this performance, won a first prize at the Conservatory in 1897 as a student of Georges Gillet (1854–1920).

63. Auguste Lenom was a bassoonist.

64. Saxophonist Marcel Mule (1901–2001) was a soloist in the Garde républicaine and formed the saxophone quartet of the Garde, which later became the Quatuor de saxophones de Paris. From 1944 to 1967, he was professor of saxophone at the Conservatory, where he taught an entire generation. Mule wrote many books of etudes and transcriptions and was the dedicatee of many works. His two sons, Pol and Jacques, each won first prizes in flute as students of Gaston Crunelle.

65. "Un *Quintette* pour flûte, hautbois, cor anglais, clarinette et basson, exécuté par M.M. Crunelle, Mercier, Brun, Cahuzac et Lenom, nous produisit un effet d'âpreté quelque peu déconcertante, peut-être parce que l'élément rythmique cessait d'y être aussi nettement accusé. Par contre, un *Quatuor* pour harpe, celesta, flûte, saxophone

et voix féminines, donné en première audition, témoigna à nouveau d'une grande richesse de rythmes, d'une extrême variété d'impressions, sans d'ailleurs poursuivre une sérieuse recherche constructive. L'équilibre sonore en est remarquable, et le début du second morceau, notamment, donne une extraordinaire impression de plénitude. Il fut exécuté par Mmes Micheline Kahn et Denise Cools, M.M. Crunelle, Mule et la Chorale Nivard." *Le Ménestrel* (April 11, 1930): p. 170.

66. Duchesnau, *L'Avant-garde musicale et ses sociétés à Paris de 1871 à 1939*, p. 295.

67. *Le Ménestrel* (May 4, 1934) announced that the concert was at the petite Salle Gaveau, but *Le Temps* (June 2, 1934) reported that it was at the Salle Chopin.

68. *Le Temps* (June 16, 1934): p. 3.

69. *L'Art musical* (December 13, 1935): p. 141. The Salle d'Iéna was a theatre from 1929 through 1955 at 12 avenue d'Iéna in the sixteenth arrondissement.

70. Lamorlette (1894–1960) was professor of oboe at the Paris Conservatory and principal oboist of the Opéra-Comique and the Société des concerts du conservatoire. In 1929, he recorded the Poulenc trio with bassoonist Gustave Dhérin and the composer at the piano.

71. Périer (1883–1947) was the author of many books of clarinet etudes, professor of clarinet at the Conservatory, and principal clarinet of the Opéra-Comique.

72. Dhérin (1887–1964) was professor of bassoon at the Conservatory and principal bassoonist in the Opéra-Comique. In 1929, he recorded the Poulenc trio with oboist Roland Lamorlette and the composer at the piano.

73. Devémy (1898–1969) was professor of horn at the Paris Conservatory from 1937 to 1969, principal hornist in the the Opéra-Comique, the Concerts Colonne, and the Garde républicaine, and a member of the Garde's wind quintet.

74. *L'Art musical* (January 17, 1936): p. 257.

75. *L'Art musical* (March 13, 1936): p. 480.

76. Pignari-Salles recorded Franck's Sonata for Violin and Piano and Brahms's Sonata in G, Op. 78 with violinist Louis Kaufmann in 1956.

77. Pasquier (1902–1986) won a first prize at the Conservatory in 1922, the same year Raymonde Crunelle won her second prize, as a student of Maurice Vieux.

78. Aïtoff (1904–2006) was a pianist and vocal coach who worked with the cabaret singer Yvette Guilbert and prepared singers for the conductors Charles Munch, Herbert von Karajan, Georg Solti, and Charles Dutoit. She is the subject of a 2008 documentary film, *La Grande Mademoiselle*.

79. "Fut accueilli par des applaudissements chaleureux. La partie musicale subséquente réunissait une pléiade d'artistes réputés . . . Le flutiste M. G. Crunelle qui, avec la talentueuse collaboration de la remarquable pianiste Mille Irène Aïtoff, mit bien en valeur la 1er Sonate." Omer Singelée, "Ce qu'on a entendu à Paris dans divers concerts et récitals," *L'Art musical* (December 25, 1936): p. 287.

80. The trio was founded in 1927 by three brothers: violinist Jean Pasquier (1903–1992), violist Pierre Pasquier, and cellist Étienne Pasquier (1905–1997). Jean and Pierre played in the Opéra-Comique with Crunelle. The trio premiered works by Jean Françaix, André Jolivet, Jean Martinon, Bohuslav Martinů, Darius Milhaud, Jean Rivier, Albert Roussel, and Florent Schmitt. In April 1946, they collaborated with

Jean-Pierre Rampal for his first commercial recording of quartets by Haydn and Mozart. The Trio Pasquier disbanded in 1974. Étienne Pasquier performed the premiere of Messiaen's *Quartet for the End of Time* in the Stalag VIII A, a prisoner-of-war camp, in 1941.

81. Aubert (1877–1968) was a composer and pianist who wrote *La Forêt bleue* (1911), performed at the Opéra-Comique in 1924.

82. Grey (1896–1979), closely associated with Ravel, performed the premiere of his *Chansons madécasses* in 1926.

83. In its first iteration, the Quatuor Calvet (1919–1939) consisted of violinists Joseph Calvet (1897–1984) and Georges Mignot (replaced by Daniel Guilevitch in 1929), violist Léon Pascal, and cellist Paul Mas. They recorded the complete quartets of Beethoven and the Debussy and Ravel quartets.

84. "Le dessus du panier des orchestres parisiens," *L'Art musical* (March 19, 1937): p. 572.

85. Charles Bartsch (1907–1979) was a Belgian composer, conductor, and cellist.

86. Giuseppe (Joseph) Benvenuti (1898–1967) was an Italian-born pianist who formed the B.B.N. Trio in 1941 with violinist René Benedetti and cellist André Navarra. They recorded Ravel's Trio in A Minor for Pathé.

87. Suzanne Demarquez, "Ce qu'on a entendu à Paris dans divers concerts et récitals," *L'Art musical* (April 8, 1938): p. 706.

88. Andrade (1918–1997) toured and recorded widely as a violin soloist.

89. Merckel (1899–1973) recorded the Debussy Sonata for Flute, Viola, and Harp with Marcel Moyse and Lily Laskine in 1938 (see Chapter 6).

90. "Les interprètes surent rendre à merveille toute la saveur." Florent Schmitt, "Les Concerts," *Le Temps* (April 29, 1939): p. 3.

91. *L'Art musical* (April 21, 1939): p. 844. The Institut international de coopération intellectuelle was in the Palais Royal at 2 rue Montpensier in the first arrondissement from 1925 to 1946.

92. The pseudonym of Pierre Édouard Léon Rousseau (1889–1939). He was the first composer to write for the *ondes Martenot*.

93. "Un accident étant arrive à la harpe de M. P. Jamet, on fut privé du plaisir d'entendre le Trio." *L'Art musical* (June 2, 1939): pp. 973–74.

94. "He never had the joy of hearing it performed despite the goodwill of the interpreters who had stayed overnight in his room even during the illness that overtook him." ("Il n'a eu jamais la joie de l'entendre exécuter malgré la bonne volonté des interprètes qui avaient fait la nuit dans sa chambre même pendant la maladie qui l'a apporté.") Live broadcast of a concert in homage of the tenth anniversary of Vellones's death, July 22, 1948, Radiodiffusion française (see Appendix 1, no. 36).

95. *L'Art musical* (June 2, 1939): p. 992.

96. In a letter to the General Director of Fine Arts, the director of the Opéra-Comique Pierre-Barthélemy Guesi wrote on March 27, 1935, "Mr. Crunelle, hired on July 1, 1933 as a replacement for Mr. Moyse, having resigned ("M. Crunelle, engagé le 1er juillet 1933 en remplacement de M. Moyse démissionné"), ANF, F/21/4674. Ann McCutchan writes in *Marcel Moyse: Voice of the Flute* (pp. 138–39) that Moyse played at the Opéra-Comique throughout the 1930s, but this is inaccurate. Unfortunately,

there are no *feuilles de présence* (sign-in sheets) for the Opéra-Comique orchestra between fall 1933 and spring 1935, but those after June 1, 1935 never show Moyse's name; Crunelle's name is always there. Bibliothèque de l'Opéra, Cotes OC Arch. 20 378, 389, 508, and 576–580.

97. Hériché, "Erinnerung an Gaston Crunelle," p. 210.

98. *Le Ménestrel* (October 6, 1933): p. 388.

99. Archives of the Opéra-Comique ARCH.O.C.20 at the Bibliothèque de l'Opéra, Paris.

100. "Bien souvent je suis confronté à une partition que je n'ai jamais vu, et ça m'a beaucoup appris mon métier, de construire tout un tas de réflexes mais aussi de trouver des systèmes de doigtés qui rendent les enchaînements de notes plus facile." Bernard Pierreuse, interview by author, Liège, February 22, 2022.

101. Although the Depression started with the Wall Street market crash in October 1929, its economic effects spread around the world; the crisis was not as severe in France as in America.

102. Gromer was a member of the Quintette à vent de Paris.

103. *Le Temps* (January 9, 1935): p. 6.

104. Delécluse (1907–1995) was professor of clarinet at the Paris Conservatory (1949–78) and principal clarinetist in the Orchestre de Paris.

105. *Comœdia* (July 15, 1936): p. 4. The repertoire was not specified but was probably Jongen's *Rhapsodie*, which the same ensemble with a different clarinetist had performed for the SN on January 11.

106. *Comœdia* (October 2, 1936): p. 1. The three musicians had performed the piece on March 25.

107. *Le Figaro* (February 26, 1937): p. 7.

108. *L'Art musical* (March 26, 1937): p. 589, and *L'Art musical* (April 23, 1937): p. 667.

109. Pierre Camus (1885–1948) studied flute with Taffanel and Gaubert and composition with Fauré at the Paris Conservatory. He played in the Concerts Colonne and composed *Twelve Etudes* for flute (Paris: Alphonse Leduc, 1920).

110. "C'est l'honnêteté du texte par rapport avec ce que le compositeur à écrit," Brigette Buxtorf, interview by author, Geneva, February 15, 2022.

111. Blakeman, *Taffanel: Genius of the Flute*, p. 194.

112. "La musicalité extraordinaire," Jean Étienne, interview by Pascal Gresset, *Tempo flûte: Revue de association d'histoire de la flûte traversière* 8 (2013 no. 2): p. 4.

113. "Il avait en lui l'élégance dans l'interprétation tout en respectant quand même le texte. Et je pense que ce qui était très important c'est qu'il nous a fait comprendre, c'est de faire passer la musique avant sa propre personnalité." Maxence Larrieu, interview by author, Geneva, November 25, 2019.

114. Jean-Pierre Rampal and Deborah Wise, *Music, My Love*, p. 47.

115. His performances of Bizet's Entr'acte to Act III of *Carmen* conducted by André Cluytens in 1950, Ferdinand Zellbell's *Concerto*, broadcast in June 1955, some low register passages in Mozart's Concerto for Harp (Paumbartner recording, 1956), and Fred Barlow's *Pavane* from 1962 are the only times I have heard him play slightly flat. See Appendix 1.

116. Pierre-Yves Artaud, interview by author, March 1, 2022.

117. "Sa façon de jouer était assez serrée, très fine, très filée dans l'aigu et un peu *bastonnée* dans le grave." Michel Debost, interview by Pascal Gresset, *Tempo flûte: Revue de l'association d'histoire de la flûte traversière* 6 (2012, no. 2): p. 4.

118. Edward Beckett, interview by author, Paris, November 23, 2019.

119. "De près, il y avait beaucoup d'air, et quelques mètres plus loin il était superbe, très tendu, très vivant." Gérard Jemain, interview by author, May 11, 2022.

Chapter 4

1. Laurence Equilbey, "René Le Roy: Une époque, un interprète" (PhD dissertation, University of Paris—Sorbonne (Paris IV), 1984), p. 39.

2. Debussy's reference to Baroque models is strongest in the Sonata's middle movement, marked "Tempo di menuetto."

3. Debussy to Robert Godet on December 11, 1916. François Lesure and Roger Nichols, *Debussy Letters*, tr. Roger Nichols (Cambridge, MA: Harvard University Press, 1987), p. 320.

4. Ann McCutchan, *Marcel Moyse: Voice of the Flute* (Portland, OR: Amadeus Press, 1994), p. 94.

5. Darius Milhaud, *Notes without Music: An Autobiography* (New York: Alfred A. Knopf, 1953), p. 64.

6. Carl Swanson, "Corrections to Debussy's *Sonate pour flute, alto, et harpe*; Second Movement: Interlude," *The American Harp Journal* 24, no. 3 (Summer 2014): p. 30.

7. Féart (1878–1954) was a soprano at the Paris Opéra known for her roles in operas by Debussy and Wagner.

8. Rummel (1887–1953) was an early interpreter of Debussy's piano works.

9. Edmond Delage, "Quinttete instrumental de Paris," *Le Monde musical* 35, nos. 9–10 (May 1924): p. 190.

10. The Fonds René Le Roy in the Bibliothèque musicale La Grange-Fleuret hold many letters between Le Roy and various composers.

11. "Il y a plus d'un an, nous avions signalé, ici même, l'originalité de ce groupement instrumental, alors nouveau, son incontestable utilité pour la mise au jour d'œuvres du passé charmantes et à peu près ignorés, les possibilités qu'il offrait aux compositeurs modernes et la place de premier plan qu'il occuperait dans l'activité musicale. Nos prévisions sont devenues maintenant des réalités. Le Quintette Instrumental de Paris composé d'artistes justement réputés: René Le Roy (flûte), Pierre Jamet (harpe), René Bas (violon), Pierre Grout (alto), Roger Boulmé (violoncelle), devra durant cette saison satisfaire à de très nombreux engagements qui ne laisseront guère le loisir de se produire à Paris: Luxembourg, Belgique et provinces de l'Est (en novembre), tournée en Bourgogne, en Normandie et en Suisse (en février), la Côte d'Azur, le Midi et l'Espagne (en mars), etc. . . .

Son répertoire s'est notablement accru. Des œuvres modernes ont été écrites spécialement pour lui. Il vient de créer la Sérénade de Roussel à la S.M.I et d'inscrire à ses programmes:

Les Chansons de Bilitis de G. Dequin, le Trio de Swan Hennessy, etc. Les membres de ce remarquable groupement, participeront à la séance inaugurale de *La Musique Vivante* le vendredi 23 octobre." *Le Guide du concert* (October 23, 1925): pp. 61–62.

12. "Le *Triptyque champêtre*, de Ch. Sohy (sous ce pseudonyme, on découvre, aux œuvres, la charmante sensibilité d'une femme) respire, comme son titre l'indique, le parfum de la campagne : il en a la fraîcheur, la clarté joyeuse : c'est une « campagne de plaisance » et l'enchantement matinal est celui que procure, non point le petit jour où, sur les chemins encore gris, le paysans, mal éveillés, traînent leurs sabots, en route pour leur pénible travail de moisson, mais le tableau du jardin tout pimpant de glycines et de capucines. Les volets claquent le long du mur ; à la fenêtre apparaît une jeune femme ; elle sourit aux oiseaux qui pépient dans le peuplier voisin ; ses yeux clignent aux rayons du soleil déjà monté. Pour n'être point âpre, la pièce n'en est pas moins très vivante et très vraie," Pierre de Lapommeraye, "Société nationale," *Le Ménestrel* (January 15, 1926): p. 27.

13. Mathieu Ferey and Benoît Menut. *Joseph-Guy Ropartz, ou le pays inaccessible* (Geneva: Éditions Papillon, 2005), p. 106.

14. "Cernant de près l'écriture chambriste, il confère à la flûte, au violon, à l'alto, au violoncelle et à la harpe qui ont bien des affinités même s'ils ne sont pas tous de même famille, un rôle plus autonome. Virtuosité d'une écriture drue et sans concession mélodique, contrepoint serré, trame instrumentale légère et translucide, apportent aux *Variations* un caractère à la fois rousselien et ravelien, nuancé par la démarche personnelle de l'auteur.

Sur le mode lydien, le finale, agile et rythmé, présente, dans le style du divertissement, de solistes un jeu instrumental plein de truculence et de pétulance. Un tantinet ibérique, il s'achève, après maint détour, par une réexposition, à l'unisson, suivie d'un rappel, quasi—*recitativo*, du thème initial." Georges Masson, *Gabriel Pierné, musicien lorrain* (Nancy: Presses Universitaires de Nancy, 1993), p. 151.

15. Johns Hopkins University Libraries, https://aspace.library.jhu.edu/repositories/4/resources/1251.

16. *The New York Times* (March 2, 1934): p. 22.

17. "vivace . . . aux très personnelles recherches de timbres et rythmes," Joseph Baruzi, "Société nationale de musique (28 avril)," *Le Ménestrel* (May 4, 1934): p. 173.

18. "Triptyque musical aux soudaines lumières et aux subtiles ombres." *Le Ménestrel* (May 48, 1934): p. 173.

19. "Napées. Sur les pentes du côteau boisé les Napées, craintivement, demeurent dissimulées ; car Pan guidé par Cupidon explore la plaine. Ægipans. Parmi les roseaux et les blancs lotus du lac d'or, les Ægipans vont et viennent malicieusement amusés par l'apeurement des Dryades. Bacchantes. Vallée sauvage ; formes nues, séductrices, magiciennes ; danses orgiaques devant l'inconnu destiné au sacrifice." Jean-Paul C. Montagnier, *Catalogue des œuvres de Jules-Marie Laure Maugüé (Nancy, 1869-Paris, 1953) et autres documents sur sa vie et son œuvre* (Nancy: Jean-Paul C. Montagnier, 2019), p. 50.

20. Dushkin (1891–1976) was a Polish-born American violinist who advised Stravinsky in the composition of his Violin Concerto (1931) and later recorded it with the composer conducting. Stravinsky also wrote the *Duo Concertante* (1932) and the *Divertimento* (1934) for Dushkin.

21. *The New York Times* (March 23, 1935): p. 10.

22. "Petite suite de moins de quatre sous . . . Le premier morceau est bâti sur deux thèmes teintés d'archaïsme. Le second revêt la forme d'un scherzo à deux thèmes également. Le troisième a ceci de particulier qu'il peut être joué dans deux mouvements : *modéré* ou *lent*. Le compositeur a choisi le premier. Cette pièce comporte deux thèmes. Le quatrième mouvement, enfin, est une sorte de rondeau à refrains, en hommage à Haydn. Il est très facile." François-René Tranchefort, *Guide de la musique de chambre* (Paris: Fayard, 1987), p. 778.

23. "Le *Quintette* de M. de Manziarly pour flûte, violon, alto, violoncelle et harpe, a paru la plus remarquable des différentes œuvres données en première audition à cette séance de la Nationale. Le signe distinctif de son inspiration comme de son écriture est l'élégance, une élégance, constamment soutenue, toujours agréable et chantante, relevée dans les deux derniers mouvements par une vivacité dont l'élan fait augurer le plus favorablement des dons de l'auteur." Michel-Léon Hirsch, "Société nationale (22 février)," *Le Ménestrel* (February 28, 1936): p. 70.

24. *L'Art musical* (March 27, 1936): p. 539.

25. Georges Masson, *Gabriel Pierné, musicien Lorrain* (Nancy: Presses Universitaires de Nancy, 1993), p. 152.

26. René Dumesnil, *La musique en France entre les deux guerres, 1919–1939* (Paris: Éditions du monde, 1946), pp. 214–215.

27. Caroline Rae, "Debussyist, Modernist, Exoticist: Marius-François Gaillard Rediscovered," *The Musical Times* 152, no. 1916 (2011): pp. 59–80, www.jstor.org/stable/23037974.

28. Introduced in Chapter 3.

29. "La *Sérénade* de M. Lajtha surprend par un accent plus robuste, une décision franche et un peu grosse, dans le mouvement et la manière; il y a même dans la première partie une verve impatiente et parfois rageuse, qu'on voudrait retrouver souvent dans un ensemble fort inégal ; la conclusion emporte l'œuvre dans un pétulance railleuse qui n'est point neuve, mais dont l'effet demeure sûr," Michel-Léon Hirsch, "Le Triton (9 mai)," *Le Ménestrel* (May 20, 1938): p. 140.

30. "Pourquoi n'avez-vous rien demandé à Gabriel Fauré ?—J'étais trop jeune.—À Maurice Ravel ? Il était trop fantasque.—À Igor Stravinsky ?—Il m'aurait écrit quelque chose de pointilliste et quand on a demandé une œuvre à un compositeur on ne peut pas ensuite refuse de la jouer.—Á Béla Bartók ? Je n'y ai pensé." Claude Dorgeuille, "Que peut-on apprendre de René Le Roy," *Traversières* 72 (July–August–September 2002): p. 41.

Chapter 5

1. *Le Chagrin et la pitié* (The Sorrow and the Pity), Marcel Orphuls's 1969 film, features archival footage of this exodus.

2. Robert Paxton, *Vichy France: Old Guard and New Order, 1940–1944* (New York: Alfred A. Knopf, 1972).

3. "Les heures de Juin-Juillet 1940 au Conservatoire National de Paris," unsigned typewritten document, ANF AJ/37/402.

4. ANF, AJ/37/402.

5. Letter from Rabaud to Moyse, July 15, 1940, ANF AJ/37/402.

6. Letter from Rabaud to Moyse, October 14, 1940, ANF AJ/37/402.

7. "Monsieur, En réponse à votre lettre, j'ai l'honneur de vous faire connaître qu'il n'est pas possible de spécifier actuellement le nombre de places disponible à la classe de flûte. Nous ignorons en effet si d'ici à la date du concours d'admission, les élèves actuellement mobilisés ou résidant encore en zone libre auront repris leurs classes. Leur remplacement éventuel ne pourra donc être envisagé qu'à cette date.

   Les aspirants auront à exécuter un morceau de leur choix et à lire un morceau inédit.

   Veuillez agréer, Monsieur, l'assurance de mes sentiments distingués. LE SOUS-CHEF DU SECRETARIAT, A. BLIN," ANF, AJ/37/402.

8. Alice Pelliot (1880–1966), who had a first prize from the Conservatory in harmony, had previously taught solfège.

9. ANF, AJ/37/402.

10. Zucca, André, "Classes et concours du Conservatoire de Paris" (July 1941) https://bibliotheques-specialisees.paris.fr/ark:/73873/pf0001668482.locale = en.

11. *L'Information musicale* 38 (September 19, 1941): p. 54.

12. "En effet au dernier concours douze sur treize élèves furent récompensés. Hommages soient rendus au nouveau maître de la classe, Gaston Crunelle, qui persévère dans les belles traditions des Paul Taffanel et Philippe Gaubert." *Comœdia* (July 11, 1942): p. 5.

13. Karine Le Bail, "Logiques et paradoxes de l'antisémitisme en musique," in *La musique au pas: Être musicien sous l'Occupation* (Paris: CNRS Éditions, 2016), pp. 121–41.

14. "Ministère de l'Instruction Publique des Beaux Arts
    Conservatoire National de Musique et d'Art Dramatique
    Paris, le 25 Sept. 1942
    Le Directeur du Conservatoire National de Musique et d'art dramatique
    À Mademoiselle Gartenlaub
    J'ai l'honneur de porter à votre connaissance que par lettre en date du 21 Septembre 1942, M. le Ministre de l'Éducation Nationale m'informe que désormais « il convient de ne maintenir ou de n'admettre au Conservatoire aucun élève juif. » En application de ces instructions, je suis dans l'obligation de vous considérer comme rayé des contrôles à partir du Ier octobre prochain. Avec mes vifs regrets, je vous prie de croie, Mademoiselle, à l'expression de mes sentiments distingués.
    LE DIRECTEUR DU CONSERVATOIRE, Claude Delvincourt," ANF, AJ/37/402.

15. "Nous avions répété la *Sonatine* avec une pianiste accompagnatrice qui, étant juive, portait l'étoile jaune; entrer dans les salles de spectacle et venir nous y écouter lui étant interdit, c'est un autre pianiste nous a accompagnés le jour du concours," Jean Étienne, interview by Pascal Gresset: p. 4.

16. "Serge Blanc et son maître Jules Boucherit," https://youtu.be/euL6ZTjD7iw.

17. Marguerite Sablonnière. "Claude Delvincourt et les cadets du conservatoire: une politique d'orchestre (1943–1954)." In *Le Conservatoire de Paris: Des Menus-Plaisirs à la Cité de la musique, 1795–1995*, ed. Anne Bongrain and Yves Gérard (Paris: Éditions Buchet/Chastel, 1996), pp. 261–281.

18. "Monsieur Oubradous a empêché plusieurs jeunes musiciens de partir en Allemagne et a caché des Français recherchés par la gestapo." Claude Delvincourt, letter to the Minister of National Education (October 31, 1944), quoted in Christiane Oubradous and Pascale d'Ogna, *Fernand Oubradous: Un Artiste du xxe siècle* (Paris: La Bruyère, 2007), p. 87.

19. Rampal *père* was a brilliant flutist; he studied with Hennebains before Crunelle entered the Conservatory, served in World War I, then returned to win a *prix d'excellence* with Lafleurance in 1919, when Crunelle was away in the army. His entire career was spent in his native Marseille as principal flutist in the Radio Orchestra and professor at the Conservatory. In addition to Jean-Pierre, his students included Maxence Larrieu, Alain Marion, and Marius Beuf (1926–2018).

20. "À l'issue du concours Jean-Pierre Rampal vient saluer Gaston Crunelle, tout en lui exposant qu'il lui sera difficile de tenir sa place à la classe, étant dans l'obligation de retourner aux *Chantiers*. Mais celui-ci, tous comme de nombreux autres professeurs, sait que le Conservatoire est toujours susceptible de représenter un parfait échappatoire au Service du Travail Obligatoire (S.T.O.) pour quantité de jeunes musiciens. Le directeur Claude Delvincourt s'y emploie d'ailleurs activement. Aussi le Maître, sachant que la situation risque fort de s'aggraver, recommande-t-il à son élève de prendre un congé plutôt que de démissionner d'emblée. Qui sait ce que l'avenir réservera … ? Précieux conseil, dont Jean-Pierre Rampal allait vite mesurer la sagesse." Denis Verroust, *Jean-Pierre Rampal: La flûte universelle* (Paris: Association française de la flûte « La Traversière » and Association Jean-Pierre Rampal, 2022), p. 39.

21. Verroust, *Jean-Pierre Rampal*, p. 44.

22. Edward Beckett, interview.

23. Jane Fulcher, *Renegotiating French Identity: Musical Culture and Creativity in France during Vichy and the German Occupation* (New York: Oxford University Press: 2018), p. 72.

24. The Bibliothèque de l'Opéra has preserved the programs from the Opéra-Comique. After the Liberation, programs were printed in French and English.

25. "L'image de cette soirée du 12 septembre à l'Opéra-Comique, où se presse un public vraiment peu extraordinaire : dans les rangs d'orchestre, il y a tous ceux que Paris peut compter dans le monde du théâtre, des lettres et de la musique—et puis il y a les autres … les officiers en uniforme, que le hasard d'une soirée fait voisiner avec ceux qui bientôt se grouperont dans le « Front national », comme Désormière lui-même est au pupitre … La salle est vibrante d'une émotion qui ne cesse de croître, des interprètes au public, tout au long de l'ouvrage dont l'esprit, le mystère, n'ont jamais, semble-t-il, été plus fidèlement traduits … le frisson que chacun ressent toujours à instant, n'a jamais été aussi intense qu'en cette soirée de septembre 1940, dans un Paris occupé," Henri Dutilleux, "Au Service de tous." In *Roger Désormière et son temps*, ed. Denise Mayer and Pierre Souvtchinsky (Monaco: Éditions du Rocher, 1966).

26. Fulcher, *Renegotiating French Identity: Musical Culture and Creativity in France during Vichy and the German Occupation*, p. 71.

27. Philippe Morin and Yannick Simon, "L'Enregistrement historique de *Pelléas et Mélisande* en 1941," *Cahiers Debussy* 37–38 (2013–2014): pp. 77–111.

28. Alexandra Laederich, "Les Associations symphoniques parisiennes." In *La Vie musicale sous Vichy*, ed. Myriam Chimènes (Brussels, 2001): pp. 217–233

29. Hervé Le Boterf, *La Vie parisienne sous l'occupation, 1940–1944* (2 vols. Paris: Éditions France-Empire, 1974), p. 298.

30. *L'Information musicale* 123 (July 2, 1943).

31. Pasdeloup Orchestra archives.

32. "Je sais que Gaston Crunelle était le préféré de mon père. Et c'était vraiment un ami." Marie-Claire Jamet, interview by author, Flayosc, France, November 27, 2019.

33. Louis Vierne (1870–1937) dedicated his *Soirs étrangers* to five cellists: Jean Vaugeois, Roger Boulmé, Nelly Gauthier, Paul Bazelaire, and Gregor Piatigorsky.

34. Bergeron also played viola da gamba in the London Baroque Ensemble on their 1952 recording of the complete Brandenburg Concertos (www.discogs.com/master/1577 195-J-S-Bach-London-Baroque-Ensemble-Six-Brandenburg-Concertos-Complete).

35. Robert Orledge, *Charles Koechlin (1867–1950): His Life and Works* (London: Harwood Academic Publishers, 1989), p. 176.

36. "L'œuvre de Ch. Koechlin, *Primavera*, dont c'était la première audition, domina le programme: la jeunesse, la fraîcheur printanière, les sonorités arachnéennes du Quintette instrumental Pierre Jamet, la grâce avec laquelle elle se déroule, concourent à faire de cette délicate partition un véritable chef-d'œuvre." *L'Information musicale* (March 31, 1944): p. 251.

37. "Il faudrait le langage du poète pour parler bien de ce concert," *L'Information musicale* 45 (November 7, 1941).

38. Carol A. Hess, *Manuel de Falla and Modernism in Spain, 1898–1936* (Chicago: The University of Chicago Press, 2001), p. 178.

39. Gilbert Chase and Andrew Budwig, *Manuel de Falla: A Bibliography and Research Guide* (New York: Garland Publishing, Inc., 1986), p. 50, and Ronald Crichton, *Manuel de Falla: Descriptive Catalog of his Works* (London: J. & W. Chester, 1976), p. 42.

40. Hess, *Manuel de Falla and Modernism in Spain*, p. 178.

41. Archivo Manuel de Falla, www.manueldefalla.com/es/obras/obras-de-camara-o-para-conjunto-instrumental/psyche.

42. Michel Duchesnau, *L'Avant-garde musicale à Paris de 1871 à 1939* (Paris: P. Mardaga, 1997), p. 320. The program does not list the other performers, but probably, they were Hortense de Sampigny, violin; Sigismond Jarecki, viola; and Tony Close, cello, as they performed other works on the same program.

43. Suzanne Demarquez, "Quintette instrumental Pierre Jamet (1er juin)," *L'Information musicale* 124 (July 9, 1943). Except for de Falla's *Psyché*, the arrangements for voice and ensemble cannot be found.

44. Leslie A. Sprout, *The Musical Legacy of Wartime Paris* (Berkeley: University of California Press, 2013), pp. 86–89.

45. Doyen (1907–1982) was professor of piano at the Conservatory (1947–1977), an esteemed interpreter of French piano music, and a composer.

46. "MM. Gaston Crunelle et Étienne Ginot conjuguèrent à merveille leurs beaux talents, faisant ressortir, tout le charme et toute la fraîcheur de cette œuvrette de grande classe." *L'Information musicale* 139 (January 7, 1944): p. 150.

47. "La *Sonatine* est d'une imagination charmante, elle a beaucoup plu," *L'Information musicale* 153 (April 15, 1944): p. 261.

48. Christine Quattrocchi-Oubradous, email to author, May 18, 2022.

49. Oboist Myrtil Morel (1889–1979) was a first-prize winner at the Conservatory in 1909. Principal oboist of the Concerts Colonne, he formed the Trio d'anches de Paris (reed trio) in 1927 with Fernand Oubradous and Pierre Lefebvre.

50. Pierre Lefebvre (1898–1963) was principal clarinetist in the Opéra-Comique, the orchestra of the Garde Républicaine, and the Lamoureux Orchestra.

51. Maurice Allard (1923–2004) was principal bassoonist in the Orchestre Lamoureux and then in the Paris Opéra. He was the bassoon professor at the Conservatory from 1957 to 1988.

52. Eugène Foveau (1886–1957) was the trumpet professor at the Conservatory from 1925 to 1947.

53. Joseph Alviset won a first prize in trombone from the Paris Conservatory in 1924 and was an administrator of the orchestra of the Vichy opera.

54. "Son Orchestre symphonique de chambre, magnifique phalange où se retrouvent depuis trois ans déjà les meilleurs parmi les meilleurs des instrumentistes à vent de France: Crunelle, Morel, Lefebvre, Devémy, Allard, Greffin, Foveau, Alviset, Billard, Mule, Chevert," Henri Martelli, *L'Information musicale* (April 15, 1944), quoted in Oubradous and d'Ogna, *Fernand Oubradous: Un Artiste du xxe siècle*, p. 73. Jules Chevert was principal tuba of the Paris Opéra.

55. Clerget was cellist in the Maurice Hewitt Quartet with violinists Maurice Hewitt (1884–1971) and Pierre Lepetit and violist Jacques Boucher. The quartet was active in the 1920s and 30s.

56. Aubert (1884–1979), a student of organist Jean Huré (1877–1930), and early music pioneer Arnold Dolmetsch (1858–1940) also recorded a solo LP, *Le Clavecin français*.

57. Karine Le Bail, "Partage des ondes, partage des hommes," in *La musique au pas: Être musicien sous l'Occupation* (Paris: CNRS Éditions, 2016), pp. 45–75.

58. Julian Jackson, *France: The Dark Years, 1940–1944* (New York: Oxford University Press, 2001), p. 256.

59. Karine Le Bail, La musique au pas: Être musicien sous l'"Occupation (Paris: CNRS Éditions, 2016), pp. 50–2.

60. Yannick Simon, *Composer sous Vichy* (Lyon: Symétrie, 2009), p. 97.

61. Philippe Burrin, *France under the Germans,* trans. Janet Lloyd (New York: The New Press, 1996), p. viii.

62. Pellas-Lenom recorded with saxophonist Marcel Mule and cellist Pierre Fournier.

63. André-Chastel recorded works on harpsichord.

64. Berthomieu (1906–1991) was a French composer, poet, and dramatist. He wrote operas, orchestral music, songs, and chamber music. The *Suite romantique* is from 1941.

65. Samazeuilh (1877–1967) was a French composer, pianist, and critic. During World War II, he was a member of the Groupe Collaboration, which supported the Pétain government in Vichy. At the invitation of Heinrich Goebbels, he and other members traveled to Vienna to celebrate the sesquicentennial of Mozart's death.

66. N. Siloiroc was a composer active in the 1940s: https://data.bnf.fr/fr/documents-by-rdt/14776719/tum/page1.

67. From the *Six sonates en quatuors ou conversations galantes*, op. 12, for flute, violin, bass viol, and basso continuo (1743).

68. Lentier (1910–1998) was a French composer and Prix de Rome winner in 1937.

69. Cruque (1890–1969) was a cellist in the Paris Opéra who recorded Manuel de Falla's Harpsichord Concerto with the composer playing harpsichord; Marcel Moyse, flute; Georges Bonneau, oboe; Émile Godeau, clarinet; and Marcel Darrieux, violin in 1949.

70. Collard (1910–1979), a student of Paul Dukas, Alfred Cortot, Yvonne Lefébure, and Nadia Boulanger, was a widely recorded pianist.

71. Karine Le Bail, "L'Épuration du monde de la musique." In *De la Liberation au Domaine Musical: Dix ans de musique en France (1944–1954)*, ed. Laurent Feneyou and Alain Poirier (Paris: Librairie Philosophique J. Vrin, 2018), pp. 23–31.

72. Active from the 1930 through the 1970s, the quartet's members in 1944 were first violinist Alfred Loewenguth, second violinist Maurice Fuéri, violist Roger Roche, and cellist Pierre Basseux.

73. Created in 1928, the Quintette à vent de Paris in 1944 consisted of flutist Fernard Caratgé, oboist Louis Gromer, clarinetist André Vacellier, bassoonist Gabriel Grandmaison, and hornist René Reumont.

74. "Les artistes soussignés ont cru qu'il était de leur devoir de maintenir la réputation de la Musique Française pendant l'occupation. Qu'en serait-il advenu si le public n'avait eu sur les scènes parisiennes et à la Radio (la seule à Paris), que des artistes allemands ou pro-allemands ?" Letter to the Minister of Fine Arts, November 5, 1944, ANF, F/21/8102.

75. ANF, F/21/8102.

76. ANF, AJ/37/429.

77. Lynn Cavanagh, "Marcel Dupré's 'Dark Years': Unveiling His Occupation-Period Concertizing," *Intersections: Canadian Journal of Music* 34, No. 1–2 (2014): p. 52, https://doi.org/10.7202/1030869ar.

78. "Vous avez bien voulu me faire suivre une lettre de M. MOYSE ancien professeur au Conservatoire, demandant sa réintégration en annulation de l'arrête du 27 Décembre 1940 le déclarant démissionnaire d'office.
En vous retournant ce document, j'ai l'honneur de vous rendre compte de ce qui suit:
La mesure prise en 1940, contre M. MOYSE n'a pas été motivée par des raisons personnelles, raciales, politique ou autres, mais par le refus de l'intéressé de rejoindre son poste à l'appel de mon prédécesseur: M. MOYSE avait alors à choisir entre son enseignement et son activité à la radio, alors repliée à Marseille. Pour des raisons d'ordre matériel, il a préféré cette dernière solution, et mon prédécesseur n'a fait qu'en tirer les conséquences. Si l'on s'en tient au strict point de vue administratif il ne semble donc pas que la demande de M. MOYSE soit recevable.
D'autre part il est incontestable que M. MOYSE est un artiste et un professeur de haute valeur et que son enseignement ne peut que faire honneur au prestige de l'école française. Je ne saurais donc envisager le retour éventuel de M. MOYSE, si celui-ci doit un jour avoir lieu, qu'avec plaisir.

Il convient cependant de ne pas perdre de vue que son successeur M. CRUNELLE a été nommé régulièrement et qu'il assure depuis 4 ans un enseignement irréprochable. Je ne saurais donc voir porter atteinte à ses droits sans protester.

La solution me paraît être fournie par le fait que la nomination de M. CRUNELLE a été faite à titre temporaire et qu'à l'expiration du délai impliqué par cette clause, délai qui sera sans doute fixé ultérieurement par décision ministérielle, la question pourra de nouveau être évoquée devant l'autorité compétente qui pourra à ce moment prendre la décision qu'elle est équitable." ANF, AJ/37/429.

79. "Cher monsieur,

J'ai bien reçu votre lettre du 6 Novembre faisant suite à votre câble du 21 Octobre, par laquelle vous posez votre candidature au poste de professeur de Flûte au Conservatoire.

J'ai le regret de vous faire connaître qu'il n'y a actuellement aucune vacance en perspective pour cette classe. Néanmoins, je prends bonne note de votre candidature pour le cas où le poste deviendrait vacant, et vous prie de croire, cher Monsieur, à mon fidèle souvenir et à mes sentiments bien cordialement dévoués." Letter from Claude Delvincourt to René Le Roy, November 14, 1946, ANF, AJ/27/430.

80. "One student from the postwar years described him as 'an angry old man, a dictator.' Moyse resented the presence of another flute professor at the Conservatoire and often criticized Crunelle during lessons." Ann McCutchan, *Marcel Moyse: Voice of the Flute*, p. 165.

81. "Quand Crunelle parlait de Marcel Moyse, visiblement il avait une grande affection et une grande admiration pour lui qui n'était pas vraiment partagée." Pierre-Yves Artaud, interview by author, March 1, 2022.

Chapter 6

1. *Le Guide du concert* 34, no. 21 (July 3, 1953): p. 1090.
2. Henri Dutilleux, "Au service de tous" in Denise Mayer and Pierre Souvtchinsky, ed., *Roger Désormière et son temps* (Monaco: Éditions du Rocher, 1966), p. 119.
3. The 1946 census is available onsite at the Archives de Paris but not online.
4. Jacques Hillairet, *Dictionnaire historique des rues de Paris*, 7th ed., vol. 2 (Paris: Éditions de minuit, 1963): p. 322.
5. "Le quartier renforce un image, non pas tellement de quartier riche, mais plutôt de lieu d'habitat d'une population d'intellectuels, d'artistes, de cadres et de membres des professions libérales . . . En 1931, les enseignants se limitent à la musique, mais il y a en a encore une douzaine, très diversifiée de la flute à l'orgue!" Maurice Garden et Jean-Luc Pinol, *Seize promenades historiques dans Paris* (Paris: Éditions du detour, 2017): pp. 36–37.
6. Edward Beckett, interview.
7. There are two versions of this story. Gabriel Fumet relates that Crunelle bought his first car in 1932: Jean-Claude Thévenon, *The Music of Silence or The Fumet Dynasty*, trans. Joseph Siegel and Catherine Dufrénois (Paris: Delatour France, 2011), p. 143. Eric Groussard, however, said that it was during World War II, which would be

surprising, since few French people could drive during the war, as gas was generally unavailable and strictly rationed. Eric Groussard and Francette Venay, interview by author, Fresnes, April 1, 2022.

8. "C'était une bâtisse des années 1870. Au cœur d'une pinède, c'était très beau ; je me souviens surtout de sa terrasse," Brigitte Buxtorf, interview by author.

9. The conductor for the premiere and subsequent recording of *La Voix humaine* was Georges Prêtre (1924–2017), who like Crunelle was from Douai.

10. Berton (1924–2009) frequently appeared at the Opéra and the Opéra-Comique in the 1950s and early 60s. She taught voice at the Conservatory starting in 1966.

11. ARCH.O.C.20/370, Bibliothèque de l'Opéra, Paris.

12. *Comœdia* (August 25, 1926): p. 2.

13. Bourdin (1923–1976) won a first prize at the Conservatory in 1939 studying with Moyse. Principal flutist in the Orchestre Lamoureux, he taught at the Versailles Conservatory.

14. *Le Figaro* (March 27, 1948): p. 4.

15. "La sonate à trois qui connut jadis deux très bons enregistrements disparus des listes, nous est proposée en une version pleine de finesse des excellents artistes que sont MM Crunelle, Blanpain et Jamet. Cependant, il semblerait que ces trois interprètes fassent partie des debussystes que j'appellerais volontiers « plus debussystes que Debussy ». On a tant dit et écrit que Debussy était le maître de la réaction contre Wagner, contre Gluck, contre le « germanisme », contre le romantisme enfin, le champion d'une certaine *musique française* synonyme de « grâce », d'« élégance » et de légèreté, que son véritable message, passionné, douloureux et délirant tour à tour, comme celui de tout grand artiste, risque fort d'être, dans certains milieux, totalement méconnu. Ceci dit, il convient de me réjouir de la publication de ces disques musicalement d'un niveau très élevé, et dont la technique d'enregistrement, tout en demi-teintes, correspond parfaitement aux intentions des interprètes." *Disques* (1948), no. 23: p. 575.

16. Susan Nelson and William Shaman, "Discography." In Ann McCutchan, *Marcel Moyse: Voice of the Flute*, p. 249 and p. 264. The Italian flutist Arrigo Tassinari (1889–1988) also recorded Debussy's Sonata in 1931 for Columbia.

17. Ursula Lentrodt, "A Conversation with Pierre Jamet," trans. Mark Palkovic, *American Harp Journal* 11, no. 3 (Summer 1988): p. 29. The composer's concern for delicacy and transparency is also reported in Marguerite Long, *At the Piano with Debussy*, trans. Olive Senior-Ellis (London: Dent, 1972).

18. Carl Swanson, "Corrections to Debussy's *Sonate pour flute, alto, et harpe* Third Movement: Final," *American Harp Journal* (Winter 2014): p. 28.

19. Carl Swanson, "Footnotes to the Full Score," Claude Debussy, *Sonate pour flute, alto, et harpe*, ed. Swanson (Carl Fisher, 2014), p. viii.

20. Grimaud (1920–2012) was a pianist, composer, and ethnomusicologist. She premiered several piano works by Pierre Boulez and André Jolivet.

21. Pierlot (1921–2007) won a first prize in 1941 at the Conservatory and was a founding member of the Quintette à vent français, in which his colleagues were Jean-Pierre Rampal, clarinetist Jacques Lancelot (1920–2009), bassoonist Maurice Allard, and hornist Gilbert Coursier. He was also in the Ensemble baroque de Paris.

22. "Mlle Yvette Grimaud fait ici sa première apparition sur disque dans la périlleuse partie de soliste ; elle s'y révèle une Mozartienne accomplie et nous avons hâte de l'applaudir dans d'autres œuvres du « Divin Maître », dont elle semble pressentir parfaitement le style. Ses collaborateurs, solistes réputés et justement appréciés, cisèlent avec émotion et allégresse ce délicate chef-d'œuvre." *Disques* (January 15, 1948).

23. Ardal Powell, "Modern Editions of the Flute Sonatas and Partita by J.S. Bach," www.academia.edu/9912632/Modern_editions_of_the_flute_sonatas_and_partita_by_J_S_Bach.

24. http://ark.bnf.fr/ark:/12148/cb42826831g

25. McCutchan, *Marcel Moyse: Voice of the Flute*, p. 53.

26. "La flûte de Crunelle est plus forte, oserais-je dire plus humaine? L'instrumentiste semble s'imposer mieux : on croit l'entendre, on l'entend reprendre son souffle. L'instrument de J.-P. Rampal est plus léger, plus aérien, plus immatériel." Jose Bruyr, "Sonate en la mineur pour flûte seule," *Disques* 29 (November 16, 1950): p. 687.

27. Aubert also recorded Blavet's Sonata in D Minor, op. 2, no. 2, "La Vibray" with Marcel Moyse in 1935 (*L'Anthologie sonore* 9).

28. "M. Gaston Crunelle joue à ravir, et on sent qu'il le fait avec plaisir. Dommage que ce Jardin soit assez petit, puisqu'il tient en un seul disque. Mais on peut sans crainte en admirer l'ordonnance," Henry-Jacques, "Airs de flûte," *Disques* 33 (January 18, 1951): p. 20.

29. Chailley-Richez (1884–1973) earned a first prize in piano from the Paris Conservatory in 1898 and married violinist Marcel Chailley in 1908. They led a long musical collaboration.

30. Javier Rodriguez, "Le Quintette instrumental Pierre Jamet: Histoire et répertoire de la période 1945–1958" (Master's thesis, Conservatoire national supérieur de musique et de danse de Paris, 2017), p. 11.

31. Pérugia (1903–1992) was known for her performances of songs by Fauré. She taught at the École normale de musique and the Schola Cantorum.

32. Touraine's original name was Geneviève Tisserand (1903–1982). She gave the premiere of Francis Poulenc's song cycle *Fiançailles pour rire* (1939) and recorded French songs with her brother, the baritone Gérard Souzay (1918–2004).

33. Robin (1918–1960), known for her extremely high register, appeared in operatic roles throughout Europe and North America. Rodriguez, "Le Quintette instrumental Pierre Jamet," p. 14.

34. "Le CHANT de LINOS était, dans l'antiquité grecque, une variété de thrène: une lamentation funèbre, une complainte entrecoupée de cris et de danses." Andre Jolivet, *Chant de Linos* for flute and piano (Paris: Leduc, 1946), flute part, p. 1.

35. Suzanne Demarquez, *André Jolivet* (Paris: Editions Ventadour, 1958), p. 36.

36. Henry Dumont or Du Mont (1610-1684), born Henry de Thier, was a French composer and organist born in the Netherlands. His *Cinq Messes en plein-chant* ("Five Masses in Plainsong") was first published in 1669.

37. "Le compositeur écrivit cette œuvre pendant l'occupation, sur la demande du Quintette Pierre Jamet à qui elle est dédiée. Le titre indique le caractère religieux de la Suite. Le premier morceau *A l'église* expose et développe le thème du Kyrie d'une des *Messes royales* de Du Mont. Le no.2 est un court divertissement *intermède* sur le nom

du dédicataire J.A.M.E.T ce qui en musique donne: *do, la, mi, fa*. Le no. 3, *Angelus* est une prière à laquelle se mêlent des sons deux cloches. Le no. 4 est simplement intitulé." *Le Guide du Concert* (March 15, 1946).

38. The current location of the German Consulate in Paris.

39. The place Malesherbes, a small park at the junction of the boulevard Malesherbes and the avenue de Villiers in the seventeenth arrondissement, was renamed the Place du Général Catroux in 1977. The building at 24 place Malesherbes is next to the École normale de musique.

40. "Le *Second Quintette*, conçu pour harpe, flute, violon, alto, violoncelle—que le quintette instrumental Pierre Jamet donna avec un éclat sobre et un sentiment fin de l'équilibre sonore—exprime, à travers ses quatre mouvements la même souplesse polyphonique en même temps que le tour intime du sentiment." Paul Le Flem, "Hommage à Charles Koechlin," *Rolet* 411 (November 13, 1952), p. 2.

41. Jeunesses musicales de France, www.jmfrance.org/nous-connaitre/qui-sommes-nous.

42. "Ce Quintette peut prétendre au titre de Divertissement. Si le premier andante a du charme où la flûte de Gaston Crunelle chante dans une atmosphère vaguement debussyste, le second n'est pas aussi caractérisé. C'est dans le *Scherzo* (No. 2), et le *Rondo* (No. 4), que nous retrouvons la personnalité pleine de gentillesse et d'agréments rhythmiques de Jean Françaix . . . Les artistes de l'ensemble Pierre Jamet, Gaston Crunelle, René Bas, Georges Blanpain et Robert Krabansky, naturellement, son excellents, comme à l'habitude." Armand Panigel, "Musique de chamber," *Disques* (February 15, 1948): pp. 67–8.

43. Alarie (1921–2011) was born in Montreal, made her Metropolitan Opera debut in 1945, and then starred in various opera roles in both Europe and North America.

44. Tournus (1922–2005), cellist for the Trio à cordes français, also recorded an album of Ravel's chamber music (EMI Classics CZS 7 67217 2) in 1991.

45. Le Dentu was a harpist in the Orchestre Pasdeloup.

46. Equilbey, "René Le Roy: Une époque, un interprète," p. 74.

Chapter 7

1. Sir James Galway and Linda Bridges, *The Man with the Golden Flute: Sir James, a Celtic Minstrel* (Hoboken, NJ: John Wiley & Sons, Inc., 2009), p. 58. Galway's description of Crunelle in his earlier *Autobiography*, now out of print, is even more negative: "At the time . . . I was sure I wasn't learning anything. My teacher had his own problem (the poor man had a tumor on the brain) but it seemed to me that there were better ways to employ my time than just standing there belting out a number while he hid behind his *France Soir* and smoked interminable Gauloises. I could stand in front of a guy like that anywhere; it didn't have to be in Paris. What I expected from him was instruction . . . but he just let each of us play our piece in turn while he studied the runners at Longchamps or whatever, and then barked, 'Right, next!'" James Galway, *An Autobiography* (London: Book Club Associates, 1979), p. 103. There is no evidence that Crunelle experienced cognitive problems.

2. Galway and Bridges, *The Man with the Golden Flute*, p. 60.

3. "J'ai lu le livre de James Galway, dans lequel il reconnaît ne pas être resté très longtemps au Conservatoire de Paris de affirme n'avoir rien appris de Gaston Crunelle, qui lisait son *Figaro* en fumant ses *Gitanes bleues sans filtre.* Crunelle, qui le trouvait formidable et reconnaissait ses talents, m'a déclaré plus tard qu'il estimait avoir cependant des choses à lui dire, mais que son élève préférait s'en tenir à ses propres idées, par ailleurs très respectables. Comme *Jimmy* (James Galway) n'en faisait qu'à sa tête, ne tenait aucun compte de conseils du maître qu'il discutait même, celui-ci lisait ostensiblement son journal pour cette raison. Monsieur Crunelle avait d'instinct trouvé la seule chose qui puisse agacer le future Sir James : qu'on ne l'écoutât pas. Son départ du Conservatoire ne fut pas dû à une démission théâtrale, mais à un échec compréhensible à l'examen de solfège qui devait être franchi pour accéder au concours final. Les cours du solfège à la française posaient à vrai dire un problème au jeune musicien anglophone." Debost, interview by Gresset: p. 4.
4. His 108 students who won first prizes are listed in Appendix 4.
5. "Son ambition avouée était d'amener ses élèves au maximum au moment du concours. Beaucoup ont obtenu leur prix grâce à lui parce qu'il les gonflait à bloc." Debost, interview by Gresset: p. 4.
6. Isabelle Chapuis, interview by author, Los Altos, CA, May 16–17, 2019.
7. Beckett, interview.
8. Chapuis, interview. At the time, the publisher Max Eschig sold sheet music at at 49 Rue de Rome. La Flûte de Pan, the leading music store in Paris, is now at the same address.
9. See Appendix 5 for a list of *morceaux imposés* and *déchiffrages* from Crunelle's era. The sightreading pieces are unpublished and are in the ANF, AJ37/20150119/16.
10. Jury notebooks, Archives of the Paris Conservatory.
11. Betty Bang, "Small Classes . . . Less Teaching, More Learning," *Music Educators Journal* 57, no. 2 (October 1970): p. 49.
12. Thévenon, *The Music of Silence or The Fumet Dynasty*, p. 143.
13. See Appendix 4.
14. Larrieu, interview by author, and Chapuis, interview.
15. Chapuis, interview.
16. George Waln, "Conservatoire National de Paris," *The Instrumentalist* 12 (September 1957): p. 10.
17. Isabelle Chapuis, email to author, September 7, 2023.
18. "C'était l'homme le plus affectueux que l'on puisse imaginer," Jean-Pierre Rampal, "Adieu, Maître Crunelle," *Traversières* 15/34 (April–May–June 1990): p. 9.
19. "Il était extrêmement bienveillant et avait une grande expérience musicale et humaine de la vie, avec une paternelle bonhomie . . . il était toujours très positif et très aimable," Jean-Louis Beaumadier, email to author, December 5, 2019.
20. "Il a toujours été là quand on avait besoin de lui, au téléphone aussi," Buxtorf, interview.
21. "Très paternel avec ses élèves, sa personnalité m'a beaucoup plu et je me suis senti bien dans sa classe," Sophie Dardeau, *Pierre-Yves Artaud: Parcours d'un flûtiste pionnier* (Paris: Pippa, 2012): p. 16.

22. "Christian adorait Monsieur Crunelle parce qu'il avait perdu son père à neuf ans. Et après, il a attrapé la polio. Il avait commencé à apprendre le violon, mais quand il a écouté un concert avec Fernand Dufresne à la radio, il a dit : « Je veux faire de la flûte ». Il est allé voir Monsieur Crunelle directement qui lui a dit qu'il était doué. Il travaillait sa flûte assis sur son lit, et Monsieur Crunelle est venu lui donner des cours assis dans sur lit, et il habitait la banlieue, sixième étage à pied pour monter. Monsieur Crunelle venait lui donner des cours et ça Christian n'a jamais oublié. Ça c'était pour lui un deuxième père," Marie-Claire Jamet, interview.

23. Jean-Claude Dhinaut, interview, Puteaux, March 28, 2022.

24. "Oh, je crois bien que vous n'avez pas d'argent, alors ça ne fait rien, vous ne me payez pas, je suis content d'être avec vous." Gérard Jemain, interview by author, telephone, May 11, 2022.

25. "C'était très chaleureux, et Gaston Crunelle veillait à ce qu'il y ait une amitié qui existe entre les élèves et qu'il n'y ait pas de négativité. Ce n'était pas la peine d'être orgueilleux ; il nous disait que ça allait être dur pour tout le monde." Renaud François, interview.

26. "Nous nous sommes demandé si nous devions demander des cours privés avec Monsieur Crunelle. Nous avions économisé et lui avions demandé et il nous a répondu « Jamais ! Vous n'avez pas besoin de ça, vous avez les cours ici » Il était très honnête, il aurait pu en profiter et dire oui, mais il nous a dit qu'il ne ferait jamais ça," Brigitte Buxtorf, interview.

27. George Waln, "Conservatoire National de Paris," p. 10.

28. Alexander Murray, email to author, February 23, 2019.

29. "Il avait aussi un côté plaisantin, il avait l'habitude de raconter des petites histoires, des anecdotes comiques dans le cours pour détendre l'atmosphère, Jean-Claude Dhinaut, interview.

30. The story refers to Schmitt's *La Tragédie de Solomé*, not the famous opera by Richard Strauss. Renaud François and Paul Méfano, *Dialogues entre sons et paroles* (Paris: Michel de Maule, 2018), p. 49.

31. Isabelle Chapuis, email to author, May 9, 2022.

32. Pierre-Yves Artaud, interview by author, March 1, 2022.

33. Translated by Michel Debost as "Crunelle's Practice Philosophy," *Flute Talk* 13 no. 5 (January 1994): pp. 2, 4. The original text has not been identified.

34. Alexander Murray, interview by author, London, November 21, 2019.

35. "On ne parlait pas encore du diaphragme, ni du soutien du son par ce biais là et on développait énormément la musculature faciale, avec la tension des lèvres et cette sorte de technique qui commençait déjà à être démodé," Buxtorf, interview.

36. Documented in André Zucca's photographs from July 1941, https://bibliotheques-specialisees.paris.fr/ark:/73873/pf0001668482. locale = en.

37. Isabelle Chapuis, email to the author, May 9, 2022.

38. Michael Scott, interview by author, Skype, December 20, 2019.

39. "Comme le général de l'armée! Les morts et les blessés derrière. Continue jusqu'au but," Chapuis, interview.

40. Scott, interview.

41. Beckett, interview.

42. Chapuis, interview.

43. Dhinaut, interview.

44. Henri Altès explained this technique in his complete method, originally published in 1880. Henri Altès, *Célèbre Méthode complète de flûte*, ed. Fernand Caratgé (Paris: Alphonse Leduc, 1956).

45. "Quand on allait travailler chez lui, il utilisait un enregistreur, c'était assez rare à l'époque et il n'y en avait pas au conservatoire. Il nous demandait de jouer, nous enregistrer et nous demandait ensuite ce qu'on avait pensé de ce qu'on venait de faire avant de nous faire écouter." Pierreuse, interview.

46. Students mentioned that he did not actually teach Chaminade's *Concertino*, as it was too easy for the Conservatory.

47. The third movement was the *morceau imposé* for 1934.

48. See Chapter 8.

49. "Pour jouer le *Chant de Linos*, il faut des heures et des heures. Pour jouer Bach ou Mozart, il faut des années et des années." Michel Debost, interview by Pascal Gresset, *Tempo flûte* 6 (2012, no. 2).

50. "En général, les élèves restaient environ trois ans au conservatoire, et alors les troisièmes année, considérés comme ceux qui allaient sortir, avaient le droit de jouer un mouvement de concerto de Mozart ou de sonate de Bach, c'était comme la récompense suprême de la troisième année." Artaud, interview, March 1, 2022.

51. Blakeman, *Taffanel: Genius of the Flute*, pp. 185–86.

52. "La musique de Bach est géniale évidemment mais elle est comme la Bible : chacun possède son interprétation," Michel Debost, interview by Pascal Gresset: p. 3.

53. Michel Debost, "Gaston Crunelle (1898–1990)," *Flute Talk* 30, no. 10 (July/August 2011): p. 4.

54. "On abordait toujours la propreté du jeu, l'exactitude parfaite, le total respect du texte, c'était surtout ça ses critères," Buxtorf, interview.

55. Pierreuse, interview.

56. "Debussy c'est au-delà des notes, c'est ton âme. Il faut faire sortir ton âme," François, interview.

57. "Le concerto est de grande dimension, l'introduction est joyeuse, c'est grandiose. Tu ne peux pas le jouer de manière introvertie, timide ; tu dois jouer très ouvert !" Groussard and Venay, interview.

58. "Nous étions obsédés par le problème de la mémoire." Artaud, interview, March 1, 2022.

59. A survey of literature on memorization for musical performance finds that sixty percent of articles written between 1872 and 2006 specifically address memorization for pianists and only six percent for woodwinds. Jennifer Mishra, "A Century of Memorization Pedagogy," *Journal of Historical Research in Music Education* 32, no. 1 (October 2010): pp. 3–18. www.jstor.org/stable/20789876.

60. François, interview.

61. Roger Boutry, email to author, May 1, 2019.

62. ANF, AJ/37/479.

63. "Il disait : « Tu feras attention à la troisième page, commence ton travail par là car c'est là que ça devient compliqué ». Il nous disait ça pour nous mettre à l'aise sans dévoiler

le morceau, sans tricher, mais il nous mettait en garde pour nous guider dans notre travail," François, interview.

64. Bang, "Small Classes . . . Less Teaching, More Learning," p. 49.

65. Pierreuse, interview.

66. Groussard and Venay interview.

67. "Il essayait de nous donner les moyens de nous débrouiller tout seul, en nous donnant des conseils habiles et astucieux, et était très précieux pour ça car il donnait beaucoup de sécurité au jeu," Artaud, interview, March 1, 2022.

68. Buxtorf, interview.

69. Chapuis, interview.

70. "Vous êtes musiciens, je n'ai pas à vous dire ce qu'il faut faire, vous le savez déjà et si vous ne le savez pas vous ne le saurai jamais," Artaud, interview, March 1, 2022.

71. "Il était très attentif et suivait ses élèves. Dès que j'ai eu mon prix il m'a donné tout suite quelques contrats pour me lancer." Jemain, interview.

72. Il était un mélange entre rigueur et liberté. Artaud, interview, March 1, 2022.

73. Chapuis, interview.

74. Leone Buyse, letter to her parents, November 18, 1968.

75. Buyse, interview by author, Salt Lake City, July 31, 2019.

76. Buxtorf, interview.

77. Tim Wilson, interview by author, Skype, July 1, 2021.

78. Janet Hulstrand, "The Importance of Stability, Order, and Being Correct." In *Demystifying the French: How to Love Them, and Make Them Love You* (Winged Words Publishing, 2018), pp. 44–52.

79. Dhinaut and Murray, interviews.

80. Waln, "Conservatoire Nationale de Paris," p. 10.

81. "C'était toujours une très grande finesse de jeu et une très grande précision d'attaque et j'ai gardé ça comme une sonorité de rêve. Quand il jouait, j'ai gardé un côté angélique, une pureté de son extraordinaire . . .

Je me souviens qu'il m'avait joué en 1964 le solo de la scène des Champs-Élysées de Gluck. Nous étions seuls dans la salle de classe, et c'était comme du cristal, magnifique !" Renaud François, interview.

82. "Il a eu une sonorité superbe que nous voulions tous imiter. Quand il jouait, c'était toujours de la belle flûte, une sonorité chaude et très colorée." Florence Bellon, "Ida Ribera: 30 ans d'enseignement," *Traversières* 4/23 (April–May–June 1987).

83. "À chaque fois que Monsieur Crunelle prenait la flûte, il avait toujours une meilleure sonorité que chacun de ses élèves . . . Il ne cherchait jamais à faire des effets ou nous montrer ses capacités," Buxtorf, interview.

84. "Il était techniquement excellent et nous épatait souvent en reprennent tel ou tel passage difficile, quelquefois avec une Gitane coincée entre deux doigts de la main droite !" Pierreuse, interview.

85. An issue of *The Flutist Quarterly* (15, no. 2, Spring 1990) is devoted the "Women and the Flute." A few nineteenth-century flutists are mentioned, but none in France.

86. Bernard Duplaix, "Lucy Dragon: Les Aventures de Radiolette," *La Traversière* 47 (October 1987): pp. 64–70.

87. Duplaix, "Lucy Dragon."

88. "Je pense avoir eu beaucoup de chance. A aucun moment j'ai eu le sentiment que les filles avaient moins de chance que les garçons. Il y avait une vraie égalité, autant au conservatoire qu'à l'orchestre," Buxtorf, interview.

89. Email to author, May 9, 2022.

90. "Étant donné le mouvement général de contestation en France, étant donnée la prise de position de la grande majorité des musiciens français en faveur d'une réforme des structures de la musique en France, nous proposons la grève des cours pour une période de quinze jours, reconductible par décision d'une assemblée générale réunie à l'issue de ce délai, la création de commissions d'études à tous les niveaux en vue d'élaborer les réformes nécessaires et d'étudier les problèmes de report des concours," Noémi Lefebvre, "Mai 1968 au Conservatoire National Supérieur de Musique," p. 6, https://halshs.archives-ouvertes.fr/halshs-00382630.

91. "Réunis en Assemblée extraordinaire le 20 mai, les professeurs "s'affirment solidaires des élèves dans la lutte engagée par tous les étudiants pour l'amélioration de tout ce qui concerne leurs études et leur avenir", se déclarent "décidés à intensifier leur propre action dans les meilleurs délais en union avec leurs élèves les différentes réformes nécessaires" et "prêts à collaborer à tout travail efficace et constructif en ce sens." ANF, 19870605/55, quoted in Lefebvre, Mai 1968 au Conservatoire," p. 6.

92. "Il était fou de rage à la suite des histoires qui s'étaient passées au conservatoire en mai 1968. Il avait été, contrairement à d'autres personnes comme André Jolivet que je connaissais, fâché contre les élèves qui avaient abîmé des choses," Buxtorf, interview.

93. A national certificate qualifying students for higher education, obtained through a comprehensive exam usually taken at the end of secondary school.

94. "Si le vocable de « maître » est moins utilisé après 1968, les classes d'instrument demeurent marquées par l'autorité autocratique du professeur," Lefebvre, "Mai 1968 au Conservatoire National Supérieur de Musique," p. 25.

Chapter 8

1. "Ce n'est pas de la musique . . . Les compositeurs modernes n'étaient pas intéressants pour lui. Crunelle était le contraire, il était extrêmement ouvert. Beaucoup de musique ne lui échappaient, parce que ce n'était pas ses opinions personnelles, il ne méprisait pas." Artaud, interview, May 18, 2019.

2. "Il avait beaucoup de pouvoirs, il pouvait choisir les jurys, les œuvres, en tout cas les suggérer. Il était très malin et manipulait bien les choses," François, interview.

3. Crunelle worked under the following directors: Claude Delvincourt, Marcel Dupré, Raymond Loucheur, and Raymond Gallois-Montbrun.

4. Appendix 5 lists recordings.

5. Kathleen Roberta Cook, "The Paris Conservatory and the 'Solos de Concours' for Flute, 1900–1955" (DMA dissertation, The University of Wisconsin, 1991); Melissa Gail Colgin, "The Paris Conservatoire Concours Tradition and the Solos de Concours for Flute, 1955–1990" (DMA dissertation, The University of Texas at Austin, 1992).

6. Colgin, "The Paris Conservatoire Concours Tradition," p. 69. She identifies a fourth category, avant-garde, but this does not apply to any works written during Crunelle's tenure.

7. Colgin, "The Paris Conservatoire Concours Tradition," p. 160.

8. "Gaston a souvent influencé les compositeurs," Artaud, interview, March 1, 2022.

9. Artaud, interview, March 1, 2022.

10. Lucie Kayas, email to author, May 7, 2022. Jolivet's diary is in the Archives of the Association, Les Amis d'André Jolivet, www.jolivet.asso.fr/fr/andre-jolivet-composit eur-1905-1974/.

11. Jemain, interview.

12. Brun, *Un Andante et un Scherzo* (1948); Brun, *Pastorale d'Arcadie* (1957); Gallon, *Improvisation et Rondo* (1958); Casadesus, *Fantaisie,* op. 59 (1960); Chaynes, *Variations sur un tanka* (1962); Hugon, Sonata (1965); Rivier, *Ballade* (1966); Hubeau, *Idylle* (1967); and Bondon, *Mouvement chorégraphique* (1969).

13. Dutilleux and Glayman, *Henri Dutilleux: Music—Mystery and Memory. Conversations with Claude Glayman,* p. 21.

14. "En 1944, j'ai obtenu mon Premier Prix de flute au Conservatoire de Paris avec le *Chant de Linos.* A l'époque, les flûtistes horrifiés par la modernité et la difficulté de l'œuvre ; si bien que j'étais l'un des seuls, avec Pol Mule, à la jouer par cœur." Lucie Kayas and Laetitia Chassain-Dolliou. *André Jolivet Portraits* (Arles: Actes Sud, 1994), p. 166.

15. Verroust, *Jean-Pierre Rampal,* p. 44.

16. Kelly, B. "Jolivet, André." *Grove Music Online.* https://doi.org/10/1093/gmo/9781561592630.article.14433.

17. Roger Nichols, "Messiaen's *Le merle noir*: The Case of a Blackbird in a Historical Pie," *The Musical Times,* 129, no. 1750 (December 1988): p. 648.

18. Kyle Dzapo, *Notes for Flutists: A Guide to the Repertoire* (New York: Oxford University Press, 2016), pp. 192–94.

19. Cook, "The Paris Conservatory and the 'Solos de Concours' for Flute, 1900–1955," pp. 129–30.

20. Colgin, "The Paris Conservatoire *concours* Tradition and the *solos de concours* for Flute, 1955–1990," p. 76.

21. Alain Louvier, "Gallon, Noël." *Grove Music Online,* 2001. https://doi.org/10/1093/gmo/9781561592630.article.10580.

22. Colgin, "The Paris Conservatoire *concours* Tradition and the *solos de concours* for Flute, 1955–1990," p. 82.

23. Colgin, "The Paris Conservatoire *concours* Tradition and the *solos de concours* for Flute, 1955–1990," p. 93.

24. Paul Griffiths and Andrea Musk. "Aubin, Tony." *Grove Music Online.* 2001. https://doi.org/10/1093/gmo/9781561592630.article.01493.

25. Colgin, "The Paris Conservatoire *concours* Tradition and the *solos de concours* for Flute, 1955–1990," p. 100.

26. ANF, 20150119/15–20150119/16, *Sujets de déchiffrage flûte,* 1931–2006.

27. Chapuis, interview.

28. Marcel Bitsch, *Douze études pour flûte* (Paris: Alphonse Leduc, 1955).
29. Gabriel Grovlez, *Concertino pour flûte avec accompagnement de piano* (Paris: Gallet et fils, 1950).

Chapter 9

1. Leone Buyse, letter to her parents, October 11, 1968.
2. Conservatoire national supérieur de musique et de danse de Paris, "Diplômes," www.conservatoiredeparis.fr/fr/cursus/decouverte-des-cursus/diplomes.
3. The QS World University Rankings rated it the third [the Royal College of Music and the Royal Academy of Music are rated higher and are separate schools]-best school in the world for performing arts in 2023. www.topuniversities.com/university-rankings/university-subject-rankings/2022/performing-arts
4. Association française des orchestres, "L'égalité femmes/hommes dans les orchestres membres de l'AFO, https://france-orchestres.com/en/egalite-des-genres/
5. "René Le Roy était très bourgeois, d'un très bon monde, élégant, raffiné. Il habitait les immeubles luxueux de Paris. Il avait toujours un très beau costume et était un peu imbu de sa personne, sûr de lui, il se prenait pour un grand maître. Il n'aimait pas Gaston Crunelle, ils n'étaient pas du même monde. Gaston Crunelle était issu d'un milieu plus populaire il était plus accessible . . . Le Roy vivait dans un monde mondain, la grande société, les gens cultivés, entouré d'industriels, et il aimait ça. Crunelle était plus simple et aimait tout le monde. Le Roy avait de la sympathie pour les gens qui venaient d'un bon milieu." Renaud François, interview by author.

Appendix 2

1. Jacques Tilly, "Pierre Jamet et son Quintette," *Les Ondes: L'Hebdomadaire de la radio* 143 (January 23, 1944), p. 9.
2. In French, his name is spelled Gretchaninoff.
3. Suzanne Demarquez, *André Jolivet* (Paris: Editions Ventadour, 1958): p. 36.
4. Manuscript in the library of the Conservatoire regional du Grand Nancy. Jean-Paul C. Montagnier, *Catalogue des œuvres de Jules-Marie Laure Maugüé (Nancy, 1869-Paris, 1953.* (Nancy: Jean-Paul C. Montagnier, 2019): p. 27.
5. Bibliothèque du conservatoire royal de Liège, www.crlg.be.
6. Elles Women Composers plans to publish Sohy's work. https://elleswomencomposers.com.

Appendix 4

1. "Passing Notes: Antoinette Handy-Miller," *The Flutist Quarterly* 28, no. 2 (Winter 2003): p. 25.
2. Mary Louise Poor, *A Guide to Flute Teaching* (New York: Envolve Music, 1978).

Bibliography

Archives

Archives départementales du Nord
Archives municipales de Douai
Archives nationales de France (ANF)
   Opera-Comique, AJ13
   Conservatoire national de musique, AJ37
Archives de Paris
Bibliothèque musicale La Grange-Fleuret
   Pierre Jamet: dossier documentaire
   René Le Roy: dossier documentaire
Bibliothèque nationale de France (BNF): Bibliothèque de l'Opéra
   Archives de l'Opéra-Comique
BNF: Inathèque
   Archives de l'Institut National de l'Audiovisuel (INA)
Centre d'études généalogiques du Douaisis
Conservatoire national supérieur de musique et de danse de Paris: Archives
Musée de l'Opéra de Vichy
Orchestre Pasdeloup: Archives
Orchestre philharmonique de Monte Carlo: Archives

Interviews by Author

Artaud, Pierre-Yves, by telephone, May 17, 2019, and in person, Bourges, March 1, 2022
Beaumadier, Jean-Louis, Aix-en-Provence, November 27, 2019
Beckett, Edward, Paris, November 23, 2019
Buxtorf, Brigitte, Geneva, February 15, 2022
Buyse, Leone, Salt Lake City, July 31, 2019
Chapuis, Isabelle, Los Altos, CA, May 16–17, 2019
Dhainaut, Jean-Claude, Puteaux, France, March 28, 2022
Dias, Odette Ernest, Skype, August 5, 2020
François, Reynaud, Paris, November 30, 2019
Fumet, Gabriel, Paris, May 27, 2022
Grognet, Gérard, La Garenne-Colombes, France, April 22, 2022
Groussard, Eric and Francette Venay, Fresnes, France, April 1, 2022
Jamet, Marie-Claire, Flayosc, France, November 27, 2019
Jemain, Gérard, Le Mans, France (by telephone), May 11, 2022
Larrieu, Maxence, Geneva, November 25, 2019
Leresche, Carlos, Paris, May 23, 2022
Luypaerts, Guy-Claude, Paris, November 26, 2019
Mather, Betty Bang, Iowa City, IA, July 22, 2019
Murray, Alexander, London, November 21, 2019

Pierreuse, Bernard, Liège, February 22, 2022
Scott, Michael, Skype, December 20, 2019
Wilson, Tim, Skype, July 1, 2021

Periodicals

The American Harp Journal
Annuaire des artistes et de l'enseignement dramatique et musical
Comœdia
Le Figaro
Flute Talk
The Flutist Quarterly
Le Guide du concert
L'Information musicale
Le Ménestrel
Le Monde
Le Monde musical
Les Ondes: L'Hebdomadaire de la radio
Radio-Sélection
Revue des jeunesses musicales de France
Rolet: Revue indépendante
Tempo flûte: Revue de l'association d'histoire de la flûte traversière
Le Temps
Traversières

Books, Articles, and Dissertations

Adams, Patti. "Sir James Galway: Living Legend." *The Flutist Quarterly* 34, no. 3 (Spring 2009): pp. 18–21.

Adorján, András and Lenz Meierott. *Lexikon der Flöte*. Laaber: Laaber-Verlag, 2008.

Alten, Michèle. "Le Conservatoire de musique et d'art dramatique: Une institution culturelle publique dans la guerre (1940–1942)." *L'Éducation musicale* (February 2012), www.yumpu.com/s/61Q2KnMHUntWwstG.

Alten, Michèle. *Musiciens français dans la guerre froide (1945–1956). L'indépendance artistique face au politique*, Paris: L'Harmattan, 2001.

Annuaire officiel du conservatoire national de musique et de declamation. Paris: Maurice Senart, 1919.

Atasay, Maïté. "L'Orchestre Pasdeloup à travers son histoire et sa vie associative." CNSMDP thesis, Conservatoire National Supérieur de Musique et de Danse de Paris, 2017.

Bang, Betty. "Small Flute Classes . . . Less Teaching, More Learning." *Music Educators Journal* 57, no. 2 (October 1970): pp. 49–51.

Bauer, Harold. "The Paris Conservatoire: Some Reminiscences." *The Musical Quarterly* 33, no. 4 (October 1947): pp. 533–42.

Bernard, Élisabeth. "A Glance at the Archives of Some Parisian Orchestral Societies." *Nineteenth Century Music* 7, no. 2 (Fall 1983): p. 104.

Blakeman, Edward. *Taffanel: Genius of the Flute*. Oxford: Oxford University Press, 2005.

Bongrain, Anne. *Le Conservatoire national de musique et de déclamation 1900–1930: Documents historiques et administratifs*. Paris: Vrin, 2012.

Bongrain, Anne. *Le Conservatoire de Paris: Deux cents ans de pédagogie, 1795–1995*. Paris: Éditions Buchet/Chastel, 1999.

Bongrain, Anne and Yves Gérard. *Le Conservatoire de Paris: Des Menus-Plaisirs à la Cité de la musique, 1795–1995*. Paris: Éditions Buchet/Chastel, 1996.

Brett, Adrian. "The Other French Players." *The Flute Worker* 3, no. 1 (Winter 1985): pp. 1–8.

Brody, Elaine. *Paris: The Musical Kaleidoscope 1870–1925*. New York: George Braziller, 1987.

Bruhn, Siglind. *Messiaen's Language of Mystical Love*. New York: Garland, 1998.

Bufquin, Victor. *Histoire de Douai*. 3rd ed. Douai: Lauverjat, 1971.

Burrin, Philippe. *France under the Germans*, trans. Janet Lloyd. New York: The New Press, 1996.

Campos, Rémy. *Le Conservatoire de Paris et son histoire: une institution en questions*. Paris: L'œil d'Or, 2016.

Cavanagh, Lynn. "Marcel Dupré's 'Dark Years': Unveiling His Occupation-Period Concertizing." *Intersections: Canadian Journal of Music* 34, no. 1–2 (2014): pp. 33–57. https://doi.org/10.7202/1030869ar

Centre belge de documentation musicale. *Catalogue des œuvres de compositeurs belges: Jean Absil*. Bruxelles: CeBeDeM, 1957.

Charlton, David and Nicole Wild. *Théâtre de l'opéra-comique, Paris: Répertoire 1762–1972*, Sprimont: Mardaga, 2005.

Chassain-Dolliou, Laetitia. *Le Conservatoire de Paris ou Les Voies de la création*. Paris: Gallimard, 1995.

Chimènes, Myriam, ed. *La Vie musicale sous Vichy*. Brussels: Éditions Complexe, 2001.

Chimènes, Myriam and Yannik Simon. *La Musique à Paris sous l'Occupation*. Paris: Fayard, 2013.

Colgin, Melissa Gail. "The Paris Conservatoire Concours Tradition and the Solos de Concours for Flute, 1955–1990." DMA dissertation, The University of Texas at Austin, 1992.

Cook, Kathleen Roberta. "The Paris Conservatory and the 'Solos de Concours' for Flute, 1900–1955." DMA dissertation, The University of Wisconsin, 1991.

Cook, Mervyn. *A History of Film Music*. Cambridge: Cambridge University Press, 2008.

Coppola, Piero. *Dix-sept ans de musique à Paris*. Geneva: Slatkine, 1982.

Councell-Vargas, Martha. "Michel Debost: Teaching Artistry." *The Flutist Quarterly* 37, no. 3 (Spring 2012): pp. 26–29.

Crunelle, Gaston. "On the Management of Time in the Study of the Flute." Trans. Michel Debost, "Crunelle's Practice Philosophy." *Flute Talk* 13, no. 5 (January 1994): pp. 2, 4.

Dardeau, Sophie. *Pierre-Yves Artaud: Parcours d'un flûtiste pionnier*. Paris: Pippa, 2012.

Debost, Michel. "Gaston Crunelle." *Flute Talk* 9, no. 8 (April 1990): pp. 29–30.

Debost, Michel. "Gaston Crunelle (1898–1990)." *Flute Talk* 30, no. 10 (July/August 2011): pp. 2, 4, 6.

Delvincourt, Claude. *Rapport sur une réorganisation administrative de la musique et de l'enseignement musical en France*. Paris: Conservatoire national de musique et d'art dramatique, 1944.

Dewez, Claudine and Jean Paul. "Ascendance Crunelle." *Le Lien généalogique du Douaisis* 39 (3ᵉ trimestre 2022): pp. 18–20.

Diot, Jean-Claude. "Gaston Crunelle." *Traversières* 72 (July–August–September 2002, Q3): p. 34.

Dorgeuille, Claude. *The French Flute School, 1860–1950*, trans. Edward Blakeman. London: Tony Bingham, 1986.

Drake, David. *Paris at War: 1939–1944*. Cambridge, MA: The Belknap Press of Harvard University Press, 2015.

Drott, Eric. *Music and the Elusive Revolution: Cultural Politics and Political Culture in France, 1968–1981*. Berkeley: University of California Press, 2011.

Duchesnau, Michel. *L'Avant-garde musicale et ses sociétés à Paris de 1871 à 1939*. Paris: P. Mardaga, 1997.

Dumesnil, René. *La Musique en France entre les deux guerres, 1919–1939*. Paris: Éditions du milieu du monde, 1946.

Duncan, Élisabeth. *Inventaire de la série AJ ^{37}*. Paris: Archives Nationales, 1971.

Duplaix, Bernard. "Lucy Dragon: Les Aventures de Radiolette." *La Traversière* 47 (October 1987): pp. 64–70.

Dutilleux, Henri and Claude Glayman. *Henri Dutilleux: Music—Mystery and Memory: Conversations with Claude Glayman*, translated by Roger Nichols. London: Routledge, 2003.

Eck, Hélène. *La Guerre des ondes. Histoire des radios de langue française pendant la Deuxième Guerre mondiale*. Paris: CRPLF, 1984.

Equilbey, Laurence. "René Le Roy: Une époque, un interprète." PhD dissertation, University of Paris – Sorbonne (Paris IV), 1984.

Fair, Demetra Baferos. "Flutists' Family Tree: In Search of the American School." DMA document, The Ohio State University, 2003.

Feneyou, Laurent and Alain Poirier, ed. *De la Libération au Domaine Musical: Dix ans de musique en France (1944–1954)*. Paris: Librairie Philosophique J. Vrin, 2018.

Ferey, Mathieu and Benoît Menut. *Joesph-Guy Ropartz, ou le pays inaccessible*. Geneva: Éditions Papillon, 2005.

Fischer, Penelope Peterson. "Philippe Gaubert (1879–1941): His Life and Contributions as Flutist, Editor, Teacher, Conductor, and Composer." DMA thesis, University of Maryland, 1982.

Fletcher, Kristine Klopfenstein. "A Comprehensive Performance Project in Bassoon Literature with an Essay on the Paris Conservatoire and the Contest Solos for Bassoon." DMA thesis, University of Iowa, 1986.

Fulcher, Jane F. *The Composer as Intellectual: Musical Culture and Ideology in France 1914–1940*. New York: Oxford University Press, 2005.

Fulcher, Jane F. *Renegotiating French Identity: Musical Culture and Creativity in France during Vichy and the German Occupation*. New York: Oxford University Press, 2018.

Galway, Sir James and Linda Bridges. *The Man with the Golden Flute: Sir James, a Celtic Minstrel*. Hoboken, NJ: John Wiley & Sons, Inc., 2009.

Garden, Maurice and Jean-Luc Pinol. *Seize Promenades historiques dans Paris*. Paris: Éditions du détour, 2017.

Garrison, Leonard. "Gaston Crunelle (1892–1990)." *Le Lien généalogique du Douaisis* 39 (3e trimester 2022): p. 17.

Gee, Harry R. *Clarinet Solos de concours, 1897–1980*. Bloomington: Indiana University Press, 1981.

George, Patricia. "Lessons with the Masters: An Interview with Isabelle Chapuis." *Flute Talk* 31, no. 5 (January 2012): 12–15, 27–30.

Gervasoni, Pierre. *Henri Dutilleux*. Paris: Actes Sud, 2016.

Gosselin, Guy. *L'Âge d'or de la vie musicale à Douai 1800–1850*. Liège: Mardaga, 1994.

Gourret, Jean. *Histoire de l'Opéra-Comique*. Paris: Publications Universitaires, 1978.

Hartopp, Guy. *Paris: A Concise Musical History*. Wilmington, DE: Vernon Press, 2017.

Hennion, Antoine, Françoise Martinat, and Jean-Pierre Vignolle. *Les Conservatoires et leurs élèves, rapport sur les élèves et anciens élèves des écoles de musique agrées par l'État*. Paris: Documentation française, 1983.

Hériché, Robert. *À Propos de la flûte*. Paris: Billaudot, 1985.

Hériché, Robert. "Erinnerung an Gaston Crunelle." *Tibia* 15, no. 3 (1990): 209–210.

Hervé, Guy. *Quand opéra entre en résistance: Les Personnels de la Réunion des théâtres lyriques nationaux sous Vichy et l'Occupation*. Paris: L'Œil d'or, 2007.

Hillairet, Jacques. *Dictionnaire historique des rues de Paris*. 7th ed. Paris: Les éditions de minuit, 1963.

Holoman, D. Kern. *The Société des concerts du conservatoire 1828–1967*. Berkeley: University of California Press, 2004.

Hondré, Emmanuel. *Le Conservatoire de musique de Paris: Regards sur un institution et son histoire*. Paris: Association du Bureau des étudiants du Conservatoire national supérieur de musique, 1995

Horne, Alistair. *Seven Ages of Paris*. New York: Vintage Books, 2002.

Jackson, Julian. *France: The Dark Years*. New York: Oxford University Press, 2001.

Kaufmann, Martine. *Le Conservatoire de Paris: Une Institution en perspectives*. Paris: CNSM, 1995.

Kayas, Lucie. *André Jolivet*. Paris: Fayard, 2005.

Kayas, Lucie and Laetitia Chassain-Dolliou. *André Jolivet portraits*. Arles: Actes Sud, 1994.

Kedward, H.R. *Occupied France: Collaboration and Resistance 1940–1944*. Cambridge, MA: Blackwell Publishers, 1985.

Keegan, John. *The First World War*. New York: Alfred A. Knopf, 1999.

Launay, Florence. "Les Musiciennes: de la pionnière adulée à la concurrente redoutée." *Travail, genre et sociétés* 19 (2008): pp. 41–63. www.cairn.info/revue-travail-genre-et-societes-2008-1-page-41.htm

Lavignac, Albert and Lionel de la Laurencie. *Encyclopédie de la musique et dictionnaire du conservatoire*. Paris: Delagrave, 1927.

Le Bail, Karine. *La Musique au pas: Être musicien sous l'Occupation*. Paris: CNRS Éditions, 2016.

Le Boterf, Hervé. *La Vie parisienne sous l'occupation, 1940–1944*. 2 vols. Paris: Éditions France-Empire, 1974.

Lefebvre, Noémi. "Mai 1968 au Conservatoire National Supérieur de Musique." HAL Open Science (2008). https://halshs.archives-ouvertes.fr/halshs-00382630.

Legrand, Raphaëlle and Nicole Wild. *Regards sur l'opéra-comique: Trois siècles de vie théâtrale*. Paris: CNRS Editions, 2002.

Lentrodt, Ursula. "A Conversation with Pierre Jamet." *American Harp Journal* 11, no. 3 (Summer 1988): pp. 28–30.

Lesure, François. *Dictionnaire musical des villes de province*. Paris: Klincksieck, 1999.

Marriott, Patrick W. *Gaubert vivant!: The Life and Music of Philippe Gaubert*. Wilmington, NC: Patrick W. Marriott, 2010.

Masson, Georges. *Gabriel Pierné, musicien lorrain*. Nancy: Presses Universitaires Nancy, 1993.

Mayer, Denise and Pierre Souvtchinsky, ed. *Roger Désormière et son temps*, Monaco: Éditions du Rocher, 1966.

McCutchan, Ann. *Marcel Moyse: Voice of the Flute*. Portland, OR: Amadeus Press, 1994.

Meusy, Jean-Jacques. *Écrans français de l'entre-deux-guerres*. Paris: Association française de recherche sur l'histoire du cinema, 2017.

Milhaud, Darius. *Notes without Music: An Autobiography*. New York: Alfred A. Knopf, 1953.

Miller, Patrick. "Music and the Silent Film." *Perspectives of New Music* 21, no. 1/2 (1982): pp. 582–84. https://doi.org/10.2307/832894.

Mitchell, Allan. *Nazi Paris: The History of an Occupation 1940–1944*. New York: Berghahn Books, 2008.

Montagnier, Jean-Paul C. *Catalogue des œuvres de Jules-Marie Laure Maugüé (Nancy, 1869–Paris, 1953)*. Nancy: Jean-Paul C. Montagnier, 2019.

Morin, Philippe and Yannick Simon. "L'Enregistrement historique de *Pelléas et Mélisande* en 1941." *Cahiers Debussy*, 37–38 (2013–2014): pp. 77–111.

Nichols, Roger. *The Harlequin Years: Music in Paris, 1917–1929*. Berkeley: University of California Press, 2002.

Nichols, Roger. "Messiaen's 'Le merle noir': The Case of a Blackbird in a Historical Pie." *The Musical Times* 129, no. 1750 (December 1988): pp. 648–50.

Nord, Philip. *France's New Deal: From the Thirties to the Postwar Era*. Princeton: Princeton University Press, 2010.

Novick, Peter. *The Resistance Versus Vichy: The Purge of Collaborators in Liberated France*. New York: Columbia University Press, 1968.

Offen, Karen. *Debating the Woman Question in the French Third Republic, 1870–1920*. Cambridge: Cambridge University Press, 2018.

Offen, Karen. *The Woman Question in France, 1400–1870*. Cambridge: Cambridge University Press, 2017.

Olivier, Philippe. "The Fate of Professional French Jewish Musicians Under the Vichy Regime." The OREL Foundation. 2009. http://orelfoundation.org/journal/journalArti cle/the_fate_of_professional_french_jewish_musicians_under_the_vichy_regime.

Orledge, Robert. *Charles Koechlin (1867–1950): His Life and Works*. London: Harwood Academic Publishers, 1989.

Oubradous, Christiane and Pascale d'Ogna. *Fernand Oubradous: Un Artiste du xxᵉ siècle*. Paris: La Bruyère, 2007.

Pâris, Alain. *Dictionnaire des interprètes et de l'interprétation musicale au xxe siècle*. Paris: Robert Laffront, 1982.

Parouty, Michel. *L'Opéra-comique*. Paris: ASA, 1998.

Paxton, Robert. *Vichy France: Old Guard and New Order, 1940–1944*. New York: Alfred A. Knopf, 1972.

Paxton, Robert and Michael R. Marrus. *Vichy France and the Jews*, 2nd ed. Stanford: Stanford University Press, 2019.

Piccini, Caitrine-Ann. "French Women Perpetuating the French Tradition: Women Composers of Flute Contest Pieces at the Paris Conservatory." DMA document, University of Houston, 2013.

Pierre, Constant. *B. Sarrette et les origines du Conservatoire national du musique et de déclamation*. Paris: Librairie Delalain Frères, 1895.

Pierre, Constant. *Le Conservatoire national de musique et de declamation*. Paris: Imprimerie nationale, 1900.

Pierreuse, Bernard. *Flûte littérature: Catalogue général des œuvres éditées et inédites par formations instrumentales*. Paris: Éditions Jobert et Éditions musicales transatlantiques, 1982.

Pistone, Danièle, ed. *L'Éducation musicale en France. Histoire et méthode*. Paris: Presses de l'Université de Paris-Sorbonne, 1983.

Pistone, Danièle, ed. *Musiques et musiciens à Paris dans les années trente*. Paris: Honoré Campion, 2000.

Pistone, Danièle. *Le Théâtre lyrique français 1945–1985*. Paris: Honoré Champion, 1987.

Porcile, François. *Les Conflits de la musique française 1940–1965*. Paris: Fayard, 2001.

Poupet, Michel. *Musique et éducation musicale: problèmes généraux, bibliographie*. Paris: Institut National de Recherche et de Documentation Pédagogique, 1976.

Pryce-Jones, David. *Paris in the Third Reich: A History of the German Occupation, 1940–1944*. New York: Holt, Rinehart and Winston, 1981.

Rampal, Jean-Pierre and Deborah Wise. *Music, My Love*. New York: Random House, 1989.

Ricquebourg, Anne. "Le Quintette instrumental Pierre Jamet." *Traversières* 72 (July–August–September 2002): pp. 31–33.

Riding, Alan. *And the Show Went On: Cultural Life in Nazi-Occupied Paris*. New York: Alfred A. Knopf, 2010.

Rioux, Jean Pierre. *La Vie culturelle sous Vichy*. Paris: Éditions Complexe, 1998.

Roberts, Mary Louise. *Civilization Without Sexes: Reconstructing Gender in Postwar France, 1917–1927*. Chicago: The University of Chicago Press, 1994.

Robinson, David. *Musique et cinéma muet*. Paris: Éditions de la Réunion des musées nationaux, 1995.

Rodriguez, Javier. "Le Quintette instrumental Pierre Jamet: Histoire et répertoire de la période 1945–1958." Master's thesis, Conservatoire national supérieur de musique et de danse de Paris, 2017.

Rosbottom, Ronald C. *When Paris Went Dark: The City of Light Under German Occupation, 1940–1944*. New York: Little, Brown and Company, 2014.

Rougnon, Paul. *Souvenirs de 60 années de vie musicale et de 50 années de professorat au Conservatoire de Paris*. Paris: Éditions Margueritat, 1925.

Saint Pulgent, Maryvonne de. *L'Opéra-Comique: La Gavroche de la musique*. Paris: Gallimard, 2010.

Serba, Anne. *Les Parisiennes: How the Women of Paris Lived, Loved, and Died Under Nazi Occupation*. New York: St. Martin's Press, 2016.

Sergis, Anie. "Education in France During World War II." PhD dissertation, Loyola University Chicago, 1991. https://ecommons.luc.edu/luc_diss/2896/

Simeone, Nigel. *Paris: A Musical Gazetteer*. New Haven, CT: Yale University Press, 2000.

Simeone, Nigel. "Making Music in Occupied Paris." *The Musical Times* 147, no. 1894 (2006): pp. 23–50.

Simon, Yannick. *Composer sous Vichy*. Lyon: Symétrie, 2009.

Simon, Yannick. *Jules Pasdeloup et les origines du concert Populaire*. Lyon, Symétrie, 2011

Spotts, Frederick. *The Shameful Peace: How French Artists and Intellectuals Survived the Nazi Occupation*. New Haven: Yale University Press, 2008.

Sprout, Leslie A. *The Musical Legacy of Wartime Paris*. Berkeley: University of California Press, 2013.

Sweets, John F. *Choices in Vichy France: The French under Nazi Occupation*. New York: Oxford University Press, 1986.

Tilly, Jacques. "Pierre Jamet et son Quintette." *Les Ondes: L'Hebdomadaire de la radio* 143 (January 23, 1944). https://gallica.bnf.fr/ark:/12148/bpt6k4226274p.

Toff, Nancy. *Monarch of the Flute: The Life of Georges Barrère*. New York: Oxford University Press, 2005.

Toulet, Emmanuelle, and Christian Belaygue. *Musique d'écran: l'accompagnement musical du cinéma muet en France 1918–1995*. Paris: Réunion de Musées Nationaux, 1994.

Tuchman, Barbara. *The Guns of August*. New York: Macmillan, 1962.

Valette, Rebecca M. "The French School: What is so French About It?" *The Flutist Quarterly* 36, no. 1 (Fall 2010): 22–35.

Verroust, Denis. *Jean-Pierre Rampal: La flûte universelle*. Paris: Association française de la flute "La Traversière" and Association Jean-Pierre Rampal, 2022.

Waln, George. "Conservatoire National de Paris." *The Instrumentalist* 12 (September 1957): 9–12.

Wild, Nicole and David Charlton. *Théâtre de l'opéra-comique Paris: Répertoire 1762–1972*. Sprimont, Belgium: Mardaga, 2005.

Woldu, Gail Hilson. "Gabriel Fauré as Director of the Conservatoire national de musique et de déclamation, 1905–1920." PhD dissertation, Yale University, 1983.

Woldu, Gail Hilson. "Gabriel Fauré, directeur du Conservatoire: les réformes du 1905." *Revue de musicologie* 70, no. 2 (1984): pp. 199–228.

Wolff, Stéphane. *Un Demi-siècle d'Opéra-Comique (1900–1950)*. Paris: Éditions André Bonne, 1953.

Wolff, Stéphane. "The Opéra-Comique of Paris." *Opera* 12, no. 3 (March 1961): pp. 160–65.

Wright, Gordon. *France in Modern Times*. 3rd ed. New York: W.W. Norton & Company, 1981.

Wye, Trevor. *Marcel Moyse, an Extraordinary Man: A Musical Biography*. Cedar Falls, IA: Winzer Press, 1993.

Sources used for the discographies

Clough, Francis F., and G.J. Cuming. *The World's Encyclopaedia of Recorded Music, and First Supplement, April 1950–May–June 1951*. London: London Gramophone Corporation & Sidgwick and Jackson Ltd., 1952; *Second Supplement 1951–1952*. London: London Records Inc. and Sidgwick and Jackson Ltd., 1953; *Third Supplement 1953–1955*. London: Sidgwick and Jackson Ltd. and Decca Record Company Ltd., 1957; reprint: 3 vols., Westport, Conn.: Greenwood Press, 1970 [c1966].

Davidson, Jim. *Lyrebird Rising: Louise Hanson-Dyer of Oiseau-Lyre, 1884–1962*. Portland, OR: Amadeus Press, 1994.

Girard, Victor, and Harold Barnes. *Vertical-Cut Cylinders and Discs*, London: British Institute of Recorded Sound, 1964/1971.

The Gramophone Co. Discography A database incorporating the Gramophone Company research of Dr. Alan Kelly with more recent additions, created by Stephen Clarke and Roger Tessier. https://gramophonecompanydiscography.com

The Gramophone Shop Supplement. New York: The Gramophone Shop, 1937 (unnumbered), 1938–54 (vols. 1–17).

Kelly, Alan. *His Master's Voice/La Voix de Son Maître: The French Catalogue*. Discographies, no. 37. Westport, CT.: Greenwood Press, 1990.

Nelson, Susan. *The Flute on Record—the 78rpm Era*. Lanham, MD: Scarecrow Press, 2006.

Piris, Georges. "Colloque Roland-Manuel—Plaisir de la musique." *La Revue du Conservatoire*, no. 7 (May 2019). https://larevue.conservatoiredeparis.fr/index.php?id=2137

Le Corf, Philippe. "Colloque Roland-Manuel (novembre 2016) Plaisir de la musique . . ." *La Revue du Conservatoire*, no. 7 (May 2019), https://larevue.conservatoiredeparis.fr/index.php?id=2174

"Quarterly Record-List." *Musical Quarterly*, 1935–1952. List appearing in January, April, and October issues, compiled by Richard Gilbert (1935–1936), Philip L. Miller (1937– April 1949), and Robert Phillips (October1949–1952).
Verroust, Denis, comp. *Jean-Pierre Rampal: un demi-siècle d'enregistrements de 1946 à 1992*. Paris: La Flûte Traversière/Salvatore Faulisi, 1991.

The online catalogs and digitized collections of the BNF, the Bibliothèques patrimoniales de Paris, the Institut national de l'audiovisuel, and Worldcat: the international library database managed by OCLC.

Record catalogs used included:
Disques de longue durée. Les éditions de la revue Disques, 1960
Pathé, *Les meilleurs disques à aiguille,* July, 1929.
Pathé, *Disques à aiguille Pathé*, 1933
Pathé, *Répertoire des disques Pathé*, 1938

For Further Reading

Full references are in the Bibliography that follows.

Gaston Crunelle

There are no books in French or English on Crunelle. The fullest treatment of his life is a two-page obituary in German, Robert Hériché's "Erinnerung an Gaston Crunelle" (1990). Michel Debost wrote two short articles about him in 1990 and 2011, and Jean-Claude Diot wrote one in 2002.

Douai

Victor Bufquin's *Histoire de Douai* (1971) covers the history of the town.

World War I

There is a vast amount of literature devoted to the Great War. Barbara Tuchman's *The Guns of August* (1962) is an engaging account of the first month, and John Keegan's *The First World War* (1999) is an excellent general study.

French Flutists

Detailed monographs on other nineteenth- and twentieth-century French flutists are Edward Blakeman's *Taffanel: Genius of the Flute* (2005), Claude Dorgeuille's *The French Flute School, 1860–1950* (1986; covering Taffanel, Gaubert, Moyse, and Le Roy), Ann McCutchan's *Marcel Moyse: Voice of the Flute* (1994), Nancy Toff's *Monarch of the Flute: The Life of Georges*

Barrère (2005), and Denis Verroust's *Jean-Pierre Rampal: La flûte universelle* (2022). Patrick W. Marriott's *Gaubert vivant!: The Life and Music of Philippe Gaubert* (2010) provides basic information, while Penelope Fischer's doctoral dissertation gives more detail: "Philippe Gaubert (1879–1941): His Life and Contributions as Flutist, Editor, Teacher, Conductor, and Composer" (1982).

The Paris Conservatory

The founding of the Conservatory is detailed in Constant Pierre's *B. Sarrette et les origines du Conservatoire national du musique et de déclamation* (1895). Important documents from its first century are found in Pierre's *Le Conservatoire national de musique et de declamation* (1900). Following the same plan, Anne Bongrain's *Le Conservatoire national de musique et de déclamation 1900–1930: Documents historiques et administratifs* (2012) conveys information from the school's archives, including policies, prize and scholarship winners, and lists of *morceaux de concours*. Histories of the Conservatory include: Bongrain's *Le Conservatoire de Paris: Deux cents ans de pédagogie, 1795–1995* (1999); a collection of essays edited by Bongrain and Yves Gérard, *Le Conservatoire de Paris: Des Menus-Plaisirs à la Cité de la musique, 1795–1995* (1996); Rémy Campos's *Le Conservatoire de Paris et son histoire: une institution en questions* (2016); Laetitia Chassain-Dolliou's *Le Conservatoire de Paris ou Les Voies de la création* (1995), and Emmanuel Hondré's *Le Conservatoire de musique de Paris: Regards sur un institution et son histoire* (1995).

Harry R. Gee's *Clarinet Solos de concours, 1897–1980* (1981) was the first full description in English of the system of *concours* and *morceaux de concours* and served as the model for Kristine Fletcher's "A Comprehensive Performance Project in Bassoon Literature with an Essay on the Paris Conservatoire and the Contest Solos for Bassoon" (1986), Kathleen Cook's "The Paris Conservatory and the 'Solos de Concours' for flute, 1900–1955" (1991), Melissa Colgin's "The Paris Conservatoire Concours Tradition and the Solos de Concours for Flute, 1955–1990" (1992), and Caitrine-Ann Piccini's "French Women Perpetuating the French Tradition: Women Composers of Flute Contest Pieces at the Paris Conservatory" (2013).

Music for silent films

Several books address musical accompaniment to silent films: Mervyn Cook, *A History of Film Music* (2008), Jean-Jacques Meusy, *Écrans français de l'entre-deux-guerres* (2017), Patrick Miller, "Music and the Silent Film" (1982), and David Robinson, *Musique et cinéma muet* (1995).

Parisian orchestras

D. Kern Holoman's *The Société des concerts du conservatoire 1828–1967* (2004) is a magisterial account of the leading French orchestra for a century and a half.

Opéra-Comique

There are several good books on the Opéra-Comique: David Charlton and Nicole Wild, *Théâtre de l'opéra-comique, Paris: Répertoire 1762–1972* (2005); Jean Gourret, *Histoire de l'Opéra-Comique*. Paris (1978); Raphaëlle Legrand and Nicole Wild, *Regards sur l'opéra-comique: Trois siècles de vie théâtrale* (2002); Michel Parouty, *L'Opéra-Comique* (1998); Maryvonne de Saint Pulgent, *L'Opéra-Comique: La Gavroche de la musique* (2010); and Stéphane Wolff, *Un Demi-siècle d'Opéra-Comique (1900–1950)* (1953).

Chamber Music in Paris

Michel Duchesneau's *L'Avant-garde musicale et ses sociétés à Paris de 1871 à 1939* (1997) covers the Parisian chamber music societies thoroughly, giving details of hundreds of programs.

Music in Paris Between the Wars

The best summaries of this era are René Dumesnil's *La Musique en France entre les deux guerres, 1919–1939* (1946), Jane Fulcher's *The Composer as*

Intellectual: Musical Culture and Ideology in France 1914–1940 (2005), and Roger Nichols's *The Harlequin Years: Music in Paris, 1917–1929* (2002).

The Quintette instrumental de Paris

Currently, the only published study of this ensemble is Anne Ricquebourg's article, "Le Quintette instrumental Pierre Jamet" (2002).

Occupied Paris

The Occupation is one of the most intensely studied periods of history. An excellent brief overview is H.R. Kedward, *Occupied France: Collaboration and Resistance 1940–1944* (1985), while a detailed study is Julian Jackson's *The Dark Years* (2001). Robert Paxton's *Vichy France: Old Guard and New Order, 1940–1944* (1972) and his book co-written with Michael Marrus, *Vichy France and the Jews* (1981, 2nd edition, 2019), overturned previous thinking about the Vichy government. Other useful studies include Philippe Burrin's *France under the Germans* (1996), Hervé Le Boterf's *La Vie parisienne sous l'occupation, 1940–1944* (1974), David Drake's *Paris at War: 1939–1944* (2015), Allan Mitchell's *Nazi Paris: The History of an Occupation 1940–1944* (2008), David Pryce-Jones's *Paris in the Third Reich: A History of the German Occupation, 1940–1944* (1981), and Ronald Rosbottom's *When Paris Went Dark: The City of Light Under German Occupation, 1940–1944* (2014). Peter Novick's *The Resistance Versus Vichy: The Purge of Collaborators in Liberated France* (1968) focuses specifically on the *épuration*.

Alan Riding covers the arts in *And the Show Went On: Cultural Life in Nazi-Occupied Paris* (2010). In English, studies of music during this period include Jane Fulcher's *Renegotiating French Identity: Musical Culture and Creativity in France during Vichy and the German Occupation* (2018), Nigel Simeone's "Making Music in Occupied Paris" (2006), and Leslie Sprout's *The Musical Legacy of Wartime Paris* (2013). In French, the main sources are: Myriam Chimènes, *La Vie musicale sous Vichy* (2001); Myriam Chimènes and Yannik Simon, *La Musique à Paris sous l'Occupation* (2013); and Karine Le Bail, *La Musique au pas: Être musicien sous l'Occupation* (2016). Michèle Alten focuses on the Paris Conservatory in "Le Conservatoire de musique et d'art dramatique: Une institution culturelle publique dans la guerre (1940–1942)" (2012).

Music in post-war Paris

Laurent Feneyou and Alain Poirier cover this period in *De la Libération au Domaine Musical: Dix ans de musique en France (1944–1954)* (2018); see also François Porcile, *Les Conflits de la musique française 1940–1965* (2001).

Women in France

Karen Offen's two volumes provide an excellent history of women in France: *The Woman Question in France, 1400–1870* (2017) and *Debating the Woman Question in the French Third Republic, 1870–1920* (2018). Anne Serba writes specifically about women in the Occupation in *Les Parisiennes: How the Women of Paris Lived, Loved, and Died Under Nazi Occupation* (2016). Florence Launay discusses the experiences of women as musicians in her article, "Les Musiciennes: de la pionnière adulée à la concurrente redoutée" (2008).

Index

Tables are indicated by an italic *t* following the page number.

Printed in the USA/Agawam, MA
August 19, 2024

871271.010